Cover Photograph by Ian Potter
Designed by Penny Wood

Castle Books
New York

true life stories of...
CROOKS, CON MEN & COURTESANS

Published 1973 by
Octopus Books Pty Ltd
1 Langley Street Darlinghurst
New South Wales 2010

© 1973 Mirror Newspapers Ltd
New South Wales 2010
ISBN 70649530 6

First published 1973 for Castle Books

Distributed in the United States of America by
Book Sales, Inc
110 Enterprise Avenue
Secaucus NJ 07094

Produced by Mandarin Publishers Limited
77A Marble Road North Point Hong Kong
Printed in Hong Kong

Contents

Henry Fauntleroy: The Amorous Banker

PERHAPS Henry Fauntleroy was not a dishonest man. Perhaps his chief crime was that he was obsessed by love; an expensive hobby that required capital he did not possess.

Therefore it was probably his over-amorous nature rather than any larcenous tendencies that led him to the Newgate scaffold in England one miserably wet morning in November 1824.

As Henry reached the gibbet's platform 100,000 spectators, who had come to see the fabulous H. Fauntleroy convulse to death at the rope's end, removed their hats.

'Look,' said Fauntleroy happily to the hangman, 'notice. I pray you, the respect they show me.'

The executioner, Cheesy Cheshire, snapped back: 'Don't deceive yourself. They only uncover so that those at the back can get a better view.'

Thus the amorous banker, who had spent at least $1 million on a series of mistresses over a 10-year period, did not die happily after all.

Henry Fauntleroy was born the son of the manager of the Marsh and Company Bank in London. It was fortunate for the bank that Fauntleroy was an honest and capable manager, for the company's doddering owners left everything in his hands.

Henry was a clerk in the bank when his father died suddenly. Thus, because the 23-year-old man knew more about the banks operations than anyone else, including the owners, he was appointed to succeed his father.

And it seemed to be a wise appointment, for the bank's business boomed almost immediately. Indeed, Fauntleroy's first annual report had the ancient owners jumping in their wheel-chairs.

After that, deposits increased and so did dividends. But Henry remained the same unassuming gentleman living quietly with his mother in a small house adjoining the bank.

The year 1810 was something of a debacle for Henry Fauntleroy for in that year a firm that had borrowed $120,000 from the bank defaulted. Also Henry became the groom in a shotgun wedding.

It was the fault of the Royal Navy that Henry Fauntleroy went to the altar with Susannah Young, the sister of a naval lieutenant.

When Lieutenant Young heard that Susannah had been dishonored by the handsome banker he applied for and received compassionate leave. Then, threatening Fauntleroy with a good thrashing unless he did the right thing, he accompanied the reluctant groom right up to the altar rails.

Soon after the nuptials Fauntleroy abandoned his wife with an allowance of $4 a week, and, despite the sad state of the bank's affairs, set himself to the task of accumulating a string of mistresses.

Few of these women kept their posts for more than a month or two, but while the affairs lasted they lived in the lap of luxury.

And when their lover told them they were no longer needed their discretion was bought with the promise of an annuity from the bank's assets.

To keep the bank's owners happy Fauntleroy saw to it that each year their dividends rose. Not being aware that these dividends were being paid from capital, the owners were, of course, delighted.

The only drawback as far as Henry Fauntleroy was concerned was that the books required so much manipulation that he had to work from 6 am to 10 pm daily, thus drastically reducing the time available for his favorite hobby.

Henry Fauntleroy took up with Mary Bertram, a new and most expensive mistress, at about the time the depression that followed the Battle of Waterloo hit Britain and forced the Bank of England to stop all credit.

This was a bitter blow for Henry who had recently installed the beautiful Mary in a magnificent Brighton villa complete with extensive gardens and, so it was said, the biggest billiards room in all Europe.

And, apart from that initial outlay, Mary Bertram, determined to make hay while the sun shone, ran up bills that would have caused concern to men far wealthier than Henry Fauntleroy.

Although Fauntleroy realised he was getting more deeply involved in his financial defalcations he could not give up the lovely Mary Bertram.

The obvious solution to his problems was forgery.

At that time his bank's vaults were stuffed with government stock left there by clients for safekeeping. Thus one night when he was alone in the bank Fauntleroy selected a parcel of stock and then forged a power of attorney giving him the right to sell it.

But because the power of attorney required three signatures—the client's and two witnessing clerks'—the bank manager had to forge all the signatures himself in hands that (he hoped) were distinct.

Next morning Fauntleroy took the stock and the power of attorney to the Bank of England. The inspection of the document was cursory. The cash was then handed over. It was easy.

After that Henry Fauntleroy took a new lease of life. He dressed in the height of fashion, sported a fine carriage and pair and became the talk of Threadneedle Street.

Later, when his visits to the Bank of England with the usual parcel of stock and the forged power of attorney became regular, a bank official remarked that it was unusual for a man in his position to be his own messenger.

Fauntleroy laughed. He said he brought the stock along himself simply because he was in need of exercise.

10

The Old Bailey. Here Fauntleroy heard the black-capped judge sentence him to death by hanging.

But while it was a simple matter stealing parcels of stock and forging signatures, it was most difficult covering up these defalcations.

For instance, when a defrauded stock-holder's dividends became due Fauntleroy had to sell another parcel to pay those dividends.

And when a client died he had to sell yet another parcel to buy back sufficient bonds to satisfy the dead man's estate.

All this required titanic ledger manipulations. Thus Henry Fauntleroy often worked until the early hours of the morning gerrymandering the books, which he always kept in close custody.

11

Nevertheless, Henry Fauntleroy saw to it that his love life did not suffer unduly.

Finally getting rid of the lovely Mary Bertram with a suitable annuity paid from his bank's assets, Fauntleroy set his sights on a beautiful schoolgirl, the 15-year-old Maria Forbes.

Dazzled by the handsome banker's show of affluence the girl offered little resistance when he set out to seduce her.

Immediately after this criminal event Maria left school, was given a gift of $12,000 and was then set up in a mansion at South Lambeth.

Everything was going peacefully at South Lambeth when the rejected Mary Bertram decided a small annuity was not enough. She needed $20,000 for immediate expenses. If this was not forthcoming the business world would hear of her former lover's double life.

To raise the money Fauntleroy collected another parcel of stock from the bank's vault, forged the power of attorney and marched off to the Bank of England.

Then, just as an official was about to hand over the cash the stock's owner walked into the bank.

Quickly Fauntleroy grabbed the power of attorney from the clerk, said it had been incorrectly filled in promised to return with it in half an hour, and stuffed it into his pocket.

Then, after chatting amiably for a minute with the stock's real owner, he left the building.

But Fauntleroy's racket could not last forever. Indeed, the beginning of the end came one day in September 1824 when trustees of a deceased estate decided to reinvest $92,000 worth of government stock then held by Fauntleroy's bank.

But the money had long since been used bringing happiness to Henry Fauntleroy's long line of mistresses.

The banker tried his best to convince the trustees that it would be foolhardy to sell such gilt-edged stock, but they did not seem interested.

Indeed, he was still trying to drive his point home when one of the trustees, while on a visit to the Bank of England, discovered the stock had already been sold on a power of attorney produced by Henry Fauntleroy.

Soon after, a warrant was issued for the amorous thief's arrest and a police officer, Samuel Plank, was sent to the bank to bring him in.

But Fauntleroy was not there. Instead he was dallying with Maria Forbes, who by now was the mother of Fauntleroy's two illegitimate children.

Next morning when Fauntleroy returned to the bank Officer Plank was still waiting. In the manager's office Plank produced his warrant of arrest.

In desperation Fauntleroy opened a drawer in his desk, produced $20,000 in bank notes and offered it to Plank in return for a chance to escape.

An hour later Fauntleroy was in gaol and the clients of Marsh's Bank were in a state of shock.

While depositiors howled outside the bank demanding their money, Fauntleroy was hauled before an examining magistrate who had the mammoth task of unravelling the tangled web of Fauntleroy's and his bank's financial affairs.

Turning suddenly into a braggart, Fauntleroy happily gave details of his series of love affairs and told the magistrate he could accept his word that the bank's assets were $1,116,372 lower than they should be.

Soon after, the Old Bailey was packed to the rafters by leaders of London's society and financial institutions when Henry Fauntleroy was placed on trial.

After being sentenced to death Henry Fauntleroy was taken to Newgate Prison, where old friends had already hired a fine room for him.

Here, attended by a turnkey who acted as his valet. Fauntleroy entertained friends with the best foods and wines. Even some of his former lovers came to pay their last respects.

On the eve of his death Fauntleroy ate a fine pigeon pie baked specially for him by the tearful Maria Forbes.

Immediately after dinner a barber entered the condemned man's room and dressed his hair. Then his valet helped him dress in a quality suit.

It was not often that a corpse-elect had such a send-off for tens of thousands turned up to watch the life snuffed from the lecherous thief.

Then immediately his body had stopped convulsing the mighty crowd moved off and went about its business.

As a result the 18-year-old Joseph Harwood, who had been sentenced to death for being one of a gang who stole 50 cents, went to his end with only the executioner and a pair of officials to bid him farewell.

The Charms of Harriet Blackford

ONE evening during the Russian summer of 1872, the Grand Duke Nicholas was breakfasting in his bedchamber in his private wing of the family palace when a knock on the door sent him scurrying.

Grabbing his breakfast partner, a beautiful woman of 25 who was still dressed in her pyjamas, the Duke pulled her to the canopied bed, threw a quilt over her, drew the curtains and, looking as composed as was possible in the circumstances, opened the door.

The caller was the Duke's aged father, the Grand Duke Constantine, who brushed past his red-faced son, marched up to the bed, jerked the curtains aside, threw back the quilt and closely inspected the quaking young woman lying in a tangle of silks and satins.

Then, chuckling happily, Constantine moved to the door, bade his son "good morning" and strolled off down the hallway.

Thus was Harriet Blackford, the courtesan from Philadelphia, introduced to Russian high society.

Although when Harriet, a professional courtesan, first came to Russia she had set her hopes on snaring wealthy and noble lovers, she had never dreamed she would catch a fish as wealthy or as noble as the young Grand Duke Nicholas.

And not only did she quickly inveigle her way into the Duke's bedchamber, but in later years, Nicholas, for love of the beautiful American, was to defy the Czar and forfeit any claim he or his heirs might have to the throne of Russia.

Harriet Blackford, the first American to win fame as a courtesan, was born in Philadelphia in 1847, the daughter of a struggling clergyman.

Following her father's death in 1863, Harriet and her mother were reduced to abject poverty, a condition, Harriet vowed, she would rectify at the first opportunity.

Then one day when Harriet and her mother were travelling by train to Parkersburg to visit sympathetic relatives, Harriet got into conversation with a struggling telegraphist, Calvin Blackford.

Blackford was scarcely a good catch but to Harriet he was better than.

nothing. As a result she swamped him with affection and on the return journey the pair left the train to be married.

A year later Mrs. Blackford became a widow when her husband succumbed to a combination of tuberculosis and alcohol.

Harriet's mother did not see her daughter for almost a year after Blackford's death. But she did hear stories that the young woman was plying the harlot's trade on riverboats.

Her mother refused to believe the stories and continued to defend her daughter's reputation even when Harriet returned to Philadelphia with trunks filled with Paris gowns and moved into a mansion in Rittenhouse Square.

In time Harriet Blackford's establishment became recognised as little more

With one exception all Harriet Blackford's lovers took her for what she was—a courtesan. The exception was a Russian grand duke, determined to marry her.

than a brothel for some of the city's wealthiest citizens.

In 1867 one of Harriet's clients suggested she should try her luck in France where beautiful women of her profession had little trouble winning the patronage of men of wealth and position.

Harriet could not get to Paris quickly enough. And the decision paid dividends for she soon found that the novelty of being an American courtesan made her a sensation.

After passing through the hands of some minor dignitaries, Harriet Blackford graduated to the bedchamber of the Duke of Bodenbach.

A German who spent much of his time enjoying the fleshpots of Paris, Bodenbach was always in the market for unusual entertainment. And an American of easy virtue was most unusual.

Czar Alexander II did not approve of foreign courtesans and did everything in his power to tear the Grand Duke Nicholas away from the wanton American woman.

The Duke paid Harriet well for her favors but when he decided to return home he squared his account by leaving her what he thought was an almost worthless parcel of shares.

Convinced she had been gypped, Harriet was on the verge of throwing the share certificates away when she discovered some of the stock was in an American oil well that had just hit a gusher.

Selling the shares, Harriet bought a luxurious house on a fashionable Parisian street, filled it with expensive furniture and announced she was open for business by inviting some of the city's more wealthy rakes to visit her.

And apart from these private visits from admirers she also organised soirees which were attended by celebrities like Prince Jerome Bonaparte and Alexandre Dumas.

Then in 1870 the outbreak of the Franco-Prussian war brought a sudden end to the sensuality in which Paris had wallowed for so long.

When the Germans began the terrible siege of the city, Harriet and most of the citizens were reduced to eating dogs and sewer rats.

Finally, with the lifting of the siege, those who could afford it abandoned the city to its misery and fled to other parts of Europe where they hoped to resume their old way of life.

Harriet Blackford, who had been the mistress of several Russians, decided to try to re-establish herself in St. Petersburg, the home city of some of her former patrons.

For a time her chief support was old Prince Golitsyn who went to great pains to see his American mistress met no man under the age of 60. But he did allow her to again live a life of luxury.

Harriet Blackford was planning ways of meeting new and younger lovers when she was visited by Count Shuvalov, a high officer of Russia's secret police.

Shuvalov had an ultimatum. Unless the American would do a little spying by unearthing subversion among members of the nobility she would receive an official order to leave the country.

But because spying was not Harriet's line of business she refused. Thus, for the rest of her period in Russia, the American was constantly under the eye of the secret police.

At Christmas 1873, Harriet attended a ball which was graced by the presence of the Grand Duke Nicholas, nephew of Czar Alexander II—a monarch who had no time for foreign courtesans.

Fascinated by the American, whose reputation had preceded her, Nicholas danced all evening with her then insisted on esorting her back to her hotel after the ball.

At dawn, just before the Grand Duke left his new mistress and returned to his family castle, he made Harriet sign an unusual document.

In the document the lovely American agreed not to see or speak to another man without the permission of her "master"—the Grand Duke Nicholas.

After that Nicholas never moved without Harriet Blackford by his side.

17

Nor did the outraged Czar's anger have any effect on his ardour.

Even when necessity forced him to stay at the family palace he always moved, with the notorious courtesan, into the wing reserved for his use.

And it was there that Nicholas's father, the Grand Duke Constantine, once discovered his son's new lover hiding under a quilt.

A more tolerant man than the Czar, Constantine's only reaction was to nod approvingly at the young woman's beauty and stroll off down the hallway chuckling.

In the summer of 1874 when Nicholas went on exercises with the army, he sought some way of taking Harriet with him.

In the end he solved the problem by dressing her in male clothing and taking her along as his personal messenger boy.

When the army manoeuvres ended Nicholas set off on a tour of Europe with Harriet. In Italy he persuaded the American courtesan to pose for a nude statue in marble then had the piece sent back to St. Petersburg.

It was while the pair were enjoying the delights of Italy that news arrived that the Khan of Khiva had risen up against his Russian masters. At once Nicholas was called to the colours.

Before leaving for the campaign that finally brought the Khan to his kness, Nicholas arranged for Harriet to return to Paris and wait there until the war's end.

Then when the last shot had been fired the lovers rushed to Samara where their reunion celebrations dragged on for weeks.

Finally, blinded by love, Nicholas sent a message to the Czar asking for permission to marry Harriet Blackford. But all that happened was that Alexander flew into a towering rage.

He told Nicholas by messenger that under no circumstances must he marry the American harlot. Then, relenting a little, he added that he would have no objection to his nephew continuing to use her as his mistress.

Desperate now, Nicholas fled with Harriet to Vienna where they instructed a clergyman to marry them. The clergyman's reaction was to report the request to the Russian Embassy.

Soon after, Nicholas's father arrived in Vienna with a message from the Czar. Nicholas must return unmarried to Russia immediately. Then six months later Alexander would reconsider the question of marriage. So Harriet and Nicholas returned to St. Petersburg.

Now Alexander's plot to break up the romance thickened. Harriet was arrested by the Russian secret police and lodged in gaol until she agreed to hand over her private papers which she had left in the care of the US Ambassador.

Immediately she wrote the authorisation to collect the papers, she was put on a train to Paris and told never again to cross Russia's borders.

After that the Czar arranged for a group of doctors to declare Nicholas insane. He was then put under restraint.

Fretting for her lover in Paris, the almost-penniless Harriet tried to earn some money by publishing her memoirs. But before they could be put on

18

sale French authorities succumbed to Russian pressure and banned them.

Not long after, Harriet Blackford was told she was no longer welcome in France. As a result she packed what was left of her possessions and crossed the border into Italy.

But her troubles were not over. Unprepared for trouble with Russia, the Italian Government saw to it that a passage to America was booked for her on the first available ship.

Just 11 years later, when the scandal of the Grand Duke and the courtesan had been forgotten, Harriet Blackford returned quietly to Europe and settled at Nice.

There in 1885, her once-beautiful body emaciated by tuberculosis, the tragic odyssey of Harriet Blackford came to an end. She was 38.

Just 32 years later, in January 1918, the Grand Duke Nicholas lay dying in his palace at Tashkent, Turkestan. For days he just stared at the marble statue of a beautiful nude woman in the corridor outside his bedchamber.

And he was still staring when he drew his last breath.

Hare's Harem

ONE day late in 1825 the schooner Hippomenes dropped anchor off one of the islands in the Cocos group to discharge the strangest bunch of migrants ever to sail the Indian Ocean.

First ashore was the group's leader, the handsome, swashbuckling, London-born go-getter and despot, Alexander Hare. He was followed by scores of slaves who had been tricked into believing that they were the legal property of the Englishman.

Finally the ship's boat brought ashore the piece de resistance—Hare's 80-strong harem that included a hand-picked selection of the beauties of many countries of the East.

There were strongly-built Zulu girls, slender Chinese, giggling belles from Bali, elf-like beauties from Sumatra and even child-like concubines from Papua.

Now Hare, ensconced in his island paradise, was at last free to enjoy the delights of his harem without interference from the various island authorities who regarded him as nothing more than a lecherous thief.

But the venture did not work out quite as Alexander Hare expected. Other men with an eye for beauty began raiding his stronghold and carrying off the women until in the end not one remained.

Alexander Hare, one of the most remarkable rogues in the history of the Indian Ocean, was born in London in the late 1780s, the son of a wealthy watchmaker.

Unlike his three younger brothers who lived a life of suburban respectability, Alexander revolted against family discipline and went out of his way to disgrace his religious-minded father.

The young and handsome Hare first showed signs of the sensuality that was to dominate his later life when, in his mid-teens, he won a reputation as a roue.

When his family made it obvious he would be more appreciated out of England, he joined the East India Company and sailed to Calcutta as its representative.

Later, still representing the company, he moved on to Malacca where, without the restraint of conservative English companions, he was able to indulge his eccentricities to the full.

Dressed in strange regalia, Hare took to visiting the market places accompanied by a major domo who entered the purchases in a book as his master bought up an assortment of attractive slave girls.

Meanwhile, as Hare selected the nucleus of his harem, a British expedition was busy annexing Java. When the fighting ended the Sultan of Banjarmassem in Borneo asked for a British resident to be attached to his kingdom. Hare got the job.

Delighted with the handsome Englishman, the Sultan gave him a grant of land and an open order to select 200 slaves. The Englishman did the selecting himself. Practically all were young and attractive girls.

With the power to impose taxes, regulate customs duties and create

Prison Island in the Cocos group where Hare built a stockade to defend himself from the robbers who swooped on his harem beauties.

monopolies, Alexander Hare went enthusiastically to work building up his personal assets.

Sending the East India Company only a fraction of the money he collected, Hare used every wile he knew to exploit foreign businessmen and local potentates.

Nevertheless he did create a facade of honesty by undertaking some public works like improved harbour facilities at Banjarmassem.

But before the harbour works could get under way Hare needed a competent man to supervise the project. And that was when he met John Clunies-Ross, skipper of the government ship, Olivia, which was then being used as a patrol boat.

At Hare's invitation Clunies-Ross not only took over the harbour works,

21

but built a 400-ton vessel, the Borneo, which he and Hare jointly operated in the lucrative spice trade.

The trading enterprise prospered. And with this income added to his more dishonest activities, Alexander Hare found himself a wealthy man.

But even as Hare was counting his ever-increasing fortune, directors of the East India Company were trying to ascertain why their income from Banjarmassem had fallen so sharply.

Finally the company sent investigators to check on its representative's business activities. And at the same time the British Government was wondering how Alexander Hare could possibly use so many female slaves for household duties.

Hare knew he had reached the end of his reign in Banjarmassem. He loaded a ship with some household effects and the pick of his harem and set out for Java, since returned to the Dutch after five years of British rule.

The Dutch, Hare soon found out, were more understanding. They were not concerned if an Englishman wanted to establish a harem and thus he was able to buy new inmates in any quantity he wished.

But if Alexander Hare's domestic life was satisfactory, his business enterprises were not. Indeed, the spice trade to Cape Town in South Africa fell off so alarmingly that he determined to sail to South Africa and investigate that end of the business.

Resolving that he would not arrive friendless in a strange country, Hare decided to take his harem with him. The only trouble was that the British authorities insisted the members of the harem should receive emancipation certificates.

Hare had no intention of emancipating the beauties who would probably flee immediately they received the documents, so he devised a plan.

Packing his dusky belles aboard the Borneo, he sailed to Bencoolen, a port in Java, and read the emancipation documents to them. The girls could not read so their master had to interpret.

The receipt of these documents, they heard, would make them and their children their master's property for life.

After that it was a simple matter to coerce the girls into making their marks on the documents.

Hare and his girls caused quite a furore when they arrived in Cape Town. Indeed, some citizens organised protest meetings at which motions were carried demanding the sensualist's expulsion from the colony.

To add to his worries he received a bundle of letters from English business houses asking him to return home at once so that he might help clear up a number of financial irregularities that had been worrying them since his sudden departure years earlier.

By now Hare was tired of financial affairs. He just wanted to be left alone to enjoy his harem. The only solution to this problem, he decided, was some idyllic and deserted island which he could build into a private kingdom.

In 1825 Hare returned to the East and immediately chartered the Hippomenes, a vessel commanded by Robert, John Clunies-Ross's younger

Balinese beauties. Bali was one of the islands from which Alexander Hare recruited his harem of 80 slave girls.

brother.

Although Hare intended setting up his love kingdom on Christmas Island, he refused to nominate their destination to Clunies-Ross until they were well at sea.

Clunies-Ross might have completed the voyage had not members of the crew decided that no one man could possibly find use for so many beauties.

The result was a near mutiny that decided Clunies-Ross to land his passengers on Direction Island in the Cocos group.

It was an odd court that the king of the Cocos led ashore—the 80 girls of the harem, about 20 male slaves, a handful of harem attendants and a small group of Oriental musicians.

At once the group set to work building a harem and living quarters for the king and his male subjects. When all was finished the male slaves set to work catching fish, picking bananas, killing wild pigs and extracting oil from coconuts.

Alexander Hare left the harem on occasions to make sure his workers were not slacking.

Meanwhile, John Clunies-Ross had been looking for a suitable island where he could store spices and other tropical products pending a price rise for these commodities in Europe.

Thus in 1827 Clunies-Ross with his wife, children and a group of European and Asiatic sailors landed on Home Island in the Cocos.

Not having seen his brother Robert in the meantime, Clunies-Ross got the shock of his life when he found Hare already established on nearby Direction Island.

Almost immediately Clunies-Ross's sailors were beset by overpowering temptations.

They were completely without female companionship while the Englishman on the adjoining island had so many concubines he could not possibly have use for all of them.

The inevitable happened quickly. Clunies-Ross's sailors, under cover of darkness, covered the distance between the two islands, grabbed a girl or two, then returned with the prizes to Home Island.

Indeed, some of the sailors were so anxious to fill the void in their lives that they actually swam to Direction Island, returning to their base with one of Hare's concubines in tow.

To protect his valuable property from the raiders, Hare built a stockade around the harem and set watches by day and night. This reduced the number of kidnappings to a mere trickle.

Hare imposed rigid restrictions on the female members of his kingdom.

When children were born, for instance, they were taken from their mothers. The boys were confined until they were old enough to work while any girl who showed potential beauty was returned to the harem and allowed to develop.

Finally with his harem dwindling rapidly under renewed onslaughts from Home Island, Hare decided to move his headquarters to another Island.

This time he selected the island of Pulu Bras, now known as Prison Island, and as speedily as possible moved the 40 wives that remained to a stockade he had built on his new domain.

But actually his move had played right into the raiders' hands for at low tide it was possible to wade from Home Island to Pulu Bras.

One by one the girls disappeared. But what was worse, those who remained seemed intrigued by the thought of becoming the mistress of a man other than Alexander Hare.

Hare tried to pacify the raiders with gifts of rum and pork. They took the gifts, but then returned later for the more acceptable gifts that waited behind the stockade.

In the end Hare wrote to Clunies-Ross: "Dear Ross: I thought that when I sent rum and pork to your sailors that they would stay away."

Standing on his island, Clunies-Ross roared across the water to Hare: "Don't you know that rum and roast pig are not a sailor's sole idea of heaven."

Alexander Hare's paradise began falling to pieces one night in 1835 when all his male slaves deserted to the enemy.

The following night they returned, bound their former master hand and foot, and took the last few inmates of the harem back to Home Island with them.

Unaccustomed to the life of a bachelor, Hare stayed on for only a few weeks before sailing for Batavia where he knew pretty girls could be had for the asking.

It took time, but in the years that followed Hare managed to restore his financial position and re-establish a harem.

He was still one of Batavia's best-known, if most despised residents, when he died leaving scores of dusky-skinned descendants from one end of the East to the other. Today his great-grandchildren can probably be numbered in the thousands.

Prince William's Notorious Actress

ONCE when the famous actress Dorothy Jordan was touring the English provincial towns she received a plaintive note from her royal lover, the Duke of Clarence, asking her to accept a large reduction in the annual allowance he made her.

Dorothy replied briefly by sending him a strip of paper torn off the bottom of a play-bill. It read: "Absolutely no money returned after the rising of the curtain."

In fact Dorothy might have retorted that it was she who chiefly financed the household where she, Duke William and their illegitimate brood lived in what one contemporary called "a snug hodge-podge of debts, domesticity and scandal".

Few stars in Drury Lane history earned more than Dorothy Jordan, the "glorious child of nature with a voice like the twang of Cupid's bow".

However, her admirers had to accept the fact that regularly once a year an "indisposition" compelled her to disappear from the stage for several months.

Ten times this happened, until 10 small royal bastards had romped through the nursery at Bushy Park—including the ancestors of many noble families decorating the pages of Debrett's Peerage today.

All the ducal sons of old, half-mad, half-blind King George III had mistresses but none aroused a greater mixture of public derision and adulation than the fair Dorothy Jordan.

Byron called her "an exquisite being". Sir Joshua Reynolds, who painted her, said she "ran upon the stage as a playground in the sheer wildness of delight".

She was also the target of savage caricatures, ballads and some of the most lurid stories in the scurrilous, uninhibited newspapers of the time.

Her end, anyway, must have satisfied the moralists for she died in lonely misery, forgotten even by the family she had reared.

The daughter of an obscure Irish actress known as Grace Phillips or Mrs Frances, Dorothy was born near Waterford in Ireland in 1762.

In later life she fostered a romantic tale that her father was a dashing army captain. More probably he was a stage hand named Bland at Dublin's Smock Alley Theatre.

Dorothy herself was a plump, pretty and precocious girl of 15 when she made her debut on the boards in Dublin.

Almost inevitably she was soon seduced by the manager, Richard Daly, a notorious lecher who specialised in lending young actresses money and then demanding repayment on other terms than cash.

Dorothy bore him at least one child before she determined to escape his clutches by running off to seek her fortune in England.

Early in 1782, penniless and hungry, she arrived in the Yorkshire town of Leeds and begged for a job with a touring theatrical company then playing there.

"What can you do—comedy, tragedy or opera"? the manager asked her. "All of them", said Dorothy in desperation.

She was hired at half a guinea a week and for the next three years, now calling herself Mrs Dorothy Jordan, she toured the north of England acquiring a considerable local reputation especially in frivolous comedy roles.

When Daly, having heard of her success, threatened to sue her for $500 he claimed to have lent her, Dorothy was no longer the innocent girl of her Dublin days.

She speedily found a protector, a rich brewer who was glad to pay Daly off in exchange for a monopoly of the beautiful actress's favors.

However, the generous brewer did not enjoy his bargain for long. Within a year Dorothy was in London and signing a contract with the most famous theatre in England.

Sarah Siddons, the stately reigning tragedy queen, regarded the provincial newcomer with supreme contempt. But the shrewd lessees of Drury Lane knew what they were doing.

From the moment of her first appearance in The Country Girl on 18 October 1785, Dorothy Jordan's triumph on the comedy stage was never in doubt.

She was hailed as the most sparkling and bewitching star since Kitty Clive. A year later she was earning $60 a week, almost as much as the divine Sarah Siddons herself.

She had lovers for the taking before she finally settled on Sir Richard Ford, the wealthy son of King George's court physician, an ardent fan of the theatre and pursuer of pretty actresses.

Her decision may have been influenced by the fact that Ford held a mortgage of $60,000 over Drury Lane and it was thus unwise to repel his advances.

Despite all temptations from suitors of more exalted rank she remained faithful to Ford for five years, during which she bore him four children at regular intervals.

This maternal instinct distinguished Dorothy Jordan from many of the other courtesans of history, few of whom cared to encumber their liaisons with the cares of the nursery.

Mrs. Dorothy Jordan.

During her career Dorothy was blessed by at least 16 known offspring, including 10 by the royal Prince William who appeared in her life for the first time in the summer of 1791.

William, the third son of George III, had recently been created Duke of Clarence and been given an establishment of his own when he laid eyes on the fascinating actress.

The future King William IV was three years Dorothy's junior. He was a portly, ruddy-faced young man who had served in the navy and acquired a large stock of naval oaths and a hearty roughness of manners.

Like his brothers he had been involved in many amorous scrapes, ranging from the daughter of a Spanish admiral to a "humorous strumpet" named Polly Finch from a London tavern.

By early in 1792 all London was buzzing with the news that the Duke of Clarence was laying siege to Mrs Jordan and trying to woo her away from the tenacious Sir Richard Ford.

Months later a newspaper satirically announced the royal victory: "We hear on the best authority that a certain illustrious Naval Officer has at length succeeded in passing the Ford that stood in his path."

According to one account Ford received a handsome present of cash and gold plate before agreeing to relinquish his delectable prize.

Dorothy's view of the transaction was not revealed. But by 1793 she was installed at Bushy Park, the duke's country retreat near Hampton Court on the Thames.

There she remained for 18 years, appearing regularly at Drury Lane each season and temporarily retiring with equal regularity to produce another pledge of her affection for her royal lover.

No one could cast a shadow of doubt on her fidelity. Even old King George growled that "William's actress" was a damned sight better than the disreputable mistresses of his other sons.

However, this did not stop the wits and gossip-mongers from spreading stories that grew in scurrility with the passing years.

Cartoonists depicted William docilely dragging a cart-load of children around the royal estate while Dorothy walked by his side studying her latest theatrical role.

Only a few of the duke's naval cronies and Dorothy's friends were invited to Bushy Park, where the parties were enlivened by gambling, deep drinking and impromptu performances by the stage visitors.

Dorothy was reputed to fine her lover a dram of rum every time he let loose a nautical oath. She also tried to stop him losing a large slice of his income over the card tables.

However, despite their disorderly and sometimes riotous household, both Dorothy and William were devoted parents and the increasing tribe of children were brought up with genuine affection.

The main problem was money, for not even the duke's allowance from parliament could meet his mounting debts and the cost of the army of servants, tutors and nurses at Bushy Park.

Several times Dorothy announced her retirement from Drury Lane only to be driven back to the stage by the pressing need for cash to pay the domestic bills.

Until the early 1800s she was still unchallenged as the most popular comedy actress in London and the theatre was crowded night after night with the fashionable world.

But age and child-bearing were catching up with her. Her once "deliciously rounded" figure coarsened and grew fat, though she stubbornly refused to play anything but girlish parts.

In 1804 when the customary announcement was made from the stage that Mrs Jordan was absent because of an "indisposition", the audience burst into hoots of derision.

Engagements at Drury Lane became fewer and Dorothy had to set off on long, exhausting provincial tours to help meet her lover's insatiable demands for money.

However, it was a dynastic crisis in 1811, when George III went permanently mad and the Prince of Wales became regent, that finally broke up the menage at Bushy Park.

The regent had only one child, Princess Charlotte, who died a few years later. None of his brothers showed any sign of producing a legitimate heir to the throne.

The Duke of Clarence seemed settled for life with Mrs Jordan. The Duke of Kent—later to father Queen Victoria—was also living with a mistress and the Duke of Sussex had married a commoner.

The Dukes of York and Cumberland were both childless. Only Charlotte stood between the House of Hanover and extinction unless the rest of the

Dorothy Jordan, her lover the Duke of Clarence, and the first three of their illegitimate brood of ten on their way to Bushy Park—Caricature by James Gillray.

royal dukes could produce more heirs.

William was the first to yield to government pressure and agreed to look for a suitable bride among the unattractive lot of German princesses available to him.

Dorothy was acting at Cheltenham when in December, 1811, she received a letter from the duke sorrowfully declaring that they must part forever.

The children, he assured her, would be well provided for and he had managed to extort from the regent a promise that she would be granted a generous pension.

Dorothy accepted her fate without rancor but her last five years were a tragic epilogue to her life as a royal mistress.

Battened on by a horde of greedy relatives, including the man who had wed her daughter by Richard Daly, she sank rapidly into debt and obscurity.

In 1814 she made her last stage appearance. A year later she fled to Paris to escape her creditors and settled in a dirty, dilapidated old house at Saint-Cloud.

There, "sighing upon a sofa", she remained, almost completely forgotten and waiting feverishly for some sign of reconciliation with her former lover.

On 3 July 1816, after sending for letters and being told there were none, she fell back on her pillows sobbing hysterically and died.

She was buried without a gravestone in the cemetery of Saint-Cloud, though for years afterwards rumours persisted that she was not dead but had returned to England under an assumed name.

One of her old friends claimed that he saw her wailing along Piccadilly and that she dropped a veil over her face and hurried on when he tried to accost her.

It was said she had come to London for one last glimpse of the Duke of Clarence before he was married off to his German princess in July 1818.

Mrs. Leveson:
Blackmailer,
Procurer
and Charlatan

M RS. Sarah Rachel Leveson's two daughters shed tears when their aged mother died in England's Woking Prison in 1880. But they were probably the only two people in the country who did.

Mrs. Leveson was not the type to attract affection. Completely without morals, she was willing to go to any length to fatten her already bloated bank account.

Blackmailer, procurer and charlatan, she wallowed in every evil that paid dividends.

But it was as a beauty treatment specialist that Mrs. Leveson is best remembered. Catering to vain, wealthy society women whose beauty was fast fading, she was able to sell them worthless treatments for thousands of pounds.

With her beauty business and its blackmail and procuring sidelines. Mrs. Leveson, or Madame Rachel as she was known, was able to enjoy an income far in excess of $40,000 a year.

Then one day a blackmail victim turned against her tormentor. Legal action followed. It was the end of one of the most vicious charlatans England has known.

Sarah Rachel was born in a Manchester slum in 1811. Because she never attended school she was to spend the rest of her life plagued by illiteracy.

In her mid-teens she married a chemist's assistant and was able to get plentiful and cheap supplies of the cosmetics then available.

When her husband died, Sarah Rachel found she had inherited a little capital. Moving now to London she bought into a number of businesses which included a fish and chip shop.

Then in 1860 she married Leveson, a businessman of ample means.

It was not long after the wedding that Mrs. Leveson was afflicted by typhoid fever. When the disease had cleared she was without a hair on her head.

In desperation she tried a number of so-called hair restorers. She was using one which had been given to her by a physician when she noticed the hair sprouting again. Finally it returned to its full luxuriance.

Mrs. Leveson was not foolish enough to believe the lotion had restored her hair. But she did think her original desperate faith in its efficacy might have had something to do with it.

A section of London's New Bond Street where Madame Rachel opened her infamous beauty parlor.

So she reasoned that there must be thousands of other women who would put faith in any colored fluid attractively bottled.

Now calling herself Madame Rachel, she opened a beauty shop in Brighton where clients were subjected to various treatments, all guaranteed to restore beauty.

Everything went well until one client developed a facial rash and refused to pay the high bill. Madame Rachel sued for the money but lost the case and was later convicted of false pretences.

On her release from a short term in Whitecross Prison, Madame Rachel opened another beauty shop in London's New Bond Street.

Although beauty treatment was then regarded as the mark of street women, wealthy women were soon surreptitiously entering the shop to sample the wonders Madame offered.

Among her specialities was Magnetic Rock Dew Water, "fresh from the Sahara Desert and bought at enormous cost from the Sultan of Morocco."

The concoction was guaranteed to increase vital energies, restore the color of greying hair, and bring back youth.

Another speciality was the Royal Arabian Toilet of Beauty. This, Madame said, was an Eastern secret formula as administered to the Sultan of Turkey.

Clients could partake of this toilet for prices ranging from $200 to $2,000.

But the less wealthy clients were not neglected. They could have the Bridal Toilet Cabinets or the Venus Toilets for as little as from $50 to $200.

Madame also supplied a special face powder of a shade which is still known as Rachel.

Three years after opening in New Bond Street, Madame owned a luxurious house in Lennox Street, a carriage and a $800 a year box at the opera.

As a sideline she also took to stealing the jewellery clients left in the dressing room while taking an Arabian Bath.

When one victimised woman threatened to take action. Madame silenced her with: "How would you like your husband to know about the gentlemen who visit you here?"

Madame Rachel's beauty parlor lent itself ideally to blackmail activities, for her wealthy clients were anxious to keep secret their sinful indulgence in the search for beauty.

And there were others who found the parlor a convenient place to carry on clandestine love affairs, often with men who were introduced by Madame.

In September 1867, with her income soaring above $40,000 a year, Madame Rachel met a new client, Mrs. Mary Borradaile, the 54-year-old widow of an army colonel.

Realising at once that Mrs. Borradaile feared old age, Madame investigated the client's financial position. She had $10,000 capital and an army pension of $600 a year.

After assuring Mrs. Borradaile that she could make her look years younger, Madame put the woman through all her treatments. At the end of the first month the client had spent nearly $400 on Arbian Baths alone.

Inevitably the day came when Mrs. Borradaile had to admit that her finances were getting low. So Madame Rachel let her into a secret.

The beautician said that the wealthy peer, Lord Ranelagh, had fallen in love with Mrs. Borradaile and, subject to her regaining her lost beauty, wanted to marry her.

Lord Ranelagh, one of the more prominent victims of Madame Rachel's lust for money. He was supposed to have written passionate love letters to a woman he hardly knew.

But for family reasons the peer wished to carry on the courtship by correspondence and later marry by proxy. Mrs. Borradaile accepted the bait. She sold $2,000 worth of bonds and gave the lot to Madame for further treatment.

Then, with the assistance of Madame's two daughters, the office boy wrote out a series of love letters to Mrs. Borradaile. All were signed "Ranelagh."

The letters became so passionate that Mrs. Borradaile went on a trousseau shopping spree and spent several thousand pounds on articles ranging from linen to a new carriage.

Now Mrs. Borradaile had an extensive trousseau but no money to continue her beauty treatments. So Madame Rachel accepted her IOU for $3,200.

Soon after, Madame sued her client for the recovery of the $3,200. The woman could not pay and was placed in the debtors' prison.

She was released immediately she agreed to sign over her $600 a year army pension to the beauty parlor owner.

Spurred on by a relative, Mrs. Borradaile now called on Madame Rachel and demanded she hand over some of the trousseau that had been entrusted to her care.

It was then Madame said Lord Ranelagh knew nothing of the affair. She also concocted a story that Mrs. Borradaile had given her fortune to a lover named William whom she frequently met in her parlor.

Yet the threat did not deter Mrs. Borradaile. She took legal action. In August 1868 the beautician faced trial on charges of having obtained $1200 by false pretences and conspiring to defraud her former client of $6,000.

In the witness box Madame Rachel reiterated the fabricated story of the widow's paid lover William.

Lord Ranelagh was there too and had to contain his anger as his alleged love letters to Mrs. Borradaile were read to the court.

In one note the writer referred to Mrs. Borradaile's "pretty little feet with which she could kick her ugly old donkey."

Called to give evidence the peer denied he had written the letters and said he never had any intention of marrying the woman.

When, after a five hour retirement, the jury foreman announced no agreement could be reached Madame Rachel said loudly: 'Sensible men! If you send your wives to me I'll beautify them for nothing'.

But there was a second trial. This time the jury's wives got no free treatment offer. Madame Rachel got five years.

Released on parole after serving four years, she at once opened another beauty parlor in Duke Street. This time she called herself "The Arabian Perfumier to the Queen."

Soon business was booming as clients rushed to try her new rejuvenation lotion, Jordan Water.

Then in 1876 the bottom fell out of Madame Rachel's evil world. In that year Mrs Pearse, the wife of an unsuccessful stockbroker, ran short of money during a course of treatment.

But again the beautician had a solution to a client's problem. She suggested

Mrs. Pearse should leave her jewellery with her as security for further treatment.

As a result Mrs. Pearse gave the beautician some jewellery pieces. saying they were presents from her father, Mario, the once-famous opera singer who had fallen on hard times.

At once Madame suggested a private subscription fund should be opened to aid the old singer. She would ask her clients to contribute.

Shortly after Mrs. Pearse had deposited the first contributions in a bank, she told Madame Rachel that she could no longer afford to buy Jordan Water.

It was then the old charlatan quietly suggested she should draw the money from the subscription fund bank account.

Aroused to anger Mrs. Pearse told her husband the whole story. He at once visited the beauty shop and demanded the return of his wife's jewellery. Every piece had been pawned.

Madame Rachel threatened to expose, what she called, his wife's illicit love life if action was taken. But Pearse refused to believe her.

In April 1878 Madame Rachel heard an Old Bailey judge sentence her to five years gaol. She was still there two years later when she died.

During the trial one of the beautician's assistants gave evidence of mixing some of the famous beauty treatments.

Facial washes, she said, consisted of hydrochloric acid, water, fullers earth, starch and carbonate of lead.

The Arabian Bath was a mixture of a thin bran mash and water. Jordan Water was always fresh. It came from the backyard pump.

Hunt for a Husband

THE Duke of Hamilton took one look at the ravishingly beautiful Elizabeth Gunning and at midnight, just 40 hours later, dragged the 17-year-old Irish redhead off to London's Mayfair Chapel where he married her.

Indeed it was all done with such haste that the nobleman could not find time even to buy a wedding ring. So he used a brass bed curtain hoop instead.

When news of the nuptials seeped into the clubs and salons, a great wail of despair rose from the throats of a thousand young blades all of whom had been madly in love with the beauteous Elizabeth.

Their one consolation was that her even more gorgeous sister Maria was still fancy free and still prowling exclusive circles in search of a husband.

Then just a fortnight later when Maria Gunning was still being followed all over London by crowds of lovelorn swains, their quest came to an abrupt end. She married the Earl of Coventry.

Which was not bad for a couple of teenagers who, just four years earlier, had been living in near poverty in the ramshackle old Castle Coote in Ireland's County Roscommon.

Their father John Gunning was a squire and an alcoholic rake who interrupted his whisky guzzling and milkmaid-chasing only to indulge in a little fox hunting.

But the girls' mother Bridget was of different mettle. The daughter of Viscount Mayo, she was fascinated by her two daughters' rapidly-developing

Maria Gunning was regarded as the most gorgeous of the two fabulous sisters. Although completely scatter-brained and amoral she was able to hold King George II in the hollow of her hand.

beauty even when they were children and dedicated herself to capitalising on this asset.

And she succeeded so well that practically every young (and old) male in Britain fell desperately in love with them. King George II himself vied for their attention with the noblemen of his court.

Never has England had to contend with such a bizarre social upheaval as that caused by the fabulous Gunning sisters; the dazzling Elizabeth and the even more breath-taking Maria.

Maria was born on her father's decaying property of Castle Coote in 1734, Elizabeth a year later.

Although Bridget Gunning had four other children—three daughters and a son—none ever possessed anything like the ethereal good looks of Maria and Elizabeth.

In 1748 when Maria and Elizabeth were 13 and 14 respectively, Bridget decided to abandon her husband to his whisky and milkmaids and move with her children to a comfortable house in Dublin's Britain Street.

It was inevitable that the creditors would catch up with her for Bridget had practically no income. Thus when they began threatening legal action she appealed to her brother Viscount Mayo for financial help.

His lordship offered no money, only advice. Bridget should go back to her husband, he said.

It was not long after this reverse that fate, in the form of the bailiffs and the actress Anne Bellamy, came to the aid of the destitute Gunning family.

The bailiffs were in the process of evicting the family and their furniture when Anne Bellamy rode past in her carriage. Attracted by the children's wails, she stopped the vehicle and crossed the street to the house.

Her eyes alighted at once on the incredible beauty of the weeping Maria and Elizabeth.

After hearing Mrs Gunning's tale of woe and of her expectations of money from her noble brother Anne Bellamy moved the entire family into her own house.

For weeks on end the actress spent hours daily teaching the two lovely sisters the arts of make-up, dressing and deportment. Then she went off on a stage tour of England leaving the Gunnings destitute again.

Came the evening in 1751 when Maria and Elizabeth, armed with a letter of introduction left them by Anne Bellamy, walked into a Dublin theatre and asked for the play's star, the famous and notorious Peg Woffington.

Peg Woffington read the letter from her fellow actress then carefully studied the two girls. Like everyone else she was astounded by their loveliness. Yet she advised them against a stage career.

Next day Miss Woffington called on Bridget Gunning. "Get the girls to London," she advised, "and half the peerage of the city will be fighting duels over them."

But first Maria and Elizabeth had to break into Dublin society. Peg Woffington footed the bill for this and arranged for them to be presented to the Lord-Lieutenant of Ireland.

And the actress carefully studied the reaction of the young bloods when they first faced the dazzling sisters. She knew then she was right about the English peerage fighting duels over them.

When Anne Bellamy returned to Dublin she and Peg Woffington contributed enough money to get Mrs Gunning and her two daughters to London. The other children were sent back to their father.

By the time the Gunnings' ship pulled into Liverpool Maria and Elizabeth's reputation had preceded them. Thus a large crowd packed the dock to get a glimpse of the famed Irish beauties.

And when they entered the London coach, male passengers had to alight and clear a way through the crowd with their swords so the horses could proceed.

The summer season of 1751 was overwhelming for Maria and Elizabeth as hostesses fought for the honour of having them grace their salons.

At night crowds of men congregated outside their hotel roaring out pleas for the girls to show themselves just once more on their balcony.

At the same time there were those who condemned the sisters as fortune hunters and who labelled them "the beautiful Irish paupers".

Some newspapers published derogatory cartoons and one editor was forced into a duel because he criticised "an indecently low" dress worn by Maria.

One who probably would have been willing to duel with the editor was King George II who was constantly inviting the sisters to his palaces so that he could once more feast his eyes on them.

Then on 12 February 1752, the spendthrift, grog-loving Duke of Hamilton saw Elizabeth Gunning for the first time.

It is said that on the night of that meeting the duke lost $2,000 at cards through "paying violent court to Elizabeth at one end of the room while supposed to be playing faro at the other".

They were married in such a hurry that the wedding ring consisted of a small brass hoop taken from the duke's bed curtains.

A fortnight later the even lovelier, but scatter-brained, Maria led the Earl of Coventry to the altar in one of the most spectacular weddings London had seen for years.

Actually Maria was so stupidly tactless that the king could not restrain himself from repeating the story of how he had asked her at a masquerade ball if she enjoyed such functions.

Maria said: "No. They bore me. What I would really like to see is a coronation." It never entered her head that a prequisite for such a ceremony was the death of the man to whom she was talking.

Not content with her position as the Countess of Coventry, Maria began a series of clandestine affairs with such noble and royal lovers as Lord Bolingbroke and Frederick, Prince of Wales.

And if that was not hard enough on her husband she spent his money with reckless abandon, running up bills for $34,000 in one year for jewellery

The Duke of Hamilton was in such a hurry to marry the lovely 17-year-old Elizabeth Gunning that, not having time to buy a ring, he used a brass curtain hoop.

and clothes alone.

Among the countess's many complaints was the staring crowds who followed her when she took the air in the parks.

George said: "If necessary I will devote the entire British Army to protect the most beautiful woman in the land."

The result was that when she took the air after that incident she was always accompanied by six soldiers marching ahead to push aside the crowd while another 12 with two sergeants followed close behind.

And all the time the countess became increasingly obsessed with her own beauty. Indeed the walls in her London mansion were practically covered with mirrors and so were the interiors of her coaches.

In Paris, during one of her visits, a doctor warned her against the excessive use of cosmetics which at that time contained white-lead.

The gorgeous countess ignored the advice but soon after her return to London she was afflicted by a ghastly skin disease. And tuberculosis was also diagnosed.

When visitors called she ordered the curtains of her bedroom drawn and all lights extinguished so that her disfigured face could not be seen.

Later, when her face really was repulsive to look on, she had curtains pulled right across the bed leaving only her hands visible. She died on 1 October 1760, at the age of 26.

Meanwhile in 1759 Elizabeth had become a widow leaving her old suitors to renew their love assaults on her. But she quickly made it obvious that no one below the rank of duke need apply for her hand.

For a time she was engaged to the wealthy but plain and dumpy Duke of Bridgewater. She cast him aside for the handsome Duke of Argyll and married him on 3 March 1759.

Already the mother of two sons who became Dukes of Hamilton and a daughter who became the Countess of Derby, Elizabeth had two more sons who became Dukes of Argyll.

Elizabeth's beauty never seemed to fade. Indeed in her late 40s when she made a quick visit to York more than 700 people sat up all night just to catch a glimpse of her next morning as she left the inn at which she stayed.

Yet this almost angelic beauty hid a tough character that often set admirers back on their heels.

During the Wilkes riots in London in March 1768 she leaned from a first floor window and hurled a barrage of gutter-like curses and insults at a mob below trying to break into her house.

Just a year earlier the famous Douglas Case was heard to determine the legitimacy of a claimant to the estate of the Duke of Douglas.

The claimant won his case. Had he lost, the estate would have gone to the Duchess of Argyll's son.

During the hearing Elizabeth suggested to a nobleman that he should go into the witness box and give false evidence for her son.

The nobleman looked startled for a moment. Then he said: "Madam, you are very handsome. Old as I am I would be very happy to be wicked with you. But I will not be wicked for you."

When Elizabeth, the last of the famed Gunning sisters, died in her ducat mansion in Argyllshire in 1790, she was a baroness in her own right. It surprised no one that she left the then enormous estate of more than $2 million.

Ada Everleigh

The Wages of Sin

I N February 1902 the United States received a semi-official goodwill visit from the distinguished Prince Henry of Prussia, brother of the German ruler Kaiser Wilhelm II.

A crowd of reporters greeting him on his arrival in New York asked him all the usual questions including what places in America he particularly wanted to visit.

To this question they received a most unusual answer. The Prince said: "Above all else in America, I would like to see the Everleigh Club in Chicago."

Diplomatically the reporters did not mention the Prince's wish in their accounts of his arrival for the Everleigh Club was, as one social historian had aptly termed it, "a house of ill—but very great—fame".

For just on 12 years at the beginning of the century Chicago's Everleigh Club was the most notorious, most luxurious and most consistently profitable bordello in the U.S.

Even European visitors marvelled at its gaudy splendour for it eclipsed anything to be found in Paris and, as Prince Henry's interest proved, was an internationally renowned resort.

The Everleigh Club was a glittering palace of sin with furnishings that cost $250,000 and a retinue of 30 beautiful and ladylike hostesses whose favours were priced from $50 upwards.

And over it all presided the two most famous madams in American history, Ada and Minna Everleigh.

For them the wages of sin were luxurious retirement while still in their 30s with a fortune of well over $1 million.

Their real name was Lester and they were the daughters of a prosperous Kentucky lawyer.

Ada was born in February 1876 and Minna in July 1878. Both girls received the typical finishing-school education of well-brought-up Southern gentlewomen.

In 1896 the sisters married two brothers in their home town but both marriages broke up within a year and neither married again.

Their husbands, the girls said afterwards, were "brutes". They claimed they were "cruel, suspicious and jealous".

The younger sister, Minna, was a blue-eyed red-head and always the stronger and more ambitious character. Ada was a quietly-spoken brunette who worshipped Minna.

After leaving their husbands the girls were reunited and tried stage careers with small-time travelling drama companies.

By early 1898 they were in Omaha, a rip-roaring western city where a mammoth Trans-Mississippi Exposition was soon to open and was expected to draw big crowds.

In their travels Ada and Minna had repeatedly heard of fortunes being made in the vice trade and so with $35,000 they had inherited from their father they decided to open a brothel in Omaha to cash in on the visitors.

Neither of the sisters had any experience of the business of prostitution and in fact had never even entered a bawdy house.

But they were shrewd and businesslike and knew how necessary it was to grease the right political palms so they could operate such an establishment without police hindrance.

To protect their family they changed their name to Everleigh which was inspired by an elderly aunt who always signed her letters "Everly Yours".

The Everleigh brothel in Omaha was well-conducted with the best of food and wines available as well as the services of an attractive bevy of harlots.

Free-spending males attending the exposition soon found their way to the love bowers of these girls and cheerfully paid the two madams the high fees they demanded.

Raid on a Chicago bawdy house. Until 1910 the police ignored the activities of the Everleigh Club.

By the time the exposition closed Ada and Minna Everleigh had increased their capital to $75,000 and decided to move on to bigger things in Chicago.

At 2131 South Dearborn Street, they found a 50-room mansion that had been built in 1890 at a cost of $125,000 and had always operated as a brothel.

The incumbent madam, Effie Hankins, wished to retire and she offered the huge seraglio to the Everleigh sisters for a mere $25,000, a sum that included the furnishings, the girls on the premises and a longterm lease at a rental of $500 a month.

Ada and Minna Everleigh at once put themselves heavily in debt to re-furnish elegantly from top to bottom.

Indeed during their sojourn at Dearborn Street they spent more than $250,000 to create an opulent bordello that made even the most luxurious rival establishments seem squalid hovels by comparison.

Newcomers were astounded by the magnificence of the Everleigh brothel with its curtains and hangings of golden silk, great divans and easy chairs upholstered in silk damask, thick oriental rugs and carpets and the 20 gold-plated spitoons worth $650 each.

The Everleigh Club, as the sisters called it, opened on 1 February 1906, and despite freezing weather grossed $1,000 in takings for the evening.

Later, as it became better known, there were occasions when the brothel customers paid out $5,000 in a night but the average was about $2,000.

Beer and spirits were barred in the club but wine was freely available at $15 a bottle.

Clients could dine on the premises and drink as much champagne as they liked for a down payment of $50. Feminine company cost extra.

Visitors were met in the foyer by Minna Everleigh who always wore a trailing gown of silk and was weighed down with jewellery.

She considered herself undressed unless she had on her diamond collar, half a dozen bracelets, a ring on each finger and a great stomacher of diamonds, emeralds and rubies.

On the ground floor there was a picture gallery, a library, a music room, a ballroom and a dining room seating 50.

Above on the first floor were a dozen elegant parlours where clients were introduced to the girls available and could sit and converse while drinking.

The inmates were given firm orders about impolite language, trying to cheat and rob customers and over-indulgence in drink.

From the first floor twin mahogany stairways swept upwards to the bed-rooms where the atmosphere, it was said, was of "refined hush, broken only by soft music and the faint splash of perfumed fountains".

The girls of the Everleigh Club were carefully chosen and this was Ada's department.

"A girl must have worked somewhere else before coming here," she was quoted as saying in 1910.

"We do not like amateurs. Inexperienced girls and young widows are too prone to accept offers of marriage and leave."

48

Other requirements were "a good face and figure, perfect health and ability to act like a lady".

The basic fee for an interlude of love at the Everleigh Club was $50. Half of this was retained by the courtesans who were taught how to flatter and persuade clients to open their purse strings even more.

"Your beauty is all you have", Ada used to lecture the girls. "Always remember that one free-spending gentleman is less wearing and can be just as profitable as five cheapskates."

The Everleigh girls were taken periodically to theatre matinees and picnics by the two sisters. The open-air picnics were considered beneficial to their complexions.

Sunday evenings the brothel was closed to paying clients and the girls were permitted to entertain their own true loves.

"Their boyfriends used to come into the club proudly", Minna once recalled in later years, "bearing bouquets, perfume and candy."

Everleigh Club girls were at the top of their profession and much in demand at other brothels through the country.

Only one of them ever figured in a scandal, or made headlines, after she left the sisters' employ.

This was the slim and beautiful Belle Schreiber who became notorious as the flaunted white mistress of Jack Johnson, heavyweight boxing champion of the world.

In 1912 Johnson was indicted by the U.S. Government on a technical charge of white slavery following allegations that he had taken the girl from Pittsburg to Chicago for "immoral purposes".

Sentenced to a year's imprisonment the boxer fled the country but ultimately served his time in Leavenworth Penitentiary after he returned to the U S in 1920 and surrendered.

From the beginning the Everleigh Club catered particularly to men of wealth. As a regular clientele became established it grew more and more exclusive and strangers were not admitted.

The sisters' profits were enormous although they employed a domestic staff of 25, including an English butler named Edward, and also a full-time orchestra.

To operate the club the sisters cheerfully paid out at least $10,000 a year in graft and as a result the world-famous institution was never named in the annual police list of Chicago bawdy houses.

But trouble came when a vice commission was set up in 1910 by the City Council following pressure by church interests.

In its report the commission named the Everleigh Club as the most profitable of the city's 1020 brothels.

But nothing was done about the report until a new election put a reform-minded mayor, Carter Harrison, into office late in October 1910.

A few days later Mayor Harrison ordered aghast police to close the Everleigh Club as a warning to the city's vice traffickers.

All appeals were in vain and at 2.45 am on October 25 the doors of

America's leading bordello closed for the last time.

Within 24 hours all the girls had departed to accept some of the hundreds of job offers that had poured in from other madams all over the country.

Within a week Ada and Minna Everleigh had also gone, taking with them $1 million in cash and jewellery worth $200,000.

The contents of the building later realised another $150,000 although they kept much of the best furniture and all the pictures and books for themselves.

Reverting to their maiden name of Lester the two former madams retired to a large house they bought on West 71st Street in New York.

Although they lost heavily in the Wall Street crash of 1929 they continued to live there comfortably as ladies of independent means until Minna died in 1948.

Ada then moved to a luxury rest home in her native Kentucky where she died on 3 January 1960.

One obituary referred admiringly to the sisters' ability to collect a $50 fee for their girls "in an age when beer was a nickel and whisky 10 cents".

Love With an Element of Danger

IN 1661 King Louis XIV of France signed a decree ordering the banishment for three years of a courtier, Philibert de Gramont, for having
stolen the affections of the royal mistress.

Sailing to England, de Gramont returned to his old tricks and was soon
caught red-handed eating a midnight snack of oysters and ham pie with
the paramour of Charles II.

What made this latest indiscretion more culpable was that the pair were
closeted in the royal bedchamber.

The rest of de Gramont's career, both past and future, was nothing more
than a variation on this theme for the man was an insatible roue who made
the pursuit of love a sport and a profession.

De Gramot began his career in this field when, as a schoolboy, he paid
a hotel bill by seducing the wife of the establishment's owner.

He ended it when the brothers of the lovely Elizabeth Hamilton rammed
pistols into his neck and marched him off to the altar where he became the
reluctant spouse of the strong-willed beauty.

Philibert de Gramont was born to wealthy parents in France's Gascony
province in 1621. By the time he was 15 any local girl who was even seen in
his company at once lost her reputation.

A year later his despairing parents sent him to a boarding school at Pau
hoping to divert his mind from the one subject that seemed to interest him.

For two months de Gramont spent the days sleeping in class and the
nights (after escaping over the walls) pursuing the local belles. Then he
was expelled.

Next he was sent to a military academy in Paris in the care of an aged
tutor named Brinon who carried the 400 louis sustenance money his charge's
now-widowed mother had entrusted to him.

On their way to Paris the pair stayed overnight at a Lyons inn. While
Brinon slept, de Gramont left the inn and lost all his pocket money gambling.

Undaunted he returned to the inn, took the 400 louis from beneath
Brinon's pillow, and lost that also.

This meant no money remained to pay the bill at the inn. The 16-year-old roue solved this problem by seducing the innkeeper's wife.

He also solved the problem of Brinon's restricting influence by dumping him and riding on alone to Paris in his mother's private coach.

No sooner had be reached the city than he sold the horses and coach, won 600 louis with the proceeds at gambling, then set off to squander the lot on a team of Parisian harlots.

When almost penniless de Gramont presented himself for enrolment at the military academy and somehow managed to scrape through his exams after a two-year course.

In 1939 the 18-year-old Philibert de Gramont was attached to the staff of the ageing General de Turenne, a gentleman whose delight in female company was exceeded only by his inability to attract them.

Immediately de Gramont joined his staff things were different. The camp was overrun by a bevy of beauties from which the young aide allowed the general to take his pick.

All went well until one day de Turenne unexpectedly returned to his headquarters from the siege of Trino to find de Gramont paying indiscreet and mutual court to the general's specially-reserved paramour.

The Court of Charles II. Philibert de Gramont was banished here from Versailles, and finally coerced into marriage with Elizabeth Hamilton.

De Turenne at first wanted to shoot his aide. Then he decided to cashier him. But in the end he agreed to cut cards for the lady's future favors.

At the game's end de Gramont had not only won the lady but 16 of the general's best horses as well. He then left the camp and joined the staff of General the Prince de Conde.

When the war ended a few weeks later de Gramont returned to Paris where his pay and the proceeds from the sale of Turenne's horses soon went over the gambling tables.

His love exploits were no more successful for he foolishly wooed the wife of a champion duellist and managed to get out of Paris only inches ahead of the enraged husband's sword point.

De Gramont's flight did not end until he arrived in Turin in Italy. There he took rooms and at once began scouting for a suitable female companion.

At that time there was a strange custom in Turin which decreed that all ladies of fashion should have a lover who must wear a gorgeous uniform engraved with her name.

In no time de Gramont had become the lover of the lovely Marquise de Senaltes. The set-up suited the amorous Frenchman, particularly as the

Elizabeth Hamilton.

MISS HAMILTON.

illicit liaison had the full approval of the lady's husband.

Indeed the Marquis was so delighted with his wife's charming acquisition that he was rarely out of their company.

It was the close contact of this menage a trois that caused de Gramont to lament: "What a plaguey country this is when one can't love a woman without being in love with her husband too."

In 1657 de Gramont received word of his mother's death and the transfer of the family estate to his name. At once he bade farewell to the weeping Marquis and Marquise and returned home to take over his inheritance.

At that time France was at war with Spain, whose forces were led by the renegade Prince de Conde. De Conde was under siege at Arras by an army led by General de Turenne.

As de Gramont knew both these generals he was detailed to approach Conde and negotiate a peace with him. His mission was successful and the Peace of the Pyrennees was signed.

It was this task that brought de Gramont to the attention of King Louis XIV. The monarch met the negotiator and was so taken by his charm that he threw his court open to him.

De Gramont had never had it so easy. The court was little more than a magnificent brothel. Some of the nation's most beautiful women could be had for a mere nod.

Philibert de Gramont, 17th Century French lover of many famous women.

One by one de Gramont sampled the delights offering, coming finally to Mlle de la Motte Houdancourt, then the King's favorite.

The famed lover's fall from grace came about one day when the King announced that he would lead a party on a hunting expedition.

Mlle Houdancourt was among those invited but at the last minute she announced the onset of a headache and asked to be excused.

Louis enjoyed the hunt. And so too, apparently, did de Gramont, for the story palace spies told Louis of the goings-on between his favorite courtier and his mistress on his return caused him to have the roue paraded before him.

The King would have had de Gramont beheaded had not the ladies of the court begged for mercy. In the end he sentenced the over-amorous courtier to banishment for three years.

Arriving in England, de Gramont used the good offices of the French ambassador in London to win an introduction to the court of Charles II.

And there his success with the ladies was no less spectacular than it had been in Paris. There were few who did not willingly succumb to his advances.

It was only a matter of time before de Gramont graduated to the King's favorite mistress, the unutterably stupid but fascinatingly beautiful Frances Stewart, later Duchess of Richmond.

When Charles discovered the pair eating oysters and ham pie in his own bedchamber his reaction was the same as Louis's. Nevertheless the King agreed to forget the incident when the Frenchman bought him a magnificent coach worth 2,000 louis.

Charles accepted the coach but refused to give the donor his mistress. So de Gramont consoled himself in the arms of the queen's maids-of-honor, the Misses Wells, Fielding, Warminister and Boynton.

Miss Boynton was a peculiar case. Whenever de Gramont entered her private chamber she fainted from excitement and had to be revived with burnt feathers.

It was about this time that Philibert de Gramont met Elizabeth Hamilton, a lady of unusual beauty who had only recently joined Charles's court and who was, therefore, still virtuous.

Deciding that the Frenchman would one day be her husband, she adopted the feminine tactic of aloofness, repulsing all his impassioned advances.

De Gramont showered Elizabeth with gifts, most of which were returned. He even followed her coach on horseback shouting his love at her as they proceeded through the streets of London.

Later he hired Italian musicians to serenade her from beneath her window, a practice that stopped when the young woman's father sighted a blunderbuss at them.

But constancy was not in de Gramont's nature. As he pursued his suit with Elizabeth Hamilton he found consolation with another of Charles's mistresses, a Mrs Middleton.

Deciding to do a little match-making, Charles arranged a magnificent ball and invited both Elizabeth and de Gramont. But the strategy came to nothing for Elizabeth danced with everyone but the love-lorn Frenchman.

But in the end Elizabeth was the first to break. She fell into his arms and later accompanied him to his apartments.

The next day de Gramont's term of banishment from France ended. He had conquered the unconquerable and was content to return alone to his homeland assured that he was still irresistible.

One night late in 1664 Philibert de Gramont took a coach and headed towards Dover where a packet boat waited to return him to France.

Suddenly he heard the sound of hooves. Soon after the coach drew to a halt and two men pushed their heads through the window. They were Elizabeth's brothers, George and Anthony Hamilton.

Anthony spoke first. He said: "Did you forget something, de Gramont?"

The Frenchman sighed. He said: "Yes, sirs, I forgot to marry your sister."

De Gramont did not seem to enjoy his shot-gun wedding although King Charles himself attended. And Nell Gwynne was highly amused when the Hamiltons threatened to shoot the groom if he tried to make a run for it.

After the wedding Philibert and Elizabeth de Gramont settled in France where two daughters were born. He never strayed again, chiefly because his wife refused to let him out of her sight.

And she maintained the vigil until 1707 when Philibert, then 86, breathed his last and was lowered into his grave out of harm's way.

Burst of a South Seas Bubble

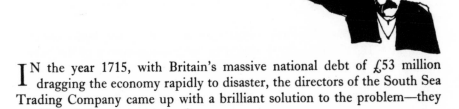

IN the year 1715, with Britain's massive national debt of £53 million dragging the economy rapidly to disaster, the directors of the South Sea Trading Company came up with a brilliant solution to the problem—they would lend the money to the Government.

Under the Prime Minister, Sir Robert Walpole, Parliament gave the offer serious thought. Some members considered the plan bordered on the ridiculous. But others favoured it.

This offer, the supporters of the scheme said, demanded a lower rate of interest than was usual. Further, it would mean the Government would have to deal with only one creditor instead of hundreds.

The only trouble with the plan (and no parliamentarian realised it at the time) was that it was loaded with all the ingredients of corruption, bribery, plot, counter-plot and plain theft.

When the loan was in the process of negotiation, the British economy soared to unprecedented heights. Money could be borrowed practically without security and the whole nation became investment-mad.

Any hare-brained scheme that offered investors good returns could not even produce enough share certificates to meet the demand.

Some companies were in such a hurry to take advantage of the bonanza that they were floated even before the directors had decided on the type of enterprise they would undertake.

Then, almost overnight, the bubble burst when corruption rumors flooded London.

South Sea's shares slumped, a run on the banks caused many to close their doors and thousands of investors found their share certificates were not worth the value of the ink on them.

History had to wait until the Great Depression of the 1920s to see the like of that economic debacle of the 18th century.

The South Sea Trading Company was formed in 1711 and held a monopoly of America and the Pacific Islands. With a capital of £11¼ million it had a reputation for integrity.

In 1715, with the problem of the huge national debt dominating every discussion in responsible circles, the company came up with its proposal to take over the £50 million burden.

If most Government members found the offer gratifying, they were further delighted when the company added that it would actually pay £3½ million for the privilege of charging the Government only £1½ million a year interest.

Now it was learned the company intended to raise the money to pay the national debt by persuading creditors of the Government to exchange their claims for company stock.

Because this stock would be issued at a high premium, a large part of the debt would be cancelled by the issue of a comparatively small amount of stock.

All the South Sea Company needed now was public confidence. It got it when, in 1718, King George I agreed to become a governor of the board. Immediately South Sea share values shot up.

Meanwhile the scheme was meeting opposition in parliament, chiefly from several members who were directors of the Bank of England.

At first these men attacked the plan as being fantastic. Then suddenly

Drawn by Thos. H. Shepherd

THE BANK OF ENGLAND

they changed their attitude and decided their bank would put forward a similar plan and outbid the South Sea's £3¼ million offer to get the contract.

Faced now with two offers to pay its debts, Parliament set a day for representatives of both the South Sea Company and the Bank of England to appear before it and bid.

With the auction date looming, the South Sea Company called a meeting of directors to consider what the loan takeover was really worth to them. They decided they would bid to £7½-million and instructed their sub-director, Sir John Fellows, to go to that figure.

Fellows got the job over very quickly. He walked into the House, bid £7½ million and the South Sea Company had the contract.

South Sea stock value skyrocketed overnight. And it leaped even further when in April 1720 royal assent was given to the Loan Bill.

This Bill, among its provisions, gave the South Sea Company power to increase its capital to nearly £40 million. Subscriptions to the new stock were invited immediately.

With investors clamoring for the stock the premium rose so high that the first £2¼ million put on the market cost buyers £300 for each £100 share.

Engraved by Wm. Tombleson

An old illustration of the Bank of England. The Bank tried to outbid the notorious South Sea Company in a scheme to take over Britain's national debt.

And following issues were sold at increasing premiums right up to £1,000 for a £100 share.

All England went into an investment frenzy. Men and women with only a few pounds to spare clamoured for shares in every company that was floated and they were being floated by the score.

The objective of one company was to import "jackasses from Spain". Another intended to turn sea water into fresh.

Then there was the company that filled its first issue although the directors had not yet decided what industry they should turn their hands to.

No one quite knew how it happened but someone or some mysterious circumstance caused the bubble to be pricked. It began deflating and South Sea stock slumped with it.

At first the fall in value was slight. Then it became more dramatic. A mild run on the banks developed into a stampede.

The banks tried to meet demands by calling up money they had lent for stock purchases. But most of it had gone forever. Many banks had no alternative but to close their doors.

The fall in South Sea stock spread like a virulent disease. Other companies, some of the highest integrity, became involved in the slump.

The whisper to sell became a thunderous roar. The trouble was that there were no buyers.

In a desperate attempt to stop the slump, the South Sea Company lent liberally on its stock and allowed six months' repayment. But this action had only a momentary effect on the falling market.

Towards the end of 1720 the South Sea Company announced it would soon pay a dividend of 30 per cent and, for the following 12 years, the annual dividend would be 50 per cent. The shares improved a little.

A week later the slump again set in and stock values fell until shares that had once changed hands for £1,000 could attract no more than a £175 offer.

By now the company had lent so much on its shares that all its cash was nearly gone. In desperation it asked the Bank of England for a loan.

With Robert Walpole urging it to help the South Sea Company the bank agreed to the loan on the understanding it would take over a large block of South Sea shares at a premium.

When news of these negotiations swept England the South Sea market firmed a little and share values rose slowly to £320 each.

Now, in an attempt to cut their losses and having no confidence in the company's future, shareholders began unloading. The market plummeted and the Bank of England, afraid it might go down with the South Sea Company, wiped its hands of the loan proposal.

England panicked. Thousands of small investors were pauperised overnight. More substantial stock holders were reduced to penury and bankrupts filled the business world.

Then ruined investors began crying for revenge. Their chief target was George I who had been rushed back from a trip to Hanover when the last crisis developed.

60

Sir Robert Walpole, Prime Minister of England when the country was swept by the wild fever of speculation.

All kinds of stories linking the King with the debacle circulated. One said his German mistresses had been bribed by the South Sea Company to win his support.

In January 1721 a secret committee appointed by Parliament began investigating the history of the South Sea Trading Company since its formation.

It also had power to follow all transactions through the company's books and to investigate the private background of all the directors including several knights, baronets and members of Parliament.

A few days after the investigation began, the committee was able to report to the House that it had discovered evidence of a colossal fraud.

False entries had been found in books, pages had been ripped out, account books were a mass of erasions and alterations and many vital documents were missing.

The committee also stated that during the period the company was negotiating to take over the Government's debt, vast quantities of stock had been issued to anonymous people, obviously as bribes to government officials.

Further, the committee said, company officers had taken large blocks of stock for themselves and by juggling it in various ways had made fortunes.

But even more startling revelations were to be put before the House as the investigation continued.

It was proved that members of the royal court had accepted bribes of stock and that when the Chancellor of the Exchequer, John Aislabie, had originally placed the loan scheme before Parliament, he had been given a gift of £800,000 worth of stock.

The Earl of Sunderland was also involved in dishonourable practices as were the Postmaster-General and the Secretary of State.

Even Walpole was found to have made a fortune by buying and selling stock although there was no suggestion of bribery.

When the committee had finished most of its work, Parliament ordered the seizure of the estates of the South Sea Trading Company's 34 directors. Also many contracts entered into by the company were cancelled.

The sales of the directors' estates raised £2-million which was paid to duped shareholders. But it did little to relieve their financial position.

Before the matter came to its inglorious conclusion, extreme anxiety had caused the deaths of the Postmaster-General and the Secretary of State, a father and son named Craggs.

In the House, Lord Stanhope, although not involved in the general corruption, became so heated during a debate on the matter that he went into convulsions and died next day.

The Chancellor of the Exchequer, Aislabie, resigned his portfolio and by order of the House was committed to the Tower.

Later Parliament found him guilty of "infamous corruption" and, after expelling him from Parliament, sent him to prison.

It was Walpole, more than anyone, who saved England's economy from complete collapse. Holding himself in dignified aloofness, he exuded an air of confidence in his country's future that pervaded the whole nation.

England found a more old fashioned way to pay its national debt and sanity slowly returned to her economy.

Nor did the South Sea Trading Company perish. With the old directors out of the way, it continued trading under the guardianship of trustees.

And it made good profits until it faded from the scene in the 19th century.

Child Actor was Hoax of London

ON the afternoon of 1 December 1804, the narrow streets round London's Covent Garden Theatre looked like the scene of a full-scale civil war. A frenzied mob surged towards the theatre portico, overturning coaches and trampling men and women underfoot. Then, above the roar of the crowd, sounded the clatter of horses' hooves as a troop of dragoons rode down Bow Street, flailing right and left with the flat of their sabres. When the mob dispersed, four people lay dead and countless injured had been carried off by their friends. Cause of all the tumult was a 13-years-old boy actor, William Betty, celebrated as the "Young Roscius".

The brief career of the young Roscius was one of the most fantastic episodes in the history of the British theatre.

For three years the fair-haired, blue-eyed boy was the subject of a torrent of adulation that completely eclipsed Mrs. Siddons, the Kembles, Edmund Kean and all the famous stars of the day.

Prime Minister Pitt adjourned the House of Commons in the midst of debates on the Napoleonic War so that members could see Master Betty play Hamlet.

Troops had to be called out to suppress the riot touched off by his first London appearance. He was flattered by royalty, feasted by aldermen and celebrated by poets and painters.

Like a meteor, the Young Roscius blazed across the dramatic sky, and, like a meteor, he vanished almost overnight. The fickle mob that had hailed his "inspired phrenzy" turned to ridicule the "baby prodigy."

But by then Betty had amassed an enormous fortune. He lived in comfortable retirement to the ripe age of 83—a cynical old man with a profound contempt for the fans who had once idolised him.

William Henry West Betty was born on 13 September 1791, son of a prosperous linen-manufacturer in Belfast, Northern Ireland.

He was a precocious boy, with a passion for mounting the family sideboard and declaiming poetry and plays, to the delight of his doting parents.

Turning point in his life came in 1802, when the famous tragedy queen, Mrs. Sarah Siddons, arrived in Belfast on a triumphal tour of the cities of Ireland.

Young Betty was overwhelmed when he saw her as Elvira in Sheridan's

Drury Lane Theatre where the precocious child actor earned $ 25 a performance.

drama, Pizarro. In two days he had learnt the whole play by heart, and was swearing passionately that he would die unless he became an actor.

Atkins, the manager of the near-bankrupt Belfast theatre, was invited to the Betty estate at Ballynahinch to hear the boy recite, and decided to use him as a stunt to revive his failing fortunes.

He was engaged to play in Hill's tragedy, Zara, and Atkins plastered Belfast with bills announcing mysteriously that the part of Osman would be taken by 'a young gentleman of but 11 years.'

Betty's success staggered even the optimistic Atkins. Taken in hand by the veteran theatre prompter, the boy quickly added Hamlet and Romeo to his repertoire—learning both parts in three days.

By November, 1803, he was in Dublin, and the star of the Crow Street Theatre, where the nightly receipts jumped from $20 to $200. In the next few months he toured Cork, Waterford and Londonderry.

Irish critics called him the Young Roscius, after the celebrated Roman actor of classical times. But Betty's fame soon spread beyond the confines of Ireland, and his father was busily planning to cash in on his son's genius.

In May, 1804, the Young Roscius was in Glasgow, where he packed the theatre for a fortnight—though Mrs. Siddons had lasted less than a week—and roused Scottish fans to a fever of adulation.

John Home, the 82-years-old author of the tragedy, Douglas, was persuaded to see Betty in the role of Norval—the romantic hero who had been a favorite of leading actors for 50 years.

As the curtain fell amid a bedlam of applause Home tottered on to the stage, weeping with emotion and vowing that for the first time he had seen Norval played as he himself imagined the character.

From Scotland the Young Roscius descended on the English provinces. In Birmingham alone his share of the profits was $3000. At Sheffield special coaches carried racegoers from Doncaster in time for each evening's performance.

Scores were injured, or had their clothes torn to ribbons and lost hats and shoes in the mad stampede for tickets in Liverpool. In Manchester, to avoid a similar riot, tickets were sold by auction a week before the Young Roscius arrived.

News of the mania soon reached London, where the managers of the two theatres, Covent Garden and Drury Lane, tumbled over each other to obtain the golden prize.

John Kemble, partner in Covent Garden with his sister, Mrs. Siddons, won the race by dashing to Leicester and signing up Betty for 20 performances at $120 guineas a night.

As soon as Betty reached London, however, his canny father negotiated a contract with Drury Lane, under which the boy also played there on alternate nights for 100 guineas a performance.

This was more than Kemble, Kean or Mrs. Siddons ever earned at the height of their fame, and rivalled even the almost legendary income of Garrick in his palmiest days.

For weeks before Betty made his Covent Garden debut in Barbarossa in December, 1804. London was agog with the wildest anticipation.

Ducal coaches, followed by mobs of cheering men and women who tried to seize his hand to kiss, carried him to and from rehearsals. A hastily hashed-up Life of the Celebrated Young Roscius sold 10,000 copies on the day of publication.

Opening night brought a hysterical pandemonium unequalled in stage annals, when more than 5000 people tried to fight their way into Covent Garden Theatre.

When every seat was filled theatre officials called on dragoons to clear the streets. They did so with ruthless efficiency, leaving a litter of dead and injured down the length of Bow Street.

Inside, the Prince of Wales led the mass of rank and fashion who crowded the boxes. The pit was so jammed with standing patrons that two men suffocated to death before they could be dragged out.

Nine days later the scenes were repeated when Betty made his first Drury Lane appearance as Norval. For 28 nights he packed the 3500-seat theatre, while $34,000 rattled into the box-office.

Throughout 1805 the Young Roscius craze raged unabated. King George summoned Betty to the royal box at Drury Lane and presented him to the Queen and princesses.

The Prince of Wales entertained him in the plush splendors of Carlton House. He was banqueted by aldermen at the Mansion House. Cambridge University offered a prize for a Young Roscius Ode.

When he appeared as Hamlet, Pitt moved the adjournment of the Commons to enable members to attend. The Whig leader, Charles Fox, solemnly consulted him about a drama he had written.

Critics vied with each other in fulsome adoration. Betty was "Garrick reborn". He had "stolen the sacred fire from Shakespeare's altar." He was "lighted up with the holy frenzy of one inspired."

Aristocratic ladies wrote begging for locks of his hair. Once his jacket was torn from his back as he left the stage-door.

Betty himself remained astonishingly unaffected by the mania. Even his enemies later conceded the 14-years-old boy's natural charm and modesty—though they denounced his much-trumpeted "genius".

By the end of 1805 criticism was beginning to mount. The poet Campbell contemptuously called Betty a "baby-faced boy" and said his popularity was "a hallucination of the public mind and a disgrace to the English theatre."

The most ferocious attacks came from Leigh Hunt's newspaper column in the News. Day after day Hunt denounced "baby theatricals" and sneered at Betty's "monotonous rant and simulated adult passions".

Celebrities like Mrs. Siddons, Edmund Kean and the Kembles were also tired of playing second fiddle to an infant prodigy.

The haughty Mrs. Siddons, after playing Ophelia and Desdemona to a teen-age Hamlet and Othello, said the Young Roscius was "a clever and pretty boy—and nothing more".

William Betty, the child actor who, for several years, dominated the London stage.

On one occasion at Stroud, when the Drury Lane company was on a provincial tour, Edmund Kean found himself billed to play Laertes to Betty's Hamlet. This he regarded as the last straw.

Swearing, "Damnation! I won't play second to any man except John Kemble!" Kean took to the woods and lived for three days on wild berries before the company could induce him to return.

When he returned to London early in 1806 the enthusiasm of even the most avid Betty fans was obviously waning. One reason was the spate of "infant prodigies" now trying to invade the stage.

Late in 1805 Kemble had introduced golden-ringleted, eight-years-old Jane Mudie at Covent Garden, billing her as the Infant Roscia in the role of Shakespeare's Juliet.

Little Jane was jeered off the stage in the first act, though Kemble himself pleaded with the audience to let her finish the performance.

For another year avaricious parents dragged their unhappy offspring round the London theatres, trying to cash in on the fading renown of Master Betty.

The Young Roscius, meanwhile, continued to tour the provinces until his final appearance as a boy actor at Bath in March, 1808.

Then, having accumulated a fortune variously estimated at between $20,000 and $60,000, he went to Cambridge to complete his education, and for the next four years disappeared from the public view.

Then the lure of the stage called him back to try his fortunes as an adult actor, only to meet disastrous and humiliating failure.

In 1812 Betty re-appeared at Covent Garden, playing Richard III and Barbarossa to echoing, almost empty houses, and completely ignored by the critics.

After that he confined himself to touring provincial theatres. He had grown into a portly, floridfaced young man, and lost all the charm and grace of the former Young Roscius.

August 9, 1824, saw his farewell stage appearance at Southampton. Then he retired to his mansion in London's fashionable Ampthill Square, to live for another 50 years on his shrewdly-invested riches.

He died on 24 August 1874—a fat, benign octogenarian, who had delighted in pouring scorn on the gullible fans who had once made his fortune.

Count Philipp Von Konigsmarck.

Murder in The
House of Hanover

AT midnight on 1 July 1694, a handsome young adventurer, Count Philipp von Konigsmarck, rode up to a side entrance of the ducal palace in Hanover to keep an assignation with his mistress, Princess Sophia Dorothea. From that moment, Konigsmarck vanished as though swept off the face of the earth and his fate has remained a grim and fascinating historical mystery ever since. The only certain fact is that he was barbarously slain with the connivance of Sophia's husband and father. The Konigsmarck scandal, with its dark implications of jealousy, illicit love and ruthless murder, haunted the House of Hanover for years after Sophia's brutal and oafish husband had become King George I of England.

Descendant of an ancient noble family, Philipp von Konigsmarck was born in March 1665, the second son of the minister-general to the King of Sweden.

When the father died in 1673, Philipp and his elder brother, Carl Johann, were handed over to their uncle, a marshal in the service of Louis XIV of France, to train for a military career.

The boys grew up as dazzling young gallants with little wealth, but a family heritage of aristocratic blood, good looks and a reckless, adventurous spirit.

Phillipp was only 15 when his uncle's influence obtained him a post at the little German court of Celle, ruled by a junior branch of the powerful electoral House of Hanover.

The Duke of Celle's main asset in the dynastic scrambles of the German princelings was his daughter. He hoped to unite the two lines of the family inheritance by marrying her off to Prince George, heir to the Elector, Ernst Augustus of Hanover.

It was to be a coldly-calculated marriage of convenience, for the gay and pretty 14-years-old Princess Sophia Dorothea had nothing in common with her cousin George, and, indeed, fell into hysterics and fainted when she first laid eyes on him.

George was a dull-witted young man, whose main passions were tinkering with clocks, gulping great quantities of sausage and Rhenish wine, and

71

seeking the favors of the fattest ladies of the court.

In 1690, the debonair Philipp von Konigsmarck descended on the stuffy, intrigue-ridden court of Celle, bringing with him an air of swashbuckling romance that swept Sophia off her feet.

Soon it was hinted that they were lovers at the precocious ages of 15 and 14, and Konigsmarck was promptly ordered by the girl's outraged father to remove himself from Celle.

A year later, armed with introductions from the Swedish king, Philipp and his brother Carl Johann appeared in London to seek their fortunes at the court of Charles II.

Their sojourn in England was brief but sensational. Philipp went to Oxford, ostensibly to study, but, in fact, to involve himself in a series of duels, amours and public scandals.

Meanwhile, Carl Johann was ardently pursuing the teenage Lady Elizabeth Percy, heiress to the vast riches of the Dukes of Northumberland and greatest matrimonial prize in England.

Alarmed by Carl Johann's threats of abduction, her guardians hastily married her off to Thomas Thynne, a Wiltshire squire known as "Tom o' Ten Thousand" from his income of £10,000 a year.

Having failed to provoke Thynne to a duel, the infuriated Carl Johann hired ruffians to drag his rival out of his coach and murder him in a London street one February night in 1682.

The assassins were seized and executed. Powerful influences at court obtained Carl Johann's acquittal, but the name of Konigsmarck was now so odious that both brothers soon fled from England.

For the next six years Philipp drifted round Europe, serving as a soldier of fortune and diplomat, and leaving a trail of conquests among frail court beauties from Portugal to Poland.

In Dresden he found his sister Aurora installed as mistress of the Elector, Augustus of Saxony, and for a while Philipp served as a major-general in the Saxon Army.

Then, in March 1688, he made the fateful decision to seek his fortune in Hanover, the first step on the road to ignominious death and a tomb within the stones of the ducal palace.

It was eight years since he had seen Princess Sophia Dorothea. She was now the wife of Prince George, son of the Elector of Hanover, and mother of the child who would one day be George II of England.

The marriage had been a disastrous failure almost from the start. At 22 Sophia was now in the prime of her beauty, romantic and passionate, and eating her heart out in bitter contempt for her husband.

George had developed from a simple-minded youth into a boorish man, who made no pretence to fidelity, and who only required of his mistresses that they should be "very willing and very fat".

The domestic affairs of the court of Hanover were more sordid than usual, as George's first mistress, Maria von Meissenburg, had been the younger sister of his father's mistress, the Countess von Platen.

72

Princess Sophia Dorothea.

In 1685 Maria was succeeded by Melusina von Schulenburg, an even more Junoesque figure, who shared her lover's taste for hearty eating and pompous court ceremonial.

The neglected Sophia greeted Konigsmarck's reappearance in 1688 with unconcealed delight, and used all her influence with the old Elector Ernst Augustus to have him offered high rank in the army of Hanover.

For a while the dashing Count Philipp basked in the favor of the whole court. The death of his uncle had brought him great wealth, he had one of the finest military reputations in Europe, and even the cloddish Prince George welcomed him as an honored guest.

But Konigsmarck made one bitter and all-powerful enemy, a woman who grew to hate him with venomous jealousy and was eventually to inspire his brutal murder.

This was the Countess von Platen, who ruled the doting old Elector, dominated Prince George by providing him with mistresses, and whose influence overawed every official in the Hanoverian court.

The countess determined to ruin Konigsmarck by exposing him as Sophia's lover, and her plot was made easy by Count Philipp's reckless display of devotion to the injured princess.

For a year he pursued Sophia with demands that she become his mistress. He wrote letters signed with his own blood. He pleaded frantically: "Are there any torments in hell as terrible as this?"

Not until he threatened to leave Hanover and fling away his life in battle did Sophia yield, and the perilous liaison of brief and stolen meetings began.

For a time the secret was well kept, mainly because of the ingenuity of Sophia's trusted confidant, Madame von Knesebeck, who arranged assignations even within the palace walls.

Once she surrendered Sophia was the more passionate of the lovers. She begged Konigsmarck to flee with her, offering to abandon her children and follow him to France or Italy, or "the world's end".

She warned him that the evil Countess von Platen had spies everywhere, that their secret could not be kept for long, that his life would be in mortal danger if the old Elector discovered the truth.

Then, early in 1693, Konigsmarck suddenly left Hanover for Dresden, telling Sophia that he intended to collect a large debt owed him by the Saxon Elector in preparation for their flight together.

The Elector could not raise the money, but he offered Count Philipp the rank of general in his army instead. To the grief and despair of his mistress, Konigsmarck promptly accepted.

Whether he intended to desert Sophia is uncertain, but he remained more than a year in Dresden, living in splendid state, indulging in numerous gallantries, and raising a crack regiment of hussars at his own expense.

Meanwhile, Sophia had openly confessed her passion to her husband and was vainly begging Prince George for a divorce so that she could join her lover in Saxony.

Threat of such a scandal threw her father-in-law, the Elector, into a frenzy of rage. The palace became her prison. Worn out with misery and frustrated hopes, she fell seriously ill from fever.

She still, however, managed to smuggle letters to Konigsmarck. Moved at last by her wretchedness, he sent a message in reply, swearing to return secretly to Hanover and snatch her from captivity.

On the night of 1 July 1694, swathed in a heavy cloak and with only two attendants, Konigzmarck rode up to an inn in Hanover. An hour later he left to make his way on foot to the ducal palace.

Only from scraps of evidence that escaped the vigilance of the Hanoverian court was it later possible to piece together the bloody chain of events that followed.

It seems that both the Elector and the Countess von Platen knew of Konigsmarck's intended return, though it remains a mystery who was responsible for the deadly trap laid for him.

Once Konigsmarck stepped within the palace walls he vanished forever. Two stories, equally grim, were later circulated about his fate.

One said he was strangled by the Elector's order, and his body stripped and thrown into a pit in the palace garden. The other made the Countess von Platen chief actor in the terrible drama.

According to this legend, guards waylaid Konigsmarck in the dimly-lit corridor outside Sophia's bedroom and hacked him to death with swords and axes, while the countess spurred them on.

Then, to complete the horror, the corpse was dragged into Sophia's own dressing-room, thrust into a sack of quicklime and buried beneath the floor boards.

The real truth will probably never be known, as the House of Hanover took care to obliterate every record of the event. The electoral palace still stands, but nobody knows what corner of it hides the bones of the gay adventurer, Philipp von Konigsmarck.

Princess Sophia, stupefied with grief, was taken to the gloomy castle of Ahlden in northern Germany. There, while her husband became George I of England she remained a prisoner till her death in 1726.

Lady Blessington, one of the most scandalous women of her era, was worth every cent of the $20,000 her husband-to-be paid for her.

The Outrageous Lady Blessington

SALLY Power was not particular whom she chose as a protector as long as he had money and a social position that would enable her to parade her fascinating Irish beauty before even more desirable suitors.

To please the first of her English lovers, Captain Thomas Jenkins, Sally regularly danced naked on a table before his guests then led the assembly, so it was said, in night-long orgies.

Nor did it concern her that the amorous captain often had to use his sword to emphasise that the delightful teenager was his property exclusively.

Five years later the captain's passion for his favorite possession had diminished somewhat and so had his bank balance. Thus he readily accepted the offer of the fabulously wealthy Earl of Blessington to purchase Sally Power from him for $20,000.

Although the earl later married the fair Sally that did not stop her becoming the mistress of Count D'Orsay, the husband of her own stepdaughter.

And it was this liaison, carried on amid social scandal and often profound poverty, that was to endure until the notorious Countess of Blessington's death in 1849.

Sally Power, who was supposed to have brought the immortal poet Lord Byron to "a fit of passionate weeping" because he could not permanently possess her, was born in Tipperary in 1789, the daughter of a squire addicted to liquor and gambling.

By the time Sally (she had actually been christened Marguerite) was a disconcertingly lovely 15, her father was on the verge of bankruptcy. To capitalise on his daughter's charm he conducted an auction for her hand among the local landowners and army officers.

The successful bidder was Captain Maurice Farmer, a drunken brute who married the girl, beat and half-starved her on the honeymoon and then for three years subjected her to a variety of vicious indignities.

Sally was 18 when she abandoned her husband and returned home to a father who welcomed her by complaining that now he had another mouth to feed.

Imbued with a gay personality despite her unfortunate marital experience, Sally could have picked as lover any one of a hundred men who haunted her father's house. But this time she decided to study the contestants before making a decision.

In 1809 the 19-year-old Sally Power accepted the advances of the rich and amiable Englishman Captain Thomas Jenkins who took her to England and set her up as his mistress in his Hampshire mansion.

Jenkins was so proud of his acquisition that he exhibited her naked to all his male guests and (so it was rumoured) allowed her to lead the orgies that were a regular part of his weekend entertainments.

Then one day in 1814 Captain Jenkins invited the fabulously wealthy Earl of Blessington to spend a short holiday at his estate. Like all the other guests the Earl was smitten by the lovely Sally Power.

But unlike them he did not resort to violence or subterfuge to win her. Instead he sat at a table with the now financially embarrassed Jenkins and discussed terms for her transfer.

The deal was sealed when Blessington finally lifted his offer to $20,000, a sum that was more than sufficient to mend the Captain's broken heart.

Four years later two events occurred almost simultaneously that allowed Blessington to make an honest woman of his charming mistress. The first was the death of his countess, the second a fatal fall from a window by Sally's husband Captain Maurice Farmer.

Soon after the nuptials in London the mansion of the Earl and Countess of Blessington became the mecca of a host of famous painters, writers, soldiers and politicians. It might have been significant that these guests were never accompanied by their wives.

On the other hand the more respectable stratum of London's society ostracised the Blessingtons by turning their backs on them when they came to London. The result was that Blessington, to escape these insults, took his wife on a Continental tour that was to last seven years.

It was an amazing cavalcade that left Paris for Italy—dozens of coaches, carts and baggage wagons all packed with the couple's entourage and their luggage.

There was even a specially fitted kitchen complete with one of Paris's most famous chefs.

Whenever the Blessingtons came across a town that pleased them they would rent a mansion, fill it with hired servants and equip it with furniture, paintings and even a stable of horses. And there they would stay until they decided it was time to move on.

At Avignon the couple were joined by the handsome, dashing Count D'Orsay who was renowned as a swordsman, athlete, painter and sculptor.

Actually after he had spent a few days studying the lovely Lady Blessington he decided to resign his army commission and accompany them to Italy.

It was almost love at first sight between the fascinating Countess of Blessington and Count D'Orsay. Yet despite their strong affection the earl, who regarded D'Orsay as a son, had no inkling of what had developed

Lord George Byron, genius of letters and love, wept so it was said, because he could not permanently possess the beautiful Marguerite Blessington.

between them.

In fact he was so blind that he quickly arranged the engagement between his own 15-year-old daughter of a previous marriage and the count.

Soon after, the earl's daughter Lady Harriet Blessington, was brought from her father's estate in Ireland to meet her future husband. And even as she travelled between England and France the Earl was rewriting his will leaving most of his assets to D'Orsay.

Within weeks of the girl's arrival she and D'Orsay were married with her husband's lover attending her during the ceremony.

In 1823 the bizarre procession reached Genoa in Italy where the handsome club-footed roue, the notorious Lord George Byron, was then staying surrounded by a court of adoring women.

The Countess met the poet and spent much time with him. Historians still debate whether or not she actually became his mistress. But it is said that that when the entourage moved on three months later Byron gave way to "a passionate fit of weeping".

In Naples (and with Marguerite Blessington still deeply involved with her step-daughter's husband) the Earl leased the magnificent Palazzo Belvidere. a palace renowned for its gardens, marble work and art gallery.

From there the caravan returned to Paris where Blessington settled in the mansion formerly owned by the Napoleonic soldier Marshal Ney. And it was here the Earl built a fantastic love bower for the wife who was betraying him.

In this bower a sunken Roman bath was surrounded by full-length mirrors, the walls of the bedroom were hung with silk and lace, the bed itself rested on huge silver swans while nearby was set a silver divan.

And it was there that the Earl of Blessington made love to his wife and the Count D'Orsay made love to his step mother-in-law. And it was there also in May 1829 Lord Blessington died.

After that Lady Blessington, D'Orsay and his young wife returned to London where they set up a scandalous household with the Count sharing his favors between the two females.

Then came the day when the shocked D'Orsay learned that Blessington had died leaving few assets.

Nevertheless they did not face penury for at the time of Marguerite's marriage the Earl had created a trust fund allowing her $4,000 a year, a handsome sum in that period.

Marguerite told the D'Orsays she would guarantee their support but did nothing to reduce her own extravagant standard of living. And apart from that she acceded to D'Orsay's every financial demand.

It was only a matter of time before Marguerite's need for an increased income became desperate and to that end she began pouring out a stream of romantic novels that were to bring her in about $6,000 a year.

But by this time Harriet D'Orsay was fully aware of the love that existed between her step-mother and her husband. There were many violent scenes which culminated in the young woman fleeing to the protection of relatives in Ireland.

While Press and stage viciously lampooned the almost incestuous relationship being carried on at Lady Blessington's Seymour Place residence the embittered Countess fought back by creating London's most brilliant salon.

To her house came men like Leigh Hunt, Bulwer Lytton, Thackeray, Dickens, Landseer, Disraeli, the Duke of Wellington, Prince Louis Napoleon always without their wives.

The still-gorgeous Marguerite, Countess of Blessington, could have chosen a husband from among a small army of the famous and the noble. But she had eyes for none but the dissolute D'Orsay.

She could not even bring herself to chide him as he spent huge sums of her money on clothing, cards, horses and prize fighting. She simply worked longer into the nights churning out her books.

In 1836 Lady Blessington, with D'Orsay trailing behind, moved from her expensive Seymour Place residence into the country district of Kensington where she took a smaller house once owned by the anti-slavery champion William Wilberforce.

D'Orsay complained that his mistress refused to spend more than $2,000 on repairs and $2,000 on furnishings in the new house. He could not seem to appreciate that his financial demands were eating deeply into her assets.

In the 1840s Marguerite's position became desperate when the potato famine dramatically reduced the income from her Irish estates. And apart from that the publisher of some of her writings died still owing her large sums for royalties.

D'Orsay whined that he now owed his creditors something like $200,000. But his mistress was unable to give him enough even to temporarily keep them quiet.

For weeks on end these creditors surrounded Lady Blessington's Kensington house waiting for the Count to show his face. Actually the law then stipulated that a writ could not be served after dark or when the creditor was on a property not his own.

Thus D'Orsay and his mistress stayed in the barren and bolted house all day and opened it at night to entertain the usual crowd of famous guests.

But this state of affairs could not continue. Something had to be done. And D'Orsay did it by fleeing to France after Marguerite promised to follow him when she had settled with her own creditors.

In May 1849 Marguerite Blessington auctioned all her furniture and objets d'art. During the auction she stood in a corner while society women who had once refused to be seen in her company swarmed about leering and gloating.

The result of the sale $24,000, allowed her to settle her debts, distribute presents to her servants and still retain $3,000. Then she set sail for France to rejoin Count D'Orsay.

Soon after they met the couple moved into a modest apartment. Neighbors often saw them walking on shopping expeditions towards the centre of Paris arm in arm. They seemed happy.

Then in June 1840, less than a month after the reunion, the Countess of Blessington died of a heart attack and was buried in the churchyard of Chambourcy.

And there almost daily for two years Count D'Orsay slaved building a beautiful mausoleum over her tomb. The work done, he died suddenly and was buried beside his mistress's remains.

Opium smokers in a Sydney dive. These places operated flagrantly and catered for European as well as Oriental clients.

Sydney's Dens of Iniquity

L ATE in August 1891 it was difficult for citizens to find even standing room in the environs of the Sydney Town Hall as the inquiry into Chinese vice in the city really began to warm up.

Primarily the commission which was called to conduct the probe was concerned with the oriental gambling dens that dotted Sydney from Goulburn Street to Lower George Street.

But now it found that opium smoking and prostitution represented an even greater menace.

And even as the inquiry heard evidence of the vice that was being carried on right under the noses of the police, a young girl sat in the Town Hall vestibule drawing on an opium-charged pipe.

Indeed the vestibule reeked with an atmosphere of decadence, with sinister-looking Chinese mingling with obvious dope addicts and prostitutes.

But inside at the hearing the evidence set the five-man commission back on its heels, as a witness told of the discovery of an opium-bemused young woman lying in a bunk in a Goulburn Street dive surrounded by 30 Chinese drug-addicts.

Then there were the local girls who calmly admitted living in vermin-infested, humanity-packed tenements with one or more of their Chinese lovers.

And there were the girls who did not turn a hair as they told the startled commissioners that they preferred Chinese men for they were better lovers and treated their women with more consideration than Europeans.

But the Chinese were not the only ones on trial, for the Sydney police had to face a barrage of allegations that they had been bribed to turn a blind eye to oriental vice.

The story of the sensational inquiry began on 14 July 1891, when a group of Sydney businessmen met in George Street's Fortune of War Hotel and formed the Anti-Chinese Gambling League under the presidency of J. Armstrong.

Certainly these men had grounds to complain, for at the time it was estimated that the income of at least 700 Chinese came exclusively from pak-a-pu and fan-tan gambling rackets.

The more industrious element of the Chinese population worked market gardens around Rushcutters Bay, Alexandria, Mascot and Annandale, while the social pariahs congested the slums in Goulburn and Liverpool Streets and the lower end of George Street.

In these areas wealthy Chinese had decided to add to their fortunes by establishing gambling and dope dives where the less privileged of their compatriots could temporarily escape from the boredom of life.

In time the dens came to attract Europeans, usually sailors from visiting ships, who ranged the darkened streets after visiting the dives, rolling drunks, bashing homeward-bound workers and sexually assaulting lone women.

Teenage girls, in search of an easy living, visited these joints and offered themselves to Chinese as casual pick-ups or permanent mistresses.

It was when the notorious reputations of the Goulburn Street-lower George Street areas began affecting the livehihood of businessmen that the Anti-Chinese League was formed under the merchant Armstrong.

In order to get action Armstrong thundered to the Press: "These dens which are a menace to our country, our homes and our children and a blot on civilisation must be removed.

"The police refuse to act and stand around idly watching this law-breaking. They are waxing fat on bribes and it is our duty to make them act."

Among the first to offer support to Armstrong's league was a group of 25 Chinese businessmen who were anxious to eradicate the elements bringing discredit on their native country.

Indeed it was these Chinese who alleged that threepence in every pound collected by the gambling operators was earmarked to bribe police into inactivity.

Then when the league was backed by newspapers and the newly-formed Labor Party, Inspector A. Atwill of No 4 police division led 20 detectives against Sydney's biggest den, Ah Ping's in George St, a little north of Bridge St.

The detectives smashed their way in, arrested a number of Chinese caught gambling and, for later identification, marked those playing fan-tan with one chalk stroke and those playing pak-a-pu as well as the organisers, with two chalk marks.

After the raid one newspaper commented on the fact that the dive's proprietor and a large number of players had left the premises just before the police broke in. It suggested these people had been tipped off.

On 30 July a number of officials from the anti-gambling league told the Premier, Sir Henry Parkes, that in George St between Bridge St and Circular Quay, Chinese occupied 36 shops.

And, they said, hoping to impress on Parkes the seriousness of the situation, at least 30 of these shops were cover-ups for gambling and opium dens.

The league's secretary R. Kelly told the Premier that the owner of one of these joints was openly boasting that he netted about $120,000 a year in commission from pak-a-pu and fan-tan winnings.

NSW's Premier Sir Henry Parkes heard evidence of the existence of vice in certain city quarters and immediately instituted a royal commission.

A Labor politician who was also present at the interview told Parkes that many believed the police were being bribed with money, gold watches and diamond rings to steer clear of the gambling and dope dives.

Parkes wasted no time taking action and less than three weeks after the interview the Governor Lord Jersey announced the appointment of a Royal Commission.

The commission, consisting of five members under the Lord Mayor W. P. Manning, was called to investigate charges of gambling and police bribes. It would also look into immorality associated with gambling activities.

On the night of 27 August the commissioners made a lightning raid on the Chinese quarters around Wexford (now Wentworth Avenue), Campbell and George Streets.

Actually there was no need for them to break into the premises for from the street itself they were able to see both Europeans and Chinese playing pak-a-pu and fan-tan.

And apart from this blatant display of illegal gambling some of the dives even had notices on the footpaths advertising that games were in progress.

When the commission assembled in session next day several witnesses said only some of the gambling schools had been open the previous night. The rest were closed because they had been tipped off about the com-

An opium smoker.

missioners' raid.

The ironmonger from George Street, Thomas Nock told the commission he had seen Detectives Carson and Beadman displaying expensive jewellery.

He had also seen them dining with owners of gambling dens and joking with patrons at the entrances to some of these gaming houses.

Then Nock dropped a bombshell. He said a Chinese friend had told him he had been asked to pass on a warning to him that he would be murdered unless he left the gambling dives alone.

Another witness called by the commission, Loung Yow, admitted under intense questioning that his lodging house in Goulburn Street had been used for gambling and opium smoking.

Then a second Chinese witness, Long Pen, startled the commission with his story of the secret Loon Yee Tong organisation which demanded a percentage of the winnings from all gambling houses.

He said the money was used to bribe police and pay the legal costs of gambling dive owners and patrons who were arrested and charged.

Long Pen said that once, after he gave evidence against an opium vendor, the Loon Yee Tong had offered a $600 reward for his death.

Later, he said, he was viciously attacked by several Chinese at Waterloo. He had managed to escape and soon after, his assailants were each sentenced to four months' gaol.

He believed that during these gaol terms each prisoner was paid six dollars weekly by the Loon Yee Tong.

After that a reporter from a Sydney newspaper told the commission he had learned of a fund created by the gambling and opium den proprietors to pay off police.

Then a procession of police officers entered the witness box; Carson, Beadman, Constable Adair, Sergeant Higgins and Inspector Atwill. All denied having received bribes and gave explanations for their possession of jewellery and gold watches.

Following these policemen came a number of young white girls who were questioned on opium smoking and immorality.

Some said they were employed by Chinese to work as prostitutes. Others said they were the mistresses of Chinese and had borne their children. All agreed that the Chinese were better lovers than Europeans and treated them with much more consideration.

Later, by visiting some of the tenements in which Chinese kept white women, the commission learned that while some of these girls and young women lived comfortably enough, others wallowed in foul overcrowded conditions.

During this inspection the commissioners found one opium-befuddled woman lying on a filthy bunk in a Goulburn Street room. Around her were 30 Chinese addicts all in various hypnotic states.

On 4 February 1892, the commissioners' report was tabled in Parliament. In it they said that of Sydney's 3,500 Chinese, at least 700 relied entirely on gambling for a living.

Many of the gambling dives were run by syndicates which included well-known shopkeepers as sleeping partners.

The report made clear the fact that the vast majority of the city's Chinese population was thoroughly law-abiding but it was concerned with the number of orientals who were gambling and opium addicts.

The commissioners refused to accept the allegation that one Chinese made $120,000 a year from gambling commissions and would not condemn the females who lived with Chinese in preference to Europeans.

The worst facet of these girls' lives, the report went on, was that invariably they were introduced to opium addiction.

The girls, as well as Chinese, the commissioners said, were able to buy their opium supplies openly from shopkeepers as well as lodginghouse owners.

Not a single allegation about police accepting bribes, the report said, could be substantiated. The report also suggested that the Government

should give police wide powers to raid suspected gambling and opium premises without warrants.

The report concluded: "Police should make frequent visits to gaming houses in addition to organised raids to harass those who make their livings by gambling or who gamble for amusement."

Following this report several newspapers accused the commission of whitewashing the police despite what they called "substantiated accusations of bribery against them".

In the face of these bitter attacks Sydney police rolled up their sleeves and let the Chinese gambling and opium principals have it.

The raids went on without letup. The notorious houses closed and the schools were forced to go underground. In time police activities became too hot even for these operators.

The era of Sydney's infamous oriental gambling dives and opium dens had at last come to an end.

Police raiding a Sydney opium den in the 1950s.

Thomas Parr.

The Shameless Farmer of Winnington

THE citizens of Winnington, a village in Shropshire, talked of little in the early months of 1588 except that "dirty old man" Thomas Parr.

Not only was he lazy in his personal habits but he drank to excess and seduced any young wench he could get his hands on. What made it worse was that the villagers loved his long-suffering wife Jane.

People turned their backs on Parr, the drunken lecher, when they passed him in the streets while the parsons, their arms waving wildly in their pulpits, called down the wrath of heaven on his dissipated head.

Not that Thomas Parr was unduly concerned, for his 106th birthday was pending and the fun he was having could not last for ever.

Actually the fun was to go on for another 46 years (give or take a few years) before one of the oldest men in English history succumbed, not to decaying old age, but to a surfeit of good living at the age of about 152.

Nevertheless, despite his scandalous past, Thomas Parr had become such a legend at his death that, with due ceremony, his body was carried to Westminister Abbey for burial.

And there it was entombed near the remains of the nine monarchs he had outlived—Edward IV, Edward V, Richard III, Henry VII, Henry VIII, Edward VI, Mary, Elizabeth and James I.

Thamas Parr, the man who was to live through several great eras of history, was born, in Winnington, probably in February 1483, the son of a village farmer.

At 17 he was doing most of the heavy work on the farm while devoting his leisure hours to the pursuit of the village maidens and younger matrons.

In 1518, Parr senior died, leaving his son the small plot be called a farm. There Thomas worked hard earning a living and still doing his share of wenching until, not long before his 80th birthday, he staggered the villagers by abandoning his bachelorhood.

It was surprising enough that old Thomas should marry at such a late stage of his life. What was more suprising was that the pretty Jane Taylor, almost young enough to be his great grand-daughter, should have accepted his proposal.

91

But the real shock was not to come until the following year when Jane presented her husband with a son. Nevertheless the boy lived only 10 weeks while a daughter who followed survived just three weeks.

At the age of 103 Old Parr, as he was now known, was just as active as ever. Yet he must have realised there was a limit to his longevity for he let it be known that he intended forsaking his frivolous ways and saving for his old age.

A year later it became apparent that he had no intention of turning over a new leaf.

He began dressing more carefully than usual, combed his long grey hair incessantly, and was often seen talking to that scandalous village wench, Katharine Milton.

Even at church he left the side of his distraught wife and moved across the aisle to sit close up against Miss Milton. There was much rubbing of knees and touching of hands and the worshippers followed every move.

In 1588 the talk in every British village, town and city (with one exception) was of the threatened Spanish invasion. The exception was Winnington, where the sole topic was the child the hussy Milton had produced to the

degenerate Old Parr.

The villagers spurned the old roue while the vicars lambasted him in their churches.

What made the sin worse, the villagers said, was that Old Parr should choose the year of his marriage's silver anniversary to flaunt his immorality.

In the end anti-Parr anger became so intense that the people called a special meeting and decided the ancient reprobate must endure the punishment of the stocks.

After his head and wrists had been pinioned in the stocks his legs were bound so that he had practically no movement whatsoever.

Then the more youthful members of the community pelted him with rotten eggs, fruit and vegetables while the older took advantage of his situation to deliver sermons on the need for chastity.

After several hours of this treatment Old Parr was released, draped with the white sheet of penance, given a lighted candle and then dragged off to the church.

There he was subjected to another sermon, this time from the parson, who assured him of the pain of hell's fires unless he mended his ways.

The cottage in which Parr spent a lifetime that spanned the reigns of nine monarchs. The great-grandson of his landlord once tried to evict him without success.

One of the results of Old Parr's public humiliation was the death (some say from sheer shame) of his wife Jane. Another was the old man's determination to carry on further clandestine relationships with more secrecy.

In 1605, when he was 122, Old Parr tired of the perennial chases that might land him back in the stocks and decided to marry the widow Jane Adda.

No children were born to the marriage but otherwise Old Parr seemed to be his usual self as he worked with the vigor of a young man on his farm.

At the age of 130 his body began declining even if his spirits remained as virile as ever. His hearing and sight faded, his hair fell out and so did his teeth. But his desires remained as youthful as ever.

He still drank and ate heartily but he had to abandon most of his farm labors and spent much time sleeping. When not in bed he usually spent his time munching with toothless gums on green cheese, garlic and onions.

The liquids he preferred included skimmed milk, ale and cherry wine.

When he was about 140 Old Parr became involved in a legal wrangle but he was more than able to hold his own.

At that time his current landlord (three others had predeceased the indestructible Old Parr) decided to see if he could get possession of the cottage.

The problem was that the landlord's great-grandfather, assuming his tenant would live a normal life span, gave Thomas Parr a lifetime tenancy.

The landlord decided the best way round the impasse was to prove that Old Parr was so blind and helpless it would be better for him if he were sent to some institution where he could get proper attention.

Hearing of the scheme, Parr told his wife to place a small pin on the floor about a yard from his feet when she heard the landlord coming up the path.

Thus when the landlord entered the cottage Parr turned to his wife and said. "Is that not a pin at my feet. Pick it up lest the landlord tread on it."

So the pin was retrieved and the landlord, realising his plan could not succeed, paid his repects to his ancient tenant and quickly took his leave.

By 1635, when he was 152, Thomas Parr was such a local legend that villagers flocked to his cottage just to watch him sitting in a chair by the fireside.

And that was the year Thomas Howard, second Earl of Arundel, heard of the ancient in Winnington and determined to exhibit him in London as one of the wonders of the age.

As a result Howard had a special two-horse carriage built for Old Parr's transport to London and sent a message to his daughter-in-law asking her to travel to Winnington and administer to the old man during his journey.

One of Howard's employees, Brian Kelly, was also ordered to ride alongside the coach and to "attend and defray all manner of reckonings and expenses" on the way.

During the painfully slow 10-day trip to London, curious crowds pressed up against the coach at various towns and villages with such vigour that Kelly almost despaired of getting his charge alive to their destination.

Arriving in London, Old Parr was installed in Arundel's town house and in September 1635 arrangements were made to present the ancient curiosity to King Charles I.

Charles was delighted with Old Parr and talked with him for more than an hour.

The King asked: "You have lived longer than any man. What have you done more than any other man?"

Thomas Parr had still not forgotten his ordeal in the stocks. He replied, "Ah sire! I did penance when I was 105 years old."

Now Charles pondered another question. At last he asked: "Tell me what do you consider the true religion?"

Quick as a flash the old man answered: "Sire! I hold it safest to be of the religion of the king and queen of the times for I know I came raw into the world and account it no point of wisdom to be broiled out of it."

Charles was so delighted by the old man's wit that he ordered Arundel to make certain his guest had whatever he wanted during his stay in London.

But Arundel was scarcely interested in the personal welfare of the man who could earn him an extra income. As a result Old Parr was put on display at the Queen's Head Inn in the Strand at twopence a look.

For an extra penny patrons could get "dead drunk" as well.

The trouble was that Old Parr took advantage of his host's hospitality to gorge himself on unfamiliar and exotic foods and drink gallons of the best wines.

And even as the drastic alterations to his normal bodily functions were quickly killing him, the great artists of the day like Van Dyck and Rubens packed into the Queen's Head painting portraits of him.

Thomas Parr died in Arundel's mansion on 14 November 1635, the victim of the "fogs and grogs of London".

Later the great medical pioneer, Dr William Harvey, conducted an autopsy on the body and then proclaimed that Old Parr should never have been moved from his native village.

He thus made the inference that Parr would have lived even longer had be not been turned into a public spectacle.

Although legends have attributed amazingly long lives to Thomas Parr's sons, grandchildren. and great-grandchildren, he actually left no heirs except Katharine Milton's illegitimate son, who did not live to any great age.

Old Parr's death presented a great opportunity for quacks to peddle some of their worthless medicines.

For instance soon after Parr's death one charlatan marketed his Old Parr Life Pills. These were guaranteed to give at least 150 years of healthy life.

As late as 1845 the Cigar and Smokers Companion claimed that smoking was obviously not injurious to health for Old Parr smoked most of his life.

This claim was dropped when research revealed that the amazing old man never touched tobacco. But the other vices he practised did not seem to worry him.

Jake (Greasy Thumb) Guzik began his crime career operating a 50 cent brothel.

"Greasy Thumb" Guzik's 50-cent Bordello

ONE day in 1906 Jake Guzik, a stocky young Sicilian-born waiter, took his older brother Harry to inspect a sleazy-looking saloon he had just bought on Chicago's Armour Avenue for the two of them.

Harry was not enthusiastic when he saw the purchase in the heart of the Levee, the city's notorious vice district. It was dirty and dilapidated and few of the passersby seemed to be entering the saloon doors.

"We won't get rich peddling booze here," said Harry Guzik finally, at which his brother looked at him with his usual unsmiling, doleful expression.

"Maybe not from booze," he said. "But as long as there are guys wanting a girl we'll do all right."

And so it proved. From the 50-cent bordello he started above the saloon, Jake (Greasy Thumb) Guzik developed into a tycoon of Chicago prostitution.

He built up a string of brothels and when he died half a century later was reputed to control about 5,000 prostitutes.

From vice Guzik branched into gambling and liquor rackets. He had a talent for business organisation and was the financial brain behind such notorious Chicago crime bosses as Johnny Torrio and Al Capone.

While these men directed the strong-arm operations, the pouchy-eyed Guzik set up the dummy companies, worked shrewd tricks with lawyers and accountants, transferred funds to Swiss banks and handled the graft.

His motto was: "Don't kill a man if you can pay him off." He believed in graft just as devoutly as he believed sex was the most saleable and profitable commodity in the world.

Guzik got his nickname of Greasy Thumb from the way the money slipped off his fingers when he counted out the monthly payments to police and other law-enforcement officers.

Born in 1886, Jake Guzik arrived in the U.S. with his Sicilian parents at the age of five. Soon after the family settled in Chicago.

Unlike most other big names of the booming ganster era between the wars Guzik had no history of juvenile delinquency.

But he did have a well-developed money sense and was more interested in a variety of boyhood business enterprises than school.

Later he worked as a factory hand, barman and waiter and at the age of 20 had accumulated enough cash to form a partnership with his brother Harry and buy the two-storey saloon on Armour Avenue.

The saloon, which was called McCarthy and Duval's, occupied the ground floor and was run by Harry Guzik.

Above the saloon was what had once been a cheap lodging house but it had not operated for years. So Jake partitioned its 20 rooms into 38 smaller ones. Now he too was ready for business.

The harlots he installed were blowsy and shopworn. But the fee was only half a dollar and the clients (mostly saloon drinkers directed upstairs by Harry) were not fussy.

Jake Guzik took the half dollar fee but his girls could keep any tips they wheedled out of the customers.

The enterprise prospered and the Guziks were soon able to open a second brothel of 16 rooms on 22nd Street. It was called Why Not and was run by one of the saloon girls promoted to madam. The fee at the Why Not was $2.

All went well until 1910 when prostitution was outlawed in Chicago. Frequent police raids and subsequent fines then began to eat into the Guzik profits.

So Jake went to Bathhouse John Coughlin and Hinky Dink Mike Kenna, two notorious grafting city politicians who specialised in providing protection from police interference for illegal gambling.

Coughlin and Kenna had recently enlarged their graft to include the now illegal brothels and for a monthly payment of $250 for each of his houses, Guzik was able to stop the police raids.

But his transactions with the grafters had opened his eyes to new possibilities of profit so he went to them with a proposition.

Guzik suggested they double their charge and instal him as their official graft collector for a fee of five per cent.

Coughlin and Kenna agreed and thereafter Jake ran their racket for them on efficient business lines.

His profits were poured back into prostitution with brother Harry acting as his manager. By the end of World War I Jake Guzik controlled 16 Chicago houses of ill-fame.

They ranged from the original 50-cent house above McCarthy and Duval's saloon to a plush mansion on Prairie Avenue run by a notorious Chicago madam, Zoe Willard. The fee was $250 a night.

As well as collecting the cash for Coughlin and Kenna, Guzik also took over the task of making the payouts to police officers who called regularly at his office on Wabash Avenue. It was there he acquired his famous nickname.

Johnny Kelley, a reporter on the Chicago Tribune, was there one afternoon when it seemed every law enforcement agency in Chicago had sent a representative to collect cash from Guzik.

"The money just rolls off Guzik's thumb as though it were greased," Kelley wrote in an ineffectual expose article in the Tribune.

98

And from that day on Jake was stuck with the name of Greasy Thumb Guzik.

Although he hated it and bi⋅terly complained when newspapers, radio stations and others used it, it was a small price to pay for the millions he coined from crime in Chicago.

Then came Prohibition and the dizzy era of the Roaring 20s with its mobsters, rum-running, hijackers and blazing guns.

Guzik saw the opportunity to extend his operations once again and tried to go into a bootlegging partnership with veteran Chicago crime boss Big Jim Colosimo.

But the ageing Colosimo had just acquired a new young wife. He was satisfied with the vice and gambling rackets he already controlled and wanted to spend more time at home instead of enlarging his business.

So Jake Guzik went to Colosimo's ambitious young nephew Johnny Torrio and they came to an agreement.

As a result on 11 May 1920, Big Jim was shot to death in his Wabash Avenue restaurant for a fee of $10,000 paid to a professional killer.

When someone took the news to Greasy Thumb Guzik he shrugged and commented: "What the hell, he wouldn't have lasted anyway. That dame he married was too young and eager for him."

So Johnny Torrio took over Colosimo's rackets and with Guzik as his background partner and financial adviser moved into bootlegging as well.

Paying off the police was again Greasy Thumb's department. He did it so efficiently that Torrio's breweries, alcohol stills and delivery trucks went unmolested.

"It's wonderful the way we can hide those six-storey breweries so the cops can't even find them," Guzik once commented wryly.

In 1922 it was Guzik who introduced a scar-faced young thug from New York named Al Capone into the organisation to handle the strong-arm side of the business.

This move was made so that Torrio could concentrate on liquor production and distribution.

Capone quickly broke the rival Genna gang and in 1924 engineered the murder of another bootleg boss Dion O'Banion in the flower shop he conducted as a blind.

But the O'Banion killing brought reprisals against the Torrio-Capone-Guzik combination from a tough, trigger-happy gangster, Hymie Weiss.

One morning Weiss's men wounded Torrio with sub-machinegun fire as he left his home. After that he decided to retire forthwith to New York with the $10 million he had accumulated.

So Al Capone became the crime czar of Chicago with Jake Guzik still lurking in the background as his closest associate.

Although he became known as Capone's secretary of the treasury there were many who believed that the mild-mannered Greasy Thumb was the real ruler of the Chicago underworld.

To support this they told of a banquet one evening at a Cicero restaurant when Capone had his aides hold Albert Anselmi and John Scalise while he battered them to death with a baseball bat.

The pair had reportedly been boasting and talking too much of the gang's affairs.

After the fatal beatings Capone screamed at the assembly:

"I don't like guys who talk too much. This should teach everyone to keep their traps shut. You guys have gotta learn loyalty."

During the violence Jake Guzik had continued imperturbably with his dinner. Now as Capone seemed likely to resume his tirade he pulled at his sleeve. "Okay, Al," said Greasy Thumb. "That's enough. You've made your point."

Capone immediately sat down without another word and consulted the menu about his dessert.

And while he was doing this the efficient Guzik ordered two gang followers to take the bodies of Anselmi and Scalise and "dump them in some vacant allotment".

The Capone-Guzik partnership continued until 1931 when Scarface Al was dragged off to Alcatraz with an 11-year sentence for income tax evasion.

Greasy Thumb continued to run the gang until Prohibition was repealed in 1933. Then he returned to his own specialty of prostitution to which he now added gambling.

The law did not catch up with him until 1938 when he received his first and only sentence of three years for income tax evasion.

Lawyers got Guzik out in 18 months after he made a cash settlement of $1½ million with the Government to clear all his past tax liabilities.

He returned to his Chicago mansion which had the windows of every room, even the attic, reinforced with heavy steel bars.

This luxury home was the only evidence of Greasy Thumb's wealth for unlike other gangsters he never boasted, never swaggered.

His brother Harry who had long acted as general manager for all his vice operations died in 1948 and after that he ran his own business.

He still owned his original saloon, McCarthy and Duval's, for which he had paid $3,600. It was finally sold in 1955 for $80,000.

After World War II Guzik gradually reduced the number of his old-style brothels and used the experienced madams who had run them to enter other forms of the vice trade.

As far back as 1926 Greasy Thumb was reputed to have set up the first call-girl ring in Chicago.

This operation was now extended and by the 1950s he was estimated to control 500 call-girl apartments in the city.

He had some 5,000 prostitutes on his books directed by at least a score of former madams. He also organised an elaborate system by which they were sent round a circuit of all the big U.S. resort hotels.

In 1952, as the mastermind of the U.S. vice trade, Guzik was subpoenaed to appear before the famed Kefauver Crime Committee.

But they got nothing out of Greasy Thumb who sat dolefully in the wit-

America's top crime tycoon, Al Capone. The only man who could handle him was his first employer Greasy Thumb Guzik.

ness box and gave the same parrot reply to 150 questions:

"I refuse to answer on the grounds that it might incriminate me or tend to incriminate me or lead by some devious ways to incriminate me."

The nonplussed committee tried to cite him for contempt but lawyers eventually wangled Guzik out of trouble and no further action was taken.

Thus Greasy Thumb was still running his empire of illicit sex with his 5,000 wantons and still guaranteeing them protection with his graft payoffs, when he died suddenly of a stroke one March night in 1956.

His will was never publicised. But a conservative Wall St financial paper estimated the Guzik wealth in investments, real estate, foreign banks and safety deposit boxes all over the U.S. amounted to $150 million.

Sir Kenelm Digby. An admirer called him "the ornament of England", while a detractor referred to him as "an arrant bragging mountebank".

An Amorous Scholar

DOCTORS at the ancient college of Montpellier in France, for centuries one of Europe's greatest centres of medical learning, had heard many famous men, but none so strange as the herculean, scar-faced Englishman who harangued them one summer's day in 1657.

The greybeards listened in growing amazement as their visitor told them about his "Powder of Sympathy", his recipes for preserving female beauty, his experiments with vipers' hearts, crabs' eyes and other grisly objects.

He concluded with a recipe for brewing tea, the new drink recently introduced from Asia. "Let the hot water remain on the leaves no longer than it takes to recite the Misere Psalm", he said solemnly.

Sir Kenelm Digby, the lecturer at Montpellier, was a man of many and varied attainments. "The ornament of England", one admirer called him. "An arrant bragging mountebank", was another, less charitable description.

Digby's career was one of history's virtuoso performances. He had been a Mediterranean buccaneer, diplomat, courtier, friend of poets and scholars, and central figure in the most tempestuous love affair of the age.

He lived to be hailed as a prodigy of scientific wisdom, though his experiments were a fantastic farrago of modern rational inquiry and the blackest dabblings in medieval astrology, alchemy and magic.

Kenelm Digby, scion of an old family of Midland squires, was born in 1603, and was a child of three when his father was beheaded on Tower Hill for his share in Guy Fawkes' Gunpowder Plot.

Most of the Digby estates were confiscated. The boy was brought up in seclusion, but he attended Oxford University and astonished his tutors by his mixture of precocious learning and full-blooded zest for living.

Digby was still only 17 when he fell passionately in love with Venetia Hanley, daughter of a rich Shropshire landowner, and described as "a girl of most extraordinary beauty, great intellect, but—alas—of a dubious kind of virtue."

Digby was now a handsome young giant, well over six feet tall, "of a presence that drew the eyes of all men and women upon him, a wonderful, graceful behaviour and a flow of language that surprised and delighted."

103

These masculine charms soon involved Digby in serious trouble. In Paris, he was introduced to the court of the Queen Mother Marie de Medici, who, despite her 47 years, became violently enamoured of the youthful Englishman and tried vainly to seduce him.

At last, fearing assassination at the order of the jealous queen, Digby spread a false report that he had died of fever and fled to Italy.

He was almost penniless when he was rescued by his cousin, Sir John Digby, recently appointed Ambassador to Spain.

Kenelm Digby reached Madrid in 1623, just as Prince Charles of England and the Duke of Buckingham arrived, under the prosaic names of Mr. Smith and Mr. Brown, to seek the hand of a Spanish princess for the prince.

The mission was a failure. Buckingham quarrelled with the haughty Madrid dons, Charles thought the princess ugly, and Digby clinched the matter by a scandalous attempted elopement with a young Spanish girl.

Digby returned to England with the royal party, a high favourite with the gay and pleasure-loving Charles, who succeeded to the throne only two years later.

However, Digby was dismayed to find that, during his four years wanderings, the reputation of the fair Venetia had sunk considerably.

Her latest "protector" was the Earl of Dorset, who allowed her 500 guineas a year, and she had had a score of other aristocratic lovers. But Digby was able to combine love and philosophy.

"Any wise and lusty man may make a virtuous woman out of a harlot," he said. In 1625 he and Venetia were married.

The marriage justified Digby's sentiments. Venetia settled down to become a loyal and devoted wife and, according to common report, a guinea pig for many of her husband's remarkable scientific researches.

Digby had a restless, inquiring mind. He brooded over old tomes of alchemy and magic, he studied botany, surgery and physics, he once kept a snake's heart beating for 12 hours on a warm plate and invited his friends to observe the spectacle on the table as they dined.

One of his favourite projects was a recipe for preserving female beauty. He fed Venetia on capons stuffed with vipers, snail soup and other concoctions, but her fidelity withstood even those grim tests.

Digby had expected lucrative preferment from the new king, Charles I, but his hopes were blasted by the jealous enmity of the all-powerful royal favourite, the Duke of Buckingham.

When the duke's attempt to invade the French coast ended in disastrous failure in 1627, Digby decided to outshine his rival by leading a naval expedition against French ships in the Mediterranean.

King Charles refused to license him as a privateer, and it was as a virtual pirate that Digby sailed from England late in 1627 with two small but heavily-armed ships, the Eagle and Elizabeth.

On 11 June 1628, a tempting array of ships were clustered in the Bay of Alexandretta—four fat-hulled French merchantmen loaded with £40,000 worth of gold, silks and spices, and three great Venetian galleys, floating

Venetia Hanley was "a girl of most extraordinary beauty, great intellect, but–alas– of a dubious kind of virtue." She became Digby's wife.

castles with 50 guns and 300 seamen in each.

At dawn, Digby's two little ships swooped into the harbour "like hawks upon a dovecote", running straight at the galleys and blasting them at point-blank range before the Venetian gunners realised what was happening.

Two hours of furious fighting ended with the galleys scattered and on fire, three French ships captured and the fourth driven ashore a blazing hulk. The action cost Digby one man dead and a handful of wounded.

While Digby cruised triumphantly in the wreck-littered bay, however, the Turkish authorities ashore seized every English merchant in the town, flung them into prison and threatened to strangle them en masse.

Only the British consul was freed to visit Digby in his ship, where he knelt on the deck and tearfully begged the conqueror to depart. With too few men to storm the town, Digby was reluctantly forced to set sail.

By February, 1629, he was back in England.

During Digby's absence, Buckingham had fallen under an assassin's dagger and there was no rival in his path. He was knighted, made a Commissioner of the Navy and forfeited family estates were restored.

For a few years Digby basked in prosperity, conducting experiments and debating with learned men whether eels were really generated by warm mud, whether ulcers were best cured by crabs' eyes or a piece of fat bacon that had been nailed to a post facing south.

In many respects Digby was a credulous child of his age, but his ceaseless practical experiments with animals and plants made him one of the most remarkable pioneers of biology and botany, and science was later to confirm many of his theories.

Then, in 1633, he was stunned by the loss of his wife Venetia. Gossip said she had at last succumbed to his search for the elixir of perpetual beauty, that she had been poisoned by "viper wine" Digby forced her to swallow.

Whatever the truth, Digby behaved like a maniac in his grief. For three years he lived as a hermit, his beard unshorn, draped from head to foot in a long black cloak.

When Digby emerged from seclusion his days of national popularity were already over. The quarrel between king and Parliament was hurrying England towards civil war, and Digby was a notorious and violent ultra-royalist.

The puritans particularly hated him for his friendship with the king's French wife, Queen Henrietta Maria. He was accused of intriguing with France and Spain to get foreign aid for the monarchy in the impending war.

In February, 1642, six months before the Civil War erupted, Digby fled to Paris. Parliament promptly seized his estates and proclaimed him a traitor.

For the next 18 years, apart from fleeting secret visits to Britain, Digby was an exile from the land that had idolised him.

It was, however, a busy exile. In Paris he published volumes on religion, chemistry and mathematics, and became a friend of the famous philosopher Rene Descartes.

He continued his experiments, especially into the "Powder of Sympathy" that spread his fame all over Europe.

106

Digby claimed to have discovered the miraculous powder when he was treating a friend wounded in a duel.

When a garter soaked in the victim's blood was placed in a solution of the powder, the wound immediately began to heal, though the injured man was several miles away at the time.

Digby's explanation was a fantastic theory of "sympathetic atoms" flying between the blood in the basin and the wounded flesh. It was typical of the age that the most learned surgeons accepted it as a serious contribution to medical knowledge.

It was not until 1657 that Digby fully expounded the magical property of the "Powder of Sympathy" in his lecture at Montpellier.

Within a few years, his lecture was printed in French, English, Dutch and Latin and the book ran through nearly 20 editions before the end of the century.

In the meantime, the Civil War in England had rolled to its foregone conclusion. Cromwell and Parliament were victorious; in January, 1640, King Charles was beheaded, and his queen Henrietta Maria, was an exile in her homeland of France.

Digby, her most ardent sympathiser, bustled with schemes to restore her and her young son, later Charles II, to the English throne. His most ambitious plan was to land in Ireland and stir up rebellion there with French and Spanish aid.

To raise funds for the desperate enterprise, Digby volunteered to go to Rome and seek a loan from the Pope.

He was plausible and ingratiating, making sweeping promises that King Charles and all his court would become converts to Catholicism as soon as the usurper Cromwell was overthrown.

Pope Innocent X was too shrewd to be taken in by such claims. Digby returned with £36,000 as a personal gift to the exiled queen, but he got little encouragement for his schemes for an Irish invasion.

His hopes dashed, Digby paid a daring visit to London and tried to open negotiations with the other side, offering to act as Cromwell's secret agent in Europe.

He was arrested, then freed and sent back to Paris after some obscure dealings that were never fully explained.

Digby's wanderings ended at last with the Restoration in 1660. Though Charles II refused to let him appear at court because of his suspected spy association with Cromwell, he was allowed to return to England and spend the last five years of his life in peace at his house in Covent Garden.

When Sir Kenelm Digby died on 11 June 1665, the grave claimed one of the most adventurous and many-sided geniuses who trod the turbulent stage of 17th century Europe.

Gaby Deslys surrounded herself with fabulous luxuries, the by-products of her beauty.

King Manoel's Indiscretion

LATE in 1910, a group of Paris society columnists were summoned to a press conference in a fashionable quarter of the capital. Their hostess was Gaby Deslys, dainty, blue-eyed toast of the boulevards and most celebrated revue actress of the age. Gaby received surrounded by the trophies of her profession—autographed photographs of princes and potentates, furs, diamonds and ropes of pearls, and even a pair of jewelled garters prominently displayed. Most of the photographs were of a handsome, sallow-faced young man who—only a week before—had been King Manoel II of Portugal, and was now a hunted exile from his country. Common gossip said his infatuation for Gaby had cost him his throne.

Gaby had summoned the society writers to denounce the slander that she was a royal mistress. In doing so, she coined an immortal phrase: "The king and I," said Gaby, "are just good friends."

If the hard-boiled journalists disbelieved her, they were too polite to say so to her ingenuous face. But the story of King Manoel and the actress remained one of the liveliest scandals of Europe in the years just before World War I.

Her stage career was as brief as it was dazzling. She died with tragic suddenness at the age of 36—but in that time she had piled up a fortune of more than £400,000.

Gaby was born of poor parents in Marseilles in 1884, and she retained the local accent of the great southern seaport to the end of her life.

Before she was 17, Gaby was singing to the sailors in the cheap cafes of the city, and her success soon encouraged her to set out to storm the theatrical world of Paris.

For a few years, Gaby did the round of small suburban revues, gradually acquiring a reputation that finally brought her starring roles at the Theatre des Capucines in the heart of the boulevards.

C B Cochran, later most famous of all British impresarios, met her about this time and described her as "resembling a fascinating little doll, with wide-open blue eyes and corn-coloured hair".

By 1908, Gaby was the reigning Queen of the Paris revue stage. The rich

King Manuel II of Portugal was willing to lose his throne, just to hold the affections of a French actress.

and famous followed her carriage through the Bois de Boulogne. Presents were lavished on her, many of which she cannily converted into cash in her bank account.

Visits to London brought her international celebrity, made her the toast of the West End clubs, and packed the Palace Theatre for months when she appeared in "naughty" Parisian revues.

She charmed British critics by declaring frankly: "I was not born to be a great actress. My singing is perhaps only mediocre, but I have youth and good looks, and more than anything—ambition.

"I was not born among the poor of Marseilles for nothing. Thank heaven, when the gaiety of the south is in the blood, it can never be extinguished."

It was in London, at a select supper party with a group of young guardsmen, that Gaby met the man whose fate was to be so romantically and dramatically entangled with her own.

Among the guests drinking Gaby's health in champagne was a shy, boyish-faced young man of 20 who, only 18 months before, had been raised by murder to become King Manoel II of Portugal.

Since his accession, Manoel had lived mostly abroad, while his capital of Lisbon seethed with stories of political corruption, republican plots and fears of revolution.

Manoel had come into an unhappy heritage. He had never forgotten the terrible day in February, 1908, when his father and brother had been shot dead before his eyes as they rode through the Lisbon streets.

King Carlos, Queen Amelie, Crown Prince Felipe and Manoel were together in the carriage when the assassin's bullets struck down Carlos and Felipe, and their blood drenched Manoel's gay uniform.

Manoel inherited the throne of the Braganzas, and also the scandals that had linked his father and monarchist politicians in devious rackets to loot the public treasury.

Cries for a republic were growing louder every week. Even the autocratic Queen Amelie was forced to promise that her son would introduce sweeping democratic reforms.

Manoel himself, however, was a broken reed. A simple, kindly youth, he was haunted by fears of revolution and a horror of the turbulent Lisbon mob.

When he emerged from the Necessidades Palace, it was in a closed carriage with cavalry clattering at his side. Promises of reform were soon forgotten by the greedy, feuding politicians who formed his government.

Manoel seized every chance to leave Portugal and "complete his education" by visits to the European capitals—chiefly in the theatres, hotels and drawing rooms of London and Paris.

Climax to this educative process was his meeting with the fascinating Gaby Deslys, and Manoel made no attempt to conceal his complete infatuation.

He showered Gaby with costly presents. He occupied a box at the Palace Theatre night after night, until theatregoers complained that police clearing a way for the royal limousine disorganised peak evening traffic.

111

Gaby welcomed the blaze of publicity, with a shrewd eye to its monetary value. No gossip writer was refused an interview and Gaby ensured that they had plenty of material.

It was whispered that the royal gifts included garters set with sapphires and diamonds, that Manoel had offered her apartments in his Lisbon palace, that he was even planning a secret wedding.

Perhaps it was the story of the jewelled garters that roused to action the management of the luxurious and highly-respectable Savoy Hotel, where Gaby was staying in London.

When Gaby fell mildly ill, the manager saw his chance. Politely suggesting that the ailment might be contagious, he asked her to transfer her quarters elsewhere.

By now, Manoel's infatuation was the talk of Europe. To the republicans plotting over their wine glasses in the Lisbon cafes, it provided a new and deadly propaganda weapon.

"The whole nation shudders with nausea at the rotten system of the monarchy!" declared Dr. Theophilo Braga, the celebrated writer, lecturer, and philosopher of the republican movement.

The court was accused of corruption, police tyranny, and of "handing over Portugal bound hand and foot to the greed of international money-lenders" to pay for Manoel's pleasures.

Gaby Deslys was denounced as a trollop, "with no code, written or un-written, to impose reticence on her intimate affairs".

One London critic also wrote that Gaby "combined a kittenish vivacity with an instinct for self-advertisement. She did not ask her royal lover to respect her secret, and showed herself no respecter of his."

Alarmed at the mounting scandal, Queen Amelie recalled her son to Lisbon. But Manoel soon showed that his passion for Gaby made him completely indifferent to public opinion.

When the actress visited Portugal, she was installed in a private suite in the royal palace, and the king rained gifts on her with undiminished ardour.

Sweeping republican gains at the elections in August, 1910, after Gaby had returned in Paris, were the prelude to the long gathering storm of revolution.

For two months longer, the monarchist government clung to power, until the political murder of a republican leader, Dr. Bombarda, sealed the fate of Manoel's crown.

Revolutionary mobs swarmed through Lisbon. Half the army joined the rebels, fighting a bloody battle with artillery and machine guns through the city against the royalist troops.

Final blow came when the crews of warships in the River Tagus raised the red and green republican flag and began shelling the royal palace at almost point-blank range.

Manoel at first romantically swore to die in the ruins. But, finding himself deserted by courtiers and servants, he was bundled into a car with Queen Amelie and driven from Lisbon.

112

From the fishing port of Ericeira, the fugitives escaped to Gibraltar, and from there they were transported to England in King George V's royal yacht.

Portugal became a republic, and Manoel remained a forgotten exile at Twickenham, near London, until his death in 1932 at the age of 42.

His romance with Gaby Deslys died with the revolution, and it is uncertain whether he ever saw her again—though she continued to be blamed for his downfall.

Gaby herself strongly denied this fatal role. Just after Manoel's flight, she told a Paris press conference that she had never been his lover and stories of his gifts were grossly exaggerated.

"Why should I have wanted his money?" she demanded. "If I needed jewelled garters I could buy them myself. My income is bigger than the king's ever was."

But the public remained sceptical. And a New York theatrical offer of 14,000 dollars a week was largely stimulated by stories of Gaby's liaison with the young king.

As co-star with Al Jolson in The Honeymoon Express, Gaby was a huge success—though one carping critic wrote: "She minces along and turns round with a little wriggle that makes her look like a large pink canary shaking its feathers after a bath."

Gaby, however, was anxious to impress the Americans favourably and told one interviewer: "I am really very serious, when I have the time. And please tell your readers I am quite religious at heart."

The two years after World War I saw Gaby at the height of her international fame. Her long train of admirers included such an unlikely character as James Barrie (of Peter Pan celebrity), who wrote a play, Rosy Rapture, for her. It was a resounding flop.

Showman C B Cochran summed up her appeal to London audiences: "She looks and behaves exactly as British people think a French actress should look and behave."

Then in February 1920, the brightest light of the revue theatre was snuffed out with tragic suddenness.

An attack of influenza developed into an infection of the throat. After the operations, Gaby refused to undergo another because she feared her neck would be scarred. On 11 February she died.

In her will, she said: "I have danced all my life for the poor." And, subject to a life interest to her mother and sister, Gaby Deslys left every penny of her £400,000 estate to the poor of her native city of Marseilles.

Bianca Capello at the age of 30. Portrait by Bronzino.

Sensual Deception at the Medici Court

ANY night in the year 1575 a procession of sinister figures might have been seen entering the courtyard of a palace in a secluded street of Florence near the River Arno.

There were grey-beard "magicians" learned in the arts of sorcery and incantations, withered old crones who peddled philtres and love potions, quack doctors, astrologers, dabblers in secret drugs and poisons.

Their patron was the loveliest courtesan in Italy, Bianca Cappello, mistress of Francesco dei Medici, who was heir to the Grand Duke of Tuscany.

To cement her hold on the wastrel young Francesco, Bianca needed a son. She was prepared to enlist the aid of any black art to achieve her aim.

When powders and magic spells failed, Bianca tried to plant a newly-born peasant child on her infatuated lover.

The deception was soon exposed. But, by a compound of sensual fascination, cunning and fortunate "accidents", Bianca was to dominate Florence as mistress or wife for 23 years.

She raised the court of the Medici to its pinnacle of wanton luxury. Poets hailed her as "the new sun of Tuscany and wonder of the age".

The common folk of Florence called her sorceress and witch, and encouraged their children to spit on the public grave into which she was finally and ignominiously shovelled.

Born in 1548, Bianca was the offsping of two of the richest and proudest families in Venice, the Cappellos and Morosinis. She was to pay bitterly for their aristocratic arrogance.

Her father, Bartolomeo Cappello, married a second time when Bianca was a child. She was brought up in strict, lonely seclusion among pious tutors and faded ladies in waiting.

At 16 Bianca was a ravishing beauty, with a pile of auburn hair, dark eyes and the traditional lily-white complexion of young Venetian women.

She was also restless and ripe for adventure when, one day, she saw a handsome youth named Pietro Bonaventuri strolling beneath her window in the square of Sant' Apollinare.

Encouraged by her glances, Pietro bribed the Cappello servants to arrange a secret meeting. Soon the lovers were exchanging letters and vows of deathless fidelity.

But there was one fatal bar to the romance. Pietro was a mere clerk, adding up ducats in the Venetian branch of the great Florentine banking house of Salviati.

Bianca know her family would be outraged by the liaison. Worse, they would probably have Pietro cut down by some hired assassin for presuming to win the heart of a Cappello maiden.

Flight was the only solution. On the night of 28 November 1563, Bianca stuffed handfuls of her mother's jewels into a casket, slipped through a side door of the Cappello palace and joined Pietro on the steps of the Grand Canal.

By next morning their boat had landed them outside Venetian territory. Through Ferrara and Bologna they made their way overland on horseback to Pietro's native city of Florence.

The Cappello fury exploded in an orgy of vengeance. Pietro's uncle was seized in Venice and flung into the Doge's prison. The wretched boatmen were tortured and finally strangled.

Angry letters went to Duke Cosimo dei Medici, ruler of Florence, demanding that the insolent Pietro be executed and Bianca sent back to be locked up in a nunnery in Venice.

Cosimo was indifferent, but rumours of Bianca's rare beauty had already reached his vicious 24-years-old son Francesco. Bianca was summoned to the palace for a personal interview.

Francesco was infatuated at first sight. He loaded Bianca with jewels, promised court employment for Pietro (whom she had just wed), and swore she should never be sent back to Venice.

A year passed, however, before Bianca yielded to become his mistress. By then she was disgusted by Pietro's blatant infidelity, and the household drudgery forced on her by his miserly family.

Late in 1564 she left Pietro's roof with her infant daughter Pellegrina and was installed in a sumptuous, but discreetly secluded, palace in a street leading down to the River Arno.

Meanwhile, for dynastic reasons, it was necessary that Francesco should marry and produce a son to continue the degenerate but still powerful rule of the Medici family in Florence.

The villa of Poggio a Caiano. Francesco died of fever here, and a few hours later Bianca, as she had foreseen, followed him in death.

The courts of Vienna and Madrid produced candidates for his bride, and the chosen victim was a daughter of the Austrian Emperor, the dumpy, devout little Princess Joanna.

In 1565, Francesco travelled to Vienna for the wedding, but spent most of the time composing sonnets to his mistress, addressing Bianca as "the shining Gem from Heaven's Treasury."

As Joanna failed to provide the necessary heir, she rapidly sank into insignificance. It was the lively Bianca who ruled Francesco's entourage of courtesans, wits and artists.

And, as old Duke Cosimo had retired to the arms of his own mistress in the country leaving his son to rule Florence, Bianca was virtual sovereign of the court of Tuscany.

Torquato Tasso, most famous Italian poet of the age, hailed her as "the sun of Tuscany". Benvenuto Cellini fashioned an exquisite silver frame for her miniature portrait.

Bianca presided over the most sumptuous revels staged in the glittering Medici palace since the days of Lorenzo the Magnificent.

A thousand guests attended the hunting parties at the Medici villa in the foothills of the Apennines.

Blanca was dressed in the radiant, jewel-hung splendor of a queen. She was attended by the proudest women in Florence, by 50 torchbearers, Negro lackeys, dwarfs, pages and dressers.

Only one shadow lay across the pageant. Through it swaggered the upstart, quarrelsome, licentious figure of Bianca's husband Pietro, with his demands for money and vulgar amours.

It was no secret that Bianca hoped eventually to wed her paramour. There were three main obstacles to that event—the unhappy Joanna, Pietro, and the fact that Bianca had also failed to bear Francesco a son.

One hot midsummer night in 1572 the obstacles were reduced to two, as Pietro, attended only by one servant, reeled home through the dark streets from visiting his current mistress.

A cloaked figure slipped from an alley, a knife flashed, and Pietro's blood trickled between the cobblestones.

It could have been a vengeful husband. It could equally have been a minion of Bianca—though she went through the pretence of pleading for justice against her husband's unknown murderer.

Two years later, Cosimo dei Medici sank into his grave under the weight of his debauches. Francesco became Duke of Tuscany, and the glory of his house flickered up in a final burst of luxury.

His need for a son was more desperate than ever. Failing that, his heir would be his brother, Cardinal Ferdinando, a silent, ruthless man who despised both Francesco and the adventuress Bianca.

Bianca knew she could expect no mercy if she outlived her lover. The sickly Joanna might die at any time, and, if Bianca could but produce a son, Francesco might well finally wed her.

So began her hunt for help in the Florentine underworld of sorcery, black magic and quackery. She dosed herself and Francesco with powders and potions. She had obscene spells recited.

All was in vain. In August, 1576, she turned to other measures, sending a trusty servant to scour Florence for women about to give birth to children.

Three healthy and ignorant peasant girls were discovered and brought to the house of a physician named Gazzi. On August 28 one of them was delivered of a male child.

Swathed in finest linen, the infant was carried secretly to Bianca's palace. Bianca herself had taken to her bed, enlisting her attendants in the plot under threat of instant execution.

Next morning the exultant Francesco was presented with his changeling "son". He was named Antonio, and guns were fired and flags flew to celebrate his birth.

Bianca's triumph was brief. The real mother had been exiled to Bologna with a bribe of gold. Within a year she repented and set out for Florence, hoping to plead for the return of her child.

She never reached the city. Ambushed on a forest road, she was carried dying to a nearby monastery with an arquebus bullet in her body.

With her last breath she gasped out her story. The monks reported it to Cardinal Ferdinando in Florence, and Duke Francesco was horrified to learn how he had been duped.

So great was his infatuation for Bianca, however, that he forgave his mistress and even provided a pension for the nameless boy.

But the ordinary citizens of Florence, convinced that Bianca had ordered the wretched mother's murder, hated the "sorceress" with a loathing that deepened with the passing years.

In 1578 the Duchess Joanna died after mysteriously falling down the palace stairs. Again the black finger of suspicion pointed at Bianca, but no proof against her ever came to light.

Other fearful tragedies lit the Medici annals with a sinister glare. Francesco's sister was strangled by her betrayed husband, and Francesco's younger brother was murdered by his wife.

Everywhere the suspicious Florentines saw the influence of the hated courtesan. Haunted by fears of assassination, Bianca determined to become Francesco's legal wife as quickly as possible.

On 5 June 1578, they were secretly wed. A year later the marriage was publicly announced. As the Duchess of Tuscany, Bianca believed herself beyond the reach of threats or calumny.

The Republic of Venice remembered its despised and rejected daughter and sent her a magnificent diamond necklace as a wedding gift.

A decree of the Venetian Senate declared her a "true and special daughter of the Republic". The Pope conferred on her the honour of the Golden Rose.

For another nine years Bianca basked in the splendours of the court of Tuscany, the patron of writers and artists, mistress of the costliest festivities Florence had ever seen.

She had no illusions about the future. "If the Duke lives, I live; if he dies, I die" she once said with bitter resignation, knowing the unbending hatred of his brother the Cardinal.

In the autumn of 1587 Francesco entertained a great hunting party at his villa of Poggio a Caiano. One day he returned soaked by icy rain and collapsed with a violent fever.

On October 19 he died. And only a few hours later, as she had sworn, Bianca followed him to death.

To silence rumors that he had poisoned her, Cardinal Ferdinando had the body opened and examined. The surgeons unromantically declared that the celebrated Duchess Bianca had perished of colic.

Mr. Fisher's 'Magic' Box

JUST before sunset one day late in 1897, two men knelt on the edge of a deserted wharf in Edgartown, Massachusetts. One, a clergyman, stared into the water while his companion, a bushy-bearded, fashionably-dressed young man, pulled gently on a rope.

The water rippled a little as a box with a small battery strapped to it broke the surface. Handling the box with great care, the younger man untied the rope, disconnected the battery and opened the perforated lid.

The clergyman looked inside. Below a disc of coiled platinum wire was a layer of silt. And glistening on the silt was a thin coating of gold dust.

The clergyman started back in amazement. "By heavens!" he cried, "It works."

Thus one of the most amazing frauds ever perpetrated on the American public had its origin. Charles Fisher's "marine gold extractor" was ready for action.

Fisher's extractor certainly collected gold, even if it was only old jewellery gold he laboriously ground to dust and placed in the box while no one was looking.

Yet the fraud was executed with such cleverness that thousands of people were hoodwinked into investing several million dollars in the marine gold mine.

Although he was simply a dupe, the clergyman, the Rev. Mr. Prescott Jernegan, was an important part of the fraud. Fisher needed a man of his reputation to give the project the imprimatur of respectability.

Charles Fisher, a former medical student and deep sea diver, had not long returned to the US after 10 years abroad, when he first met Jernegan.

The clergyman seemed just the man he wanted for his marine gold enterprise.

Pastor of a prosperous New England parish, Jernegan had been dismissed by his church elders for persistently preaching the parable of the camel and the eye of the needle to his wealthy congregation.

Jernegan was living at Edgartown when he met the plausible Charles Fisher. The two became friends and the clergyman poured out his troubles into his companion's sympathetic ear.

Money, Jernegan said, was the root of all evil. But it didn't take the

121

confidence man long to convince him that there was nothing wrong with money if it were not earned at the expense of one's fellow man.

Indeed, he added, in the right hands money could be put to many praiseworthy uses.

Then he told Jernegan about the extraordinary box he had bought during his world travels. Fisher said that when he first acquired the machine it was little more than a novelty.

Since then he had improved it so much it could now extract payable amounts of gold from the sea.

Later, Fisher showed the incredulous clergyman the wonder box. Small, it was perforated with holes, while inside was a platinum wire coil with battery terminals connected to the coil's ends.

Fisher said that when working, the box had a weak "Q current flowing through the magnetic field on the polar axis." If he installed another coil the current would be strengthened, thus allowing more gold to be collected.

Now that Fisher had the clergyman interested, he lost no time following up. One evening he invited Jernegan to his rooms where, dramatically, he produced a vial. The bottom was filled with gold dust.

He said he had collected the gold with the extractor. Perhaps he had just been lucky. He would like Jernegan to operate the electrical box and see if he, too, could make it work.

The same evening the two men went to a deserted Edgartown wharf where, after a battery had been connected to the terminals, the box was lowered into the water at the end of a rope.

Fisher said the box would need at least 24 hours to collect even a small amount of gold.

Early next morning he returned to the wharf alone, pulled up the box and salted inside with ground up jewellery gold he had bought at a pawnbroker's shop.

And the Rev. Mr. Prescott Jernegan was greatly impressed when, that evening, he saw the box's contents.

Convinced that his new-found friend had discovered the path to unlimited wealth, Jernegan agreed to approach two of his wealthy former parishioners, Andrew Pierson and Arthur Ryan.

The two men did not believe the clergyman's fantastic story. Yet, jokingly, they agreed to finance the project if it could be proved the box was really capable of producing gold from the sea.

As a result, Fisher, who kept well in the background, told Jernegan to deliver the box to Pierson and Ryan and instruct them in its operation.

He added that the men should be advised to closely watch the box during the period of its immersion. No one must be allowed to tamper with it.

One freezing night in February 1898 Pierson and Ryan approached a wharf in Providence, Rhode Island, carrying Fisher's little box.

After attaching the battery and lowering the box into the water, they retired to a shed where they had lit a coal fire. Then they prepared for their 24-hour vigil.

Charles Fisher demonstrating his wonder box to his clergyman friend the Rev. Mr. Jernegan. Using the box, Fisher was able to hoodwink thousands of people into investing millions of dollars in his 'gold from seawater' enterprise.

A little before dawn, Charles Fisher, wearing a primitive underwater breathing apparatus he had bought in England, slipped silently into the water about 100 yards from the wharf.

Feeling his way underwater by moving from pier to pier, he at last felt the rope that led to the box.

After that it took only a few seconds to open the box's lid, mix the gold dust in the silt it had already collected, close the lid and slip away.

When the box was hauled up that afternoon, Fisher had all the backers he needed. One gave his project moral tone, the others could supply capital.

Within weeks, Prescott Jernegan, accompanied by his wife and infant son, arrived in the Canadian border fishing town of Lubec in Maine. The following day they were joined by Fisher.

At the town's end was Quoddy Head, the most easterly point in the US. Past this point and into Passam-quoddy Bay flowed one of the world's highest tides.

For the first few days the clergyman and his flashily-dressed companion did little but study the bay and examine an old tidal mill near the town's perimeter.

The mill stood at the mouth of an inlet and, when in use, took its power from the tide working on a water wheel.

A week later the mystified townspeople learned that the strangers had paid the "ridiculous" price of 10,000 dollars cash for the old mill.

Lubec had hardly recovered from this shock when a gang of Canadian workmen set up camp and began erecting round the mill a high fence surmounted by barbed wire.

At every opportunity, the citizens of Lubec questioned the Canadians, but apparently the work they were doing was equally mysterious to them.

All they knew was that they had strengthened a small tidal-control dam across the mouth of the inlet and installed a 30-foot sluiceway through it.

Also, the owners had put in a 32-ampere, 600 hp dynamo which, powered by the tide, allowed them to generate their own electric current.

As the months passed, the workmen installed a number of kettle-like containers along the floor of the sluiceway. Each kettle was fitted with a wire coil which was connected to the electrical system.

Then one day early in 1898, the Canadians disappeared (except for a few who maintained an armed guard over the mill) and the dynamo began humming.

A few weeks later the Rev. Mr. Jernegan arrived at the local post office carrying a heavily sealed parcel. He told the clerk he wanted to register the parcel and have it sent to the US Mint in New York.

When asked what was in the parcel, the clergyman told the startled clerk that it contained a little more than five pounds of gold.

Then the secret of the mill came out. Jernegan said the gold had been mined from the sea. In the following months, he added, he would be sending even larger amounts to the mint.

When this news had spread over the town, Jernegan decided to take the citizens into his confidence.

He told them his partner, Fisher, had found a means of extracting gold from the sea. The high tides at Lubec had attracted them to the town.

Fisher's amazing fraud which was known as The Electrolytic Marine Salts Company, had begun operations with an initial share issue of half-a-million one dollar shares.

Now, at Fisher's request it was decided to issue a further 350,000 shares.

Thousands of dollars of this were handed over to Jernegan who in turn gave it to his partner. Fisher took large amounts of it to New York at regular intervals to "buy more equipment."

Actually, he toured pawn shops buying vast quantities of old gold which he laboriously ground to dust and used to salt the "extractors."

Later, when he found this work too tiring, he simply melted the gold and placed nuggets in the extractors.

He explained to Jernegan and the directors that since he had increased the electric power to the extractors, they were fusing the dust into nuggets.

By July 1898 when Jernegan had sent off a total of 3,000 ounces of gold to the mint, the one dollar EMS shares were being quoted at 48 dollars.

Now Fisher could see the inevitable end looming. Weekly he had to increase the amount of gold recovered as the extractors grew in number. This began eating into his profit.

He could not go on forever calling for more capital to buy more "equipment."

When the directors voted him and Jernegan royalty payments of 200,000 dollars each in lieu of salary which they had not drawn, Charles Fisher disappeared.

Jernegan took no notice of his absence for a few days assuming he had gone off to New York on another of his equipment-buying missions.

But in the end he became worried. He wired Pierson and Ryan to come to Lubec.

Then, together, the frightened men broke down the locked door that led to the extraction chamber.

They lifted the lids of the extractors which should by now be laced with gold. They contained nothing but sea water.

No trace was ever found of Fisher although Jernegan set off for Europe on a fruitless search for him.

The clergyman returned to the EMS shareholders all but 15,000 dollars which he retained for "justifiable expenses."

Then he set off first for Manila, then Hawaii where he earned a modest living as a schoolteacher.

No one knew anything of his background when, as a well-loved, retired clergyman, he died in Galveston, Texas, on February 23, 1942.

Charles II : A Jealous Philanderer

KING CHARLES II of England was deeply in love with his mistress, the beautiful Barbara Palmer. Yet that did not stop him showering his favours on other charmers who happened to catch his eye.

For instance there was the serving maid of Queen Catherine (his wife), the actress Nell Gwynne, the dancer Moll Davis and the more youthful members of the notorious brothels in Nightingale Lane.

Although the Queen Consort accepted her husband's infidelities philosophically, Barbara Palmer, inflamed with jealousy decided to bring the philanderer to heel.

Her plan was simple—she took a lover herself, a man described as having the "face of an African lemur, a hideously-large head and wobbly little pipe-stem legs".

When news of this incongruous love affair reached Charles he flew into a rage and then (as Barbara Palmer had expected) settled down to win back the love of the fascinating wanton whose charms he could not resist.

Such incidents were part and parcel of the stormy yet enduring love match between the insatiable Charles and his equally insatiable mistress.

If it was not Charles who was being unfaithful to the woman he was to create Duchess of Cleveland, it was Barbara Palmer who was cavorting with young bucks of the court who were willing to risk their necks for her love.

Barbara Palmer, Duchess of Cleveland, Baroness Nonsuch, Countess of Castlemaine and Southampton and perhaps the most sensational woman of her age, was born in 1641, the daughter of William Villiers, Viscount Grandison.

Barbara was still a child when her father lost his life and fortune fighting for the Royalists during the Cromwellian civil war. And she was only 14 when she begged the Earl of Chesterfield to elope with her.

Chesterfield would probably have agreed to this request from the lovely Barbara had not Cromwell imprisoned him in the Tower for political crimes.

In April 1659 the now exquisitively beautiful Barbara Palmer was on the verge of despair. She was without funds and faced starvation. And that was when she met and married Roger Palmer, a rich merchant's son.

Barbara Palmer, duchess of Cleveland.

Just a year later Mrs Palmer learned that Chesterfield had been released from the Tower and had fled to Holland to join the exiled King Charles.

Deciding the Earl would make a better lover than her husband, Barbara persuaded Palmer to take her to Holland on the pretext they could enjoy a second honeymoon.

A few weeks later Chesterfield's eyes fell on the dazzlingly lovely girl he had not seen since her childhood days—and so did Charles'.

The result was that within days of that meeting members of the King's court in exile accepted the fact that Mrs Palmer was the exclusive property of the monarch.

Chesterfield was delighted he was able to bring such happiness to his adored King while Palmer was so overawed by his wife's sudden rise in the social scale that he made no objection although he fumed inwardly.

Then in 1660 came the news from England—the people wanted Charles back on the throne. And when he arrived in London on 29 May 1660, one of the first to greet him was the pregnant Barbara Palmer.

Although some historians attribute the paternity of Mrs Palmer's first child, Anne, to the King, others claim the daughter was really sired by the

Earl of Chesterfield.

Nevertheless, Charles accepted his mistress's word that the expected baby was his and immediately after the Restoration entered with Barbara into an orgy of pleasure-seeking and extravagance that shocked the English middle and lower classes.

During royal balls in Whitehall, Barbara Palmer invariably sat beside the King and passionately responded to his embraces in full view of the noble guests.

Following the birth of Barbara's daughter in February 1661, Roger Palmer began to make trouble.

The King's advisers suggested that Charles might arrange for someone to pick a quarrel with his mistress's husband and then run him through with a sword.

But the King had a better plan. He created Palmer Earl of Castlemaine, a title that carried large estates in Ireland.

And as these estates required constant supervision, the new Earl would be tied up in Ireland leaving his countess to continue her royal social activities in London.

The return of King Charles II to England. One of the first to greet him was his new-found mistress, Barbara Palmer, who preceded him from Europe.

129

Then, with Barbara Palmer already dreaming of the day when one of her children would sit on England's throne, a marriage contract was signed between Charles and the Portuguese princess, Catherine of Braganza.

It was no love match but rather a political expedient by which England, apart from other privileges, secured Tangier and Bombay.

Almost immediately after the couple were married in England in May 1662, Catherine was pushed into the background away from the debaucheries of the court and Barbara Palmer was appointed the Queen Consort's Lady of the Bedchamber.

Later, although Catherine remained barren, Barbara Palmer bore the King a son who was christened Charles Palmer.

The advent of this child so delighted the monarch that he insisted his mistress should sit in the royal coach with him when he rode through the streets of London.

Nevertheless, if Barbara, Countess of Castlemaine, gave all her attention to pleasing her lover she insisted on being repaid for her efforts.

Charles gave her a yearly allowance of about $200,000 in addition to gifts of almost priceless jewellery. He also accepted her suggestion that he should pass on to her all the presents subjects seeking special favours pressed on him.

Apart from that, she took a cut from post office revenue and was allowed to sell appointments to the army and civil service.

But if money deluged into Lady Castlemaine's coffers it poured out just as quickly. She was an obsessive gambler and often lost as much as $40,000 at a sitting.

Then came the day when Barbara Palmer decided her lover was philandering outrageously and must be brought to heel.

To arouse the King's jealousy the courtesan chose as a lover an ugly untitled wastrel who hovered unobtrusively on the court's fringe.

Completely overwhelmed by the advances of the lovely Lady Castlemaine, the man, Harry Jermyn, was soon strutting about the court like a peacock boasting of his conquest.

When news of the match between the beauty and the beast reached Charles, he ordered his mistress to his private apartments and thundered at her:

"It is not consistent with my dignity that a mistress whom I have honoured with public distinction and who receives considerable support from me should appear chained to the chariot of the most ridiculous conqueror who ever lived."

Barbara Palmer was determined to continue her affair with Jermyn and arouse Charles to an even greater pitch of jealousy. But the plan collapsed when the ugly little courtier, realising his danger, fled to Scotland.

Now the royal mistress decided to use the same strategy to draw Charles from the arms of Nell Gwynne.

This time she chose as her lover a huge muscle-bound tightrope walker, Jacob Hall. But if he was physically unattractive his lovemaking was so expert that Lady Castlemaine found herself falling in love with him.

Barbara Palmer had not bargained for such an eventuality. Nor did she appreciate the bawdy jokes about her and the tightrope walker that circulated all over London.

In the end she begged Charles to forgive her indiscretion and take her back. As usual the King, longing for her companionship, agreed but stipulated she must share him with "that pitiful strolling actress" Nell Gwynne. Barbara Palmer agreed.

All went peacefully enough between the lovers until one night in 1670 when Charles was told by a courtier that his mistress (now the Duchess of Cleveland) was locked in her rooms with a young officer of the Guards, John Churchill.

Enraged by this latest example of amorous skulduggery, the King roared for his carriage and set off towards the great mansion in Westminster he had just given to the Duchess as a gift.

Stepping smartly up the mansion's elaborately-carved staircase, Charles bounded up to the bedchamber's door and turned the handle. It was locked. So he banged on the door demanding immediate admission.

A full minute passed before it was opened by the gorgeous Duchess dressed in a nightgown. Behind her a window lay open admitting the cold night air.

The King hurried to the window just in time to see a male figure jump from the ivy on the wall and run off into the darkness.

Next instant Charles shouted: "I know who you are son. But I forgive you. I know you do it for your bread."

The monarch then turned to the trembling Duchess. He cried: "Madame, I hope to live to see you ugly. Then I won't care who you love."

Within a week Lieutenant Churchill, later Duke of Marlborough, had been transferred to disease-ridden Tangier while Charles and his mistress resumed their interrupted love affair.

A year later Barbara Palmer's fifth and last child was born. Charles insisted it was the result of his mistress's alliance with Churchill but, in the face of her protestations, agreed to ackowledge its paternity.

As the years passed Barbara Palmer, Duchess of Cleveland, Baroness Nonsuch and Countess of Castlemaine and Southampton, continued dabbling in a variety of love affairs.

Nevertheless, the ageing Charles accepted her obsession and was quite ready to take her back when the current liaison had lost its attraction.

Then in 1685 Charles died. Although the Duchess had received several fortunes from the monarch during his reign, she now had to rely on the generosity of her dead lover's brother, James II, to maintain her standard of living.

And even when James fled the country in 1688 his successor, William of Orange continued to make provision for the Duchess of Cleveland.

Nevertheless, although the Duchess was now in her mid 40s she was still beautiful and was able to attract wealthy and noble lovers.

Sometimes, to bolster her income, she turned her mansion into a gambling saloon and personally attended her guests while her current lover, the actor Cardenell Goodman, acted as croupier.

In 1705, the Duchess, long since a widow and now 64, married a handsome young roue Bób Fielding who, until he announced he was already married and therefore not her legal husband, robbed her, abused her and even beat her.

In a blaze of ridicule the Duchess of Cleveland sold all her London possessions and retired friendless to Chiswick. And there, a grotesque hulk, filled with the fluid of dropsy, she died on 9 October 1709.

Cavalcade of Silken Dandies

BY 1772 Mlle Hippolyte Clarion had lost count of the number of French English, German and Russian noblemen who had been her temporary lovers. But certainly the score ran into the hundreds.

Yet, despite the never-ending cavalcade of silken, perfumed dandies who passed rapidly through her life, real love had never been a part of a single relationship.

Then came Mlle Clarion's 49th birthday and her first experience with love as an elevating emotion.

Nor did it surprise the citizens of Paris that the object of her admiration was a 16-year-old youth, for the famed courtesan and actress, despite her advancing years, still retained all the vigor and physical loveliness of her youth.

Mlle Hippolyte Clarion was a French institution from 1737, when the 14-year-old's chief occupation was deciding which nobleman should be her next supporter, until shortly before her death.

Even in her 70th year she proved she had not lost her old zest and attractiveness by seducing the Swedish ambassador to France, Baron Eric de Stael.

Rarely had Paris seen such a startling sensuous beauty as Hippolyte Clarion.

Indeed, once she enticed so many courtiers from Versailles to follow her on a provincial theatrical tour that Louis XV ordered her back to Paris so that he would have sufficient attendants on State occasions.

Some said she rivalled the royal mistress, Mme de Pompadour. But Hippolyte placed herself on even a higher plane than the historic courtesan by saying: "The Pompadour owes her position to accident. I acquired mine by genius."

Hippolyte Clarion was born in 1723, the illegitimate result of a brief affair between a seamstress and a soldier. At 12 the child was so lovely and vivacious that one of her mother's clients paid her fees to attend a theatrical academy.

At 14 she was touring the provinces as an actress, singer and dancer and had already succumbed to the dishonourable advances of a number of young

133

and noble admirers.

The girl's mother, alarmed at the course the girl's life was taking, tried to force her into marriage.

But even at that age Hippolyte had decided that a stream of wealthy admirers offer more security and excitement than a single husband.

Her first recorded lover was the Comte de Bergheic. Her second was the Baron Desplaces. Her third the Chevalier de By.

In one provincial city, authorities became so alarmed that jealousy between suitors for the beautiful Mlle Clarion's favours would flare into sword play that they sent agents to investigate.

Following several revealing interviews the agents reported back. "There is no need for alarm. Mlle Clarion knows what she is doing. All is peaceful. Everybody is satisfied."

It was in Ghent that England's third Duke of Marlborough first set eyes on the fascinating Mlle Clarion. Completely infatuated he insisted on meeting her. Scarcely had the introductions been made than he promised her a fortune if she would become his mistress.

When news of this offer spread, her French lovers rose up in a body. Marlborough's very life might have been threatened had not Hippolyte made her position clear.

"All Englishmen are odious to me," she told her enraged batch of lovers,

Hippolyte Clarion had scores of lovers before taking a boy young enough to be her grandson.

"Besides, my ambition is to win glory on the stage."

By the time she was 17 Mlle Clarion had entertained, for varying periods (and the result was seen in her gorgeous clothes and sparking jewels), at least 21 noblemen.

But now some of her current lovers became dissatisfied. The amorous actress was still touring the provinces and this entailed constant travelling for those who regularly needed her company.

The result was that a group of these nobles approached Louis XV, described her charms and persuaded him to assign her to the Comedie Francaise in Paris where she would be handy to their family mansions.

Finally installed in the Comedie Francaise and constantly invited to court, Hippolyte Clarion's pride got the better of her. She became arrogant and hurled abuse at her stage director and fellow actors.

And this, despite the fact that she rarely appeared on the stage, preferring to devote her time to her seething horde of lovers whose constant demands added to her egotism and treasure.

Among those who had yet to savour her delights was the Marquis de Ximenes, an amorous nobleman old enough to be the famed courtesan's grandfather.

For a start the marquis inundated her with sonnets of his own composition. When these failed to soften Hippolyte's attitude towards him, he sent her a huge pie with 300 gold louis pieces concealed in it.

Still his suit failed. So in desperation de Ximenes sold his huge estate in Champagne, converted the sale price into golden louis and poured the lot at Mlle Clarion's feet.

The banker Le Cindre was more successful. He simply gave her his country house and 2,000 louis and was at once admitted to her bedchamber.

Not long after Hippolyte took up residence in Le Cindre's country house. And there one day she was entertaining Jeweller de Jacourt in the privacy of her boudoir when Le Cindre burst in.

Next day Le Cindre sent a gang of workmen to demolish the luxurious house. Mlle Clarion fled before the place fell about her ears.

Then there was the famed comedian Grandval, who pawned every single asset he possessed for a few hours of Mlle Clarion's company.

Later a benefit performance was organised at the Comedie Francaise to save his destitute wife and children from eviction.

Next on Mlle Clarion's list was the aged Comte de Valbelle, a leader at the king's court and the owner of a mansion packed with priceless objets d'art.

The comte begged the actress to marry him. She declined, but agreed to become his mistress for an indefinite period.

It was during this liaison that de Valbelle had a magnificent statue executed of his mistress.

And it was this statue that a mob, during the Revolution, carried away and set up in a village as a shrine. They thought it was the statue of a saint.

The happiest period of the Comte de Valbelle's life came to an end when the influential Russian, Princess Galitzin, visited Paris and invited Mlle Clarion to appear before the royal court at St Petersburg.

The gorgeous Frenchwoman was an enormous success in Russia even if her tour came to a sudden and dramatic end when her hostess, Princess Galitzin, caught her in bed with her own favorite lover, Baron de Kervert.

When Mlle Clarion arrived back in Paris she was 49. Yet, and it was almost miraculous, she still retained the figure and face of a young girl. And the numbers of her suitors seemed to increase rather than decrease.

It was at this time she met the only true love of her life, the 16-year-old Henri Larive, a youth of a wealthy family who had stage ambitions.

Young Larive was flattered by the famous actress's initial attentions, but he was overwhelmed when she installed him as her permanent lover and began coaching him as an actor.

The letters Hippolyte wrote to the youth from Paris when he was touring the provinces oozed with the frenzied emotions of a middle-aged woman desperately in love.

Mlle Clarion even employed spies to keep a watch on the boy and protect him from designing females. But the spies were not always successful in this

last duty as one of Hippolyte's letters shows.

In it she wrote: "So you have made a conquest. And the lady is beautiful. I am not surprised, you are handsome.

"But don't be silly. A moment of pleasure is what your age requires, but not if it has to be paid for with years of pain and regret."

The incongruous union between the ageing actress and her lover, who was little more than a boy, came to an end when Henri Larive married during one of his tours.

Mlle Clarion shed tears, recovered quickly, then threw herself into the arms of the youthful Margrave of Anspach, who took her back home with him to share his palace with his invalid wife.

For 19 years all went smoothly in the menage a trois. Then the margravine died and the margrave went on a tour of Europe to forget his sorrow. And it was during this tour that he met the lovely Elizabeth, Countess of Craven.

Separated from her husband, Elizabeth accepted the margrave's invitation to accompany him to Anspach where she was set up in a sumptuous suite in the viceregal palace.

It did not take Mlle Clarion long to realise that the margrave was spending

The court of Louis XV. Many of the nobles who attended the monarch at Versailles abandoned him to follow the lovely actress Mlle Clarion when she toured the provinces.

more time in the countess's boudoir than in her own.

One day she cornered the margrave. "The overthrow of our plans and my destiny," she shouted, "your disregard of public opinion, the licentiousness of your morals, your lack of respect for your age, convinces me you are out of your mind."

Which was a strange statement for a woman who had spent 55 of her 69 years wallowing in immorality.

After that Hippolyte Clarion returned to Paris, then seething in the grip of revolution.

Still beautiful, she tried to win her way back on to the stage. But if she was only moderately successful in this quest her pursuit of love was again a triumph.

At that time the Swedish Ambassador to France, Baron Eric de Stael, was 43. Hippolyte was touching 70, but she still managed to arouse in him a passion that caused him to buy her a house and settle a substantial annuity on her.

Not that de Stael was unsophisticated in the matter of love, for his French-born wife who had fled to Switzerland to escape the Revolution was Geraldine Necker, the heiress who was the mother of five children, all by different men.

In 1801 when Napoleon Bonaparte was pulling France out of the chaos of the Revolution, de Stael lost his position while his wealthy wife drastically reduced his allowance.

No longer able to maintain his aged mistress, de Stael cut out her annuity to be at once sued in court for breach of contract.

Mlle Clarion won the case and the bailiffs invaded de Stael's house, seizing everything of value in it. Nevertheless, the sum realised on the sale of these effects was scarcely enough to keep Hippolyte Clarion from poverty.

The notorious old courtesan stayed on in the de Stael house bedridden and existing on the gifts of food old admirers brought her.

Early in January 1803 when alone in the house she fell from her bed. When they found her she was dead. She looked much younger than her 80 years.

The 'Millionaire' Insurance Clerk

L ONDON had seen nothing quite like the extravagant after-dinner parties arranged by that suave, handsome entrepreneur, stock exchange tycoon, horseflesh fancier and patron of the arts Walter Watts.

Any socialite who could persuade the elegant Mr. Watts to attend one of her soirees achieved added status overnight while gentlemen of vision vied to win invitations to sample his vintage cellar. The only trouble with Mr. Watts was that he was a fraud, one of the most blatant—and for a time most successful—in 19th century England.

A man of apparently unlimited wealth by night, he was a $8 a week insurance office clerk by day with a genius for cooking his employer's books.

Then when the law finally caught up with the amazing Mr. Watts and levelled a whole string of charges against him he beat them all—except one.

And that charge concerned the stealing of a practically valueless piece of paper.

Walter Watts was born in 1817 the son of a respectable clerk employed by the Globe Assurance Company of London.

In 1838 Watts senior, by now the company's chief cashier, asked his directors if they would consider employing his son. Called to be interviewed young Watts impressed the manager and was put on the staff.

Walter Watts had a head for figures. This, combined with a natural enthusiasm for the work, soon brought him to the attention of his superiors.

One promotion followed another until in 1843 he was put in charge of a small department on a salary of $400 a year.

Watts's responsibility consisted of keeping a check on the company's bank accounts and on the claims paid.

One morning each week the handsome young clerk was required to visit the directors and report on income, expenditure and the number of claims met.

The rest of the week he spent checking all cheques returned from the bankers against the claims. When this work was done the cheques were tied into bundles and filed.

Walter Watts began his famed nocturnal career in 1844. Completely unknown to the world of the socially elite, he burst among them dressed in the height of fashion and spending money with complete abandon.

139

In this circle no one ever did get to know who he really was or where he came from. All they knew was that he was handsome, entertaining and wealthy.

Soon he had acquired an expensive apartment in the most fashionable quarter of the West End as well as a carriage and team that were the envy of his contemporaries.

Everywhere he went he was attended by a footman-valet who was bedecked in a uniform of velvet and cloth of gold which was weighed down by rows of brass buttons.

Apart from that the footman-valet was a man who was always ready to entertain his master's guests.

London's Olympic Theatre where Watts, the mysterious entrepreneur, presented extravagant shows that staggered the city.

Now Watts rented a permanent box at the opera and saw to it that it was always cluttered with his guests.

At the end of the performance all would retire to a specially prepared room where the supply of exotic foods and vintage wines was unlimited.

Really branching out now, Walter Watts invested in a Brighton house which possessed a cellar of rare distinction.

All social London began talking of the elegant Mr. Watts the well-known patron of the arts and sport and the friend of the nobility.

But still the young $8 a week insurance clerk was not satisfied. He began working harder than ever during his time at his office to supply himself with the money needed to launch out as an entrepreneur.

At that time the Sadlers Wells Theatre was in the middle of a crusade designed to stop the downward drift in the standard of drama that was affecting the British theatre's reputation.

Watts decided to help with the good work.

He leased an obscure theatre the Marylebone, and hired Mrs. Warner, one of the great theatrical figures of the day, to direct the productions.

Following the launching of an expensive publicity campaign the theatre was packed by the cream of London's society to watch the opening night of a modern intellectual play specially written for the occasion.

It was a success and after the performance the front stalls and box audience packed back stage offering congratulations to Walter Watts, Mrs. Warner and the cast.

Next morning, as usual, Watts put aside his role as entrepreneur and socialite and after dressing in a sober suit befitting an insurance clerk, returned to his daily routine.

It happened every day. Leaving his luxurious apartment he would take a hansom cab and travel in it to a spot around a corner and several hundred yards from the Globe Assurance office.

Then he would walk the rest of the way until he finally took his place at his high desk.

Having spent the day engaged in legitimate and illegitimate employment, he would wish his fellow clerks "good evening" and return unostentatiously to his apartment to prepare himself for the night's social round.

As time passed Watts began spending on an even grander scale by investing in a whole chain of theatres and sporting enterprises.

Rumors began circulating about the financial background of the mysterious Walter Watts.

It was said he had developed a friendship with King Louis of France who had instructed his Government to keep the amiable Englishman informed of financial trends.

This information, the rumor had it, allowed Watts to bring off Rothschild-like coups on the stock exchange.

The story, of course, was not true, but Watts made no effort to deny it. Indeed he often dropped hints indicating the stories even underestimated the position.

Meanwhile the Marylebone Theatre, despite the extravagance of its performances, was on the decline. The chief reason was that the upper classes were finding the cultured modern dramas boring.

But the fabulous Mr. Watts had no intention of allowing a few thousand pounds to interfere with the success of his theatrical ambitions.

To stop the rot he signed up the beautiful American actress and socialite, Mrs. Mowatt, for a long season. Thus with Mrs. Mowatt starring in works especially written for her, the patrons flocked back.

Now at last the directors of the Globe Assurance Company heard something of their young clerk's nocturnal habits. His association with the theatre particularly upset them.

Watts was called before the board and questioned. He said he had made a fortunate investment on the stock exchange and using this money, as well as the financial support of several wealthy backers, he had made a hobby of the theatre.

The directors accepted the story. After telling Watts that they considered it not quite the proper thing for an insurance officer to associate with the theatre, they closed the matter.

Confident now that he could get away with anything Walter Watts launched out on his greatest gamble.

Some time earlier the Olympic Theatre in Wych Street, the Strand, had been burned down and replaced by a more ornate and spacious building.

Watts decided to take over the new theatre and use it to stage spectacular productions unlike anything seen before in London.

Watts did not spare himself (or the Globe Assurance Company's assets) to ensure the success of the opening night. And his confidence was not misplaced. London raved.

Using every propaganda trick to lure patrons from rival theatres, the Olympic soon had other theatre managers facing half empty houses.

Then in the midst of Watts's success a rumor swept financial circles in London. A large insurance company, it was said, had been swindled of a huge sum.

At first no names were mentioned. Then details came out. The insurance company was the Globe and the swindler was the fabulous man-about-town Walter Watts.

Called before the board and questioned by company investigators and police, Watts bluffed for all he was worth. Even when his accounting books were taken from him he shouted: "I have been disgraced before the whole office."

Finally he marched before the directors and thundered: "As a partner holding shares you can't prove me guilty in law."

And Walter Watts had something there.

It took a long time but finally company investigators had worked out the extent of the frauds.

By forging cheques and other documents, Watts had cheated the company of as much as $1,000 a time. He had also faked claims and paid the proceeds into his own account under another name.

Because he controlled all the records he was able to destroy the documents relating to forged cheques and faked claims.

In 1840 alone Watts had swindled his employers of $36,000.

At the investigation's end it was found he had taken from the company $140,000 or more than half a million in modern currency.

On 10 May 1850, Watts stood trial on a string of charges connected with

A contemporary illustration of Walter Watts awaiting transportation to West Australia. Soon after, he hanged himself.

the Globe forgeries and the faking of claims. The last charge concerned the stealing of a piece of paper (a cheque form).

Immediately the prosecution had outlined the case against Watts, the defence counsel pleaded that the charge must fall because Watts, as the holder of two Globe shares, was a partner in the company and could not be charged with stealing his own property.

As a result the judge instructed the jury to ignore the first batch of charges and try him only on having stolen the cheque form. He was convicted.

After a series of unsuccessful appeals Watts at last came up for conviction believing he could not possibly get more than 12 months' gaol.

But the judge's sentence staggered him. His Honor said: "We are sentencing you not just for stealing a piece of paper but for the frauds that lie behind it. You are to be transported for 10 years."

While awaiting transportation to West Australia, Walter Watts was held in Newgate Prison. And there one day he went berserk and was sent to the infirmary.

During the first night in the infirmary he asked to be allowed to visit the lavatory.

Alone now he stood on the closet and took a short length of rope from beneath his shirt.

He tied one end to the bars of the high window and knotted the other around his neck. Then he jumped into eternity.

Lover at Eighty-Five

PRINCE Hermann Puckler-Muskau claimed there was not a woman who could resist his amorous advances. And he was probably right as the youthful lady of letters, Ludmilla Assing, found one moonlit evening in 1870.

Fascinated by the Prince, Ludmilla wrote to him begging for a chance to "enfold you like a creeping vine in close embrace". Intrigued, Hermann insisted the young lady should test her horticultural-like brand of love-making on him without delay.

The experience under the beaming moon did not disappoint Ludmilla, which was a feather in the Prince's cap, for he had just celebrated his 85th birthday.

Actually Hermann Puckler-Muskau had always kept in training. Indeed in his late 70s he described an 18 year-old beauty as a "teasing, fascinating little animal".

Then there was the singer, young enough to be his great granddaughter, whose name in the Prince's diary carried with it the comment: "She is a complete child of nature."

But apart from his genius in the realm of love, Hermann Puckler-Muskau had other attributes. He was for instance an author of note. He also introduced horse racing to Vienna and made one of the first balloon ascents over Berlin.

Born in 1785 the son of Count and Countess Puckler of Muskau, Hermann (he acquired the Prince title in 1822) inherited the family's vast estates on his father's death in 1811.

The Napoleonic wars of 1813 gave Puckler-Muskau the opportunity to display the spirit of adventurous gallantry that pervaded his whole career.

One day when the Duke of Saxe-Weimar's army was confronted by a strong French force, a French colonel of Hussars rode out from his lines and contemptuously challenged to a duel any Prussian brave enough to meet him.

Drawing his sword and spurring his charger forward, Puckler-Muskau, with both sides cheering their champions on, rammed straight into the Frenchman, sending him flying to the ground.

Prince Hermann Puckler-Muskau.

Although he was now at liberty to put his sword through the unarmed colonel's body, Puckler-Muskau simply grinned at him and trotted back to his own lines.

When Napoleon was finally crushed at Waterloo, Puckler-Muskau was among the high-ranking Allied soldiers who rode into Paris. After that he attended Wellington's victory celebrations in London.

Puckler-Muskau really enjoyed himself in Paris and London. When his time was not taken up with expensive women or more expensive cards, he was throwing small fortunes away on racehorses that made a habit of losing.

And apart from his unsuccessful betting plunges, he threw more good money after bad by buying a string of English horses, none of which cost less than $2,000.

With all his liquid assets gone, Puckler-Muskau tried to repair the position by talking the wealthy Lady Lansdowne into marriage.

Four times the lady said "Yes" and four times she said "No".

Convinced at last that the wealthy noblewoman would never make up her mind, the handsome Prussian left England, taking with him $4,800 Lady Lansdowne had put in his care.

Back home, Puckler-Muskau began looking over the marriage market hoping he might find a bride, wealthy and attractive in that order of preference.

Soon his eye fell on Helmine, the adopted daughter of Luci, Countess of Pappenheim. Helmine seemed to have everything. She was beautiful and obviously had access to the vast Pappenheim fortune.

But when the Prussian found that the divorced Countess held a tight rein on the family coffers, be reluctantly abandoned Helmine and instead pursued the Countess, a woman who at 40 was 10 years older than her suitor.

Immediately the couple were married and Puckler-Muskau got his hands on to the Pappenheim fortune, he began spending vast sums on his family estate, hoping to turn it into a popular holiday resort.

Quickly the Pappenheim assets dwindled as the Muskau estate acquired a pump room for the spa, a gambling casino and a huge theatre.

Then, after 30 extra buildings had been added to the manor and a million trees planted, he filled place with paying guests.

In 1826 when Puckler-Muskau (now a prince by decree of King Frederick William III) discovered the Pappenheim fortune was gone, he calmly asked his wife for a divorce so that he could catch another heiress.

Luci gave him the divorce but insisted she be allowed to continue living on at Muskau.

Making for England where he was convinced lonely heiresses grew on trees, the Prince did the social rounds making notes of the eligible women he met.

At last, when the list had grown to pleasing proportions, he set himself to the task of making a final selection.

Miss Gibbons of Brighton was ruled out because she insisted her parents should live with them. The thought of sharing his manor with his new wife, her parents and Luci appalled Puckler-Muskau.

Miss Elphinstone and Miss Windham were both fabulously rich. But one was stupid and the other fearfully ugly.

Lady Garvagn would have been ideal. But she refused to divorce her husband.

Desperately the Prince wrote to Luci:"I'm tired of the whole business. If you only had 50,000 thalers I'd marry you again tomorrow."

On his way home the disappointed Prince decided to have a look around Paris to see if there was anything offering.

He spent some time courting the widow of Henry Christophe the Negro King of Haiti, but got nowhere.

Chances seemed better with the famed singer, Henriette Sontag, who enjoyed his violent courting for a week or two, then suddenly went back to her old lover, Count Rossi.

Returning finally to his estate still empty handed, the Prince made a living with his writings. The income was not great but it did support Puckler-Muskau and Luci, who was now his mistress.

By 1834 the Prince owed half a million thalers to an army of creditors who daily swarmed over his estate.

Finally while Luci held the creditors at bay, Puckler-Muskau escaped

Lady Hester Stanhope, self-styled Queen of the Arabs, was visited by Puckler-Muskau and his harem of two Abyssinian slave girls when the Prince was travelling through the East.

under cover of darkness and set off on a tour of the Middle East, hoping to earn something by writing of his adventures.

Acquiring a pint-sized harem consisting of two Abyssinian slave girls, the Prince bombarded German newspapers and publishers with accounts of his adventures. Many of his manuscripts got into print.

Complete with slave girls he even dropped in to see Lady Hester Stanhope, self-styled Queen of the Arabs.

When the Prince finally returned to Muskau six years after setting out, his harem had dwindled to one—Machbuba, an attractive but high-smelling young woman who at once aroused Luci's jealousy.

Despite Puckler-Muskau's assertion that Machbuba was nothing more than a daughter to him, Luci, who well knew her former husband's habits by this, whisked him off to Berlin out of the reach of the Abyssinian's arms.

During the pair's absence in Berlin, Machbuba, unaccustomed to the severity of European winters, died of tuberculosis. Grief stricken, the Prince returned to Muskau as fast as possible and ordered all his tenants to attend the young woman's funeral.

Puckler-Muskau was still mourning Machbuba when he was suddenly assailed by the over-amorous 60-year-old writer Bettina von Arnim.

A former lover of King Frederick IV, Beethoven, Liszt and Goethe, age had done nothing to dim the woman's hunger for men.

Petrified by Bettina's violent attentions, the frightened Prince finally begged Luci to rescue him from his predicament by acting the role of the jealous paramour.

The ruse succeeded, leaving the Prince free of the man-hungry writer but burdened by debts that now threatened to completely swamp him.

Selling Muskau, he settled on a smaller estate he owned at Branitz and, for a hobby, began making improper advances to any pretty woman who came into his sights.

After seducing Melanie, the wife of the influential Prince Metternich, he turned his attention to the Countess Ida Hahn-Hahn.

The dedicated roue delighted in the association until the Countess wrote him a love letter. Branding the document as "rude", Puckler-Muskau told the crestfallen lady he was finished with her.

After that the 60-year-old Prince broke down the defences of the young and beautiful Countess De La Rochefoucauld, a lady who, according to old Puckler-Muskau, was "as caressing as a kitten".

When the Countess's diplomat husband was away on national business, the Prince, well wrapped in a long cloak, visited the lady nightly, letting himself into the house with a duplicate key.

Meanwhile Luci, now in her 70s, continued to do all in her power to make life as easy as possible for her former husband.

Several times she gave him large sums from bequests she received from relative's estates, while there was the occasion she spent every thaler she possessed paying off a young woman who tried to blackmail the Prince.

The woman, Marie von Hochstedt, had warned that unless her silence

149

was paid for she would broadcast the information that she was the Prince's illegitimate daughter and he had committed incest with her.

When Luci died in 1859, the 69-year-old and suddenly-lonely Puckler-Muskau tried to drown his sorrow by indulging in affairs with a succession of harlots.

One, Bertha von Meerveldt, displayed such violent passion when in his company that he decided she was only assuming a pose to get more of his money.

Disgusted, the Prince broke the physical association and, after entering her in an acting academy, footed the bill for her training.

The old man's next mistress was the 18-year-old Ida von Seydewitz, daughter of his half-brother and the girl he described as a "teasing, fascinating little animal".

When he was 80, he dallied with the singer, Sarolta de Mujanovics, while in his 86th year, he entertained the writer, Ludmilla Assing, who expressed a desire to enfold him "like a creeping vine in close embrace".

After that, he served with King William I during the Austro-Prussian war, taking time off from his martial duties only to refresh himself in the company of some new and attractive conquest.

When the mighty old libertine died finally in 1871, his body was cremated and the ashes buried under a huge, pyramid-shaped tomb he had erected on one of his estates.

A mountain of love letters found among his effects were the clues historians used to piece together the story of his fantastic adventures in the realm of love.

Scheming Wanton of the Byzantine Age

TO many of her contemporaries she was "a crowned siren, a woman as lovely in face and body as Helen of Troy and even more shameless, lascivious and utterly corrupt".

She was the beloved of three successive Byzantine Emperors. She almost certainly instigated the hideous murder of one of them and was widely reputed to have had a hand in poisoning another.

She once reigned in splendour over the heart of western civilisation. And she lived to be hooted and stoned by the rabble of Constantinople who had been her adoring slaves.

Later historians were kinder to the beautiful Princess Theophano, regarding her more as a puppet of fate than the scheming wanton whose name seemed blackened beyond redemption by the chroniclers of her own age.

Yet, whatever the truth about her enigmatic character, she was the central figure in one of the bloodiest and most turbulent dramas in the long history of the Eastern Roman Empire.

The generally accepted date of Theophano's birth is A.D. 940 but her parentage and the circumstances of her early years are veiled in mystery.

When she became Empress a story was put about that she came from an impoverished branch of an ancient and noble Byzantine family.

According to her enemies, her father was a Greek adventurer named Craterus who kept a tavern and brothel much patronised by the gilded youth of Constantinople.

Theophano was a girl of about 15, and the prize of her father's establishment, when she first met the debauched wastrel destined to raise her to the imperial throne.

The Prince Romanus, son and heir to the Emperor Constantine VII, was only two years her senior but already seasoned in all the vices of the great city on the Bosphorus.

Tall, fair-haired, "handsome as Apollo and standing straight as a cypress", young Romanus repaid the doting care of his pious father with a life of the wildest licentiousness.

Hunting filled his days, whoring and drinking his nights. Around him

151

gathered a gang of parasites from nobles to favourite slaves who pandered to his most perverted whim.

However, from the time when he laid eyes on Theophano, the Prince was consumed by one passion, to make her his mistress and eventually his wife.

Probably early in 956 they were secretly betrothed. Legends were already spreading about her noble birth and when she was introduced at court even the austere Emperor Constantine was conquered.

Though she was still little more than a child, she was hailed as "a beauty beyond compare, a veritable miracle of nature surpassing all the ladies of her time".

Her behaviour was without reproach and within a few months, ignoring the warnings of his outraged counsellors, the Emperor yielded to his son's pleas and agreed to a marriage.

The wedding was celebrated with glittering pomp in the cathedral of Santa Sophia. Games were staged in the arena and for a week the citizens of Constantinople gave themselves up to riotous rejoicing.

Nobles and churchmen might whisper that the heir to Byzantium had taken a harlot as his bride. But with the Emperor on her side, Theophano

could ignore every slanderous intrigue.

A year later she gave birth to a son, the future Basil II. It was then, according to her enemies, that she began spinning her dark plots to hasten her husband's ascent to the throne.

Romanus, his passion for Theophano sated, had returned to the gross orgies that were rapidly converting him into a bloated, drunken caricature of the former princely Apollo.

The Emperor Constantine was ageing and sickly, dividing his time between pious pilgrimages to the monasteries of Greece and secluding himself with physicians in the palace.

The real rulers of the empire were the Chief imperial minister, Joseph Bringas, and the brilliant general, Nicephorus, who scourged the foes of Byzantium from Italy to the Syrian deserts.

Then in November 959 Constantine sank into the grave. His death had long been expected, despite the devotion of Theophano who often prepared his medicine with her own hands.

Romanus was Emperor. And, while he caroused with his male and female parasites, Theophano could at last drop the demure mask that concealed

The wedding procession of Theophano moves towards the church. Her spouse, Romanus, son of the Emperor Constantine VII, was already noted for his moral degradation.

153

A battle between Byzantine and Saracen armies in Syria during the reign of the usurping Emperor Nicephorus, second husband of the lascivious Theophano.

her ambitions.

Constantine's widow, the devout and much-loved Dowager Empress Helena, was driven from the court and died broken-hearted within a few months.

Romanus's five sisters were compelled to enter a convent, their heads being forcibly shaved while they wept, struggled and tore their habits in despair.

Bringas was ousted from office. Every other powerful figure in the councils of the former emperor was executed, hounded into exile or terrified into subjection.

As Romanus wallowed ever deeper in the mire of his debauches Theophano herself found consolation in the arms of lovers until the palace became "a golden sty of wickedness and corruption".

The most notorious of her paramours was the elegant, red-bearded John Tzimisces, nephew of the mighty General Nicephorus who was then reconquering Crete and Syria from the Saracens.

But many lesser nobles, dancers, charioteers and even humble grooms were reputed to share the favors of the Empress Theophano.

Whether Theophano deliberately plotted to remove her worthless husband and rule in fact as well as in name is uncertain.

However early in March 963 after returning from a wild hunting expedition with his companions, Romanus was suddenly stricken by a mortal sickness.

In a few days he was dead. Once more dark rumours spread through the palace—stories of some strange Asiatic poison mingled in the draughts prepared for him by the Empress.

Yet no voice was raised in protest when, before a great assemblage in Santa Sophia, the Patriarch Polyeuctes declared Theophano regent of Byzantium for her infant son.

The mob rejoiced in their beautiful young monarch. Revelling in her triumph Theophano only gradually became aware of the web of intrigue surrounding her within the palace walls.

The conspiracy was headed by the disgraced minister, Joseph Bringas, and soon included all those who hated the upstart who had risen from a brothel to the imperial throne.

At first Theophano ignored all warnings. Then, terrified of assassination and with her favourites deserting her every day, she turned to the one man she believed could save her.

Nicephorus was campaigning in Syria when he heard the news of Romanus's death, followed two months later by a summons from the regent to hasten to Constantinople.

The great general was then 50 years old, ugly, swarthy as a Tartar and enormously wealthy from the plunder of his endless wars around the frontiers of the Byzantine Empire.

He was the martial idol of Constantinople. Every season he returned from his victories to delight the citizens with parades of captives and costly spectacles in the arena.

In July 963, followed by a handful of cavalry, the General reached the Asiatic shore of the Bosphorus where he learned that Bringas was plotting to have him seized and blinded as soon as he entered the capital.

A month passed before the rest of the army came up. Then the soldiers marched before his tent in thousands acclaiming Nicephorus as their new emperor.

By late August Nicephorus was in Constantinope, the mob opening the gates and greeting him with frenzied jubilation while Bringas fled for his life.

For a moment Theophano's fate also trembled in the balance, for the usurping Emperor Nicephorus might well have no mercy on rival claimants to the throne.

One interview, however, assured her that she had nothing to fear. All her wanton charms were lavished on the conqueror and Nicephorus was infatuated by the spell.

Next day, clad in the purple imperial robe and leading Theophano by the hand, he entered Santa Sophia and prostrated himself before the stern figure of the patriarch at the high altar.

Polyeuctes refused to marry them and even forbade the usurper the rites of the church. In a passion of fury Theophano swore that nothing should separate her from her lover.

A more complaisant priest was found to conduct the ceremony and on September 20, to the disgust of the court nobility, Theophano became the wife of the Emperor Nicephorus.

For six years they jointly reigned while even the cynical citizens of Constantinople were revolted by the shamelessness and corruption of the imperial palace.

Every spring Nicephorus departed for the wars, leaving the Empress to revel with her paramours and enjoy the riches showered on her by her doting husband.

The treasury was looted by her minions, the highest State offices were openly bought and sold and it was reputed that a sumptuous brothel flourished within the palace walls.

John Tzimisces, despite his close kinship to the Emperor, remained Theophano's favorite partner. And it was this reeking scandal that brought the reign to its bloody climax.

By the time Nicephorus returned from his campaigns in the autumn of 969 he could no longer ignore the stories circulating everywhere about his faithless wife and his nephew.

Theophano had been hooted in the streets. She had had a woman burned alive for throwing a stone at her when she appeared at the games in the arena.

Even worse it was rumored that she was plotting his murder to put John Tzimisces on the throne.

Tormented and filled with gloomy forebodings Nicephorus quit the palace and locked himself up in the fortress of Bucoleon on the opposite side of the waters of the Bosphorus.

But already he had been marked for death. On the night of 10 December Tzimisces and a band of assassins were admitted through a gate left open on Theophano's orders.

Roused from slumber Nicephorus staggered to his feet crying "Mother of God help me!" as the murderers plunged their swords into his body.

Next day all Constantinople was in turmoil. Again the throne was vacant and, faced with complete anarchy, the nobles and clergy could only accept John Tzimisces as their ruler.

But Theophano, blamed as the real instigator of the fearful crime, had reached the end of her career of power.

As soon as Tzimisces was secure on the throne he disowned her, after a final meeting when she threw herself on him and beat him with her fists in an outburst of maniacal fury.

Early in 970, Theophano was confined in a convent in distant Armenia where she remained a prisoner until her son succeeded as the Emperor Basil II six years later.

Then, broken in health and spirit, she returned to Constantinople to live in such obscurity that the date of her death is unknown.

The Dreadful Voyage of The Peri

EARLY on 5 February 1872, the look-out in HMS Basilisk, which was sailing cautiously northwards just inside the Great Barrier Reef, rubbed his eyes in surprise as he sighted a schooner heading deliberately towards a jagged section of the reef.

Although the stranger was surrounded by black points of rock she made the passage safely and sailed steadily on into full view of the Basilisk's crew.

Only then when there was no reply to the man-of-war's hoisted ensign did it occur to Captain John Moresby that the vessel was a derelict.

Minutes later came another shock. As two boat's crews rowed over to investigate, several wild-looking figures rose up in the stern and pointed carbines straight at the oarsmen.

For a moment it looked as though the navy had walked into a trap.

But then as the vessel drifted on and the carbines continued to point harmlessly in the same fixed direction the sailors realised what had happened.

Aboard the schooner Peri were about a dozen South Seas islanders in the last stages of emaciation. The few who had evidently made one final effort to repel the imagined enemy were now slumped over the side too weak to make further resistance.

A few minutes later the sailors clambered aboard the vessel, disarmed the riflemen and began tending their comrades who lay about the deck in various stages of starvation.

The saga of the Peri had come to an end.

For five weeks, since the time 80 kidnapped natives had risen against their captors and massacred every member of the Peri's crew, the schooner had drifted 1800 miles from Fiji to the coast of Australia.

In the fierce hour-long encounter between blacks and whites, most of the Peri's supplies of food and water had been destroyed or lost overboard.

But 13 of the original 80 castaways had survived by killing their companions, eating them and drinking their blood.

The horrifying story of the Peri really began months earlier when the notorious blackbirding vessel, the Carl, owned by the sadistic former Melbourne physician, James Murray, and skippered by Joseph Armstrong, set out to kidnap islanders for the Fijian cotton plantations.

158

One special device invented by the ingenious Dr Murray to 'recruit' labor consisted of a small cannon mounted in the shrouds.

The heavy weapon was so rigged that it could be dropped overboard to smash through a canoe and then smartly hoisted back into position ready for another assault.

During one particular voyage a handful of Bougainville islanders tried to escape from the hold in which they had been imprisoned by setting fire to the coconut fibre stored nearby.

Murray's answer was to open the hatches and order his crew to fire indiscriminately down into the hold until the mutiny stopped.

Seventy natives were killed while 35 who were seriously wounded were thrown overboard to drown.

Later the Carl set out on another recruiting voyage beginning this time at the island of Malaita in the eastern Solomons.

Possibly the most daring and courageous of all the Solomon islanders, the Malaitamen knew enough about occasional European visitors to distrust them.

But desire for adventure and hopes of trade usually overcame their fears.

As the Carl hove to off the tiny islet of Leli, three canoes bearing 30 men paddled out to do business. Cautiously two circled round the 250-ton brig while the third stood farther out.

Soon however the circling canoes drifted within range and the kidnappers seized their chance.

Two heavy bars of iron ballast suddenly hurtled down shattering both canoes. At once the startled occupants began swimming frantically towards the third canoe.

All but one of the swimmers appeared to make it safely to the canoe which by now was being chased by the Carl as it fled towards the beach.

Firing steadily as they drew nearer, the brig's marksmen picked off man after man until the canoe suddenly slewed around in the vessel's path and was swamped in her wash.

Twenty-five islanders, some showing ugly bruises where the iron bolts had grazed them, were packed into the hold.

After this episode Murray sailed on to Gaudalcanal and Isabel. At the end of three weeks he had "recruited" 180 more laborers, both men and women, for the plantations of Fiji.

According to one of the Leli men who was lucky enough to survive and reach Australia, some of the Malaita captives had worked out a plan of escape even before the Carl had left the Solomons.

But they were deterred from leaving the vessel by the thought of what might happen to them if they swam ashore and landed among the cannibals of Gaudalcanal and similar islands.

So the Carl's return voyage to Fiji was uneventful—except for the fact that Dr Murray decided his skipper Armstrong was trying to poison him and determined to turn King's evidence when they reached port.

Shortly after the Carl arrived at Levuka in Fiji, Murray handed the police

The notorious slave brig Carl stands to awaiting to be boarded by a naval party. The Peri escapees were once imprisoned in the Carl's hold.

a long statement describing the massacre of the previous voyage down to the last agonising detail.

Armstrong and his first mate were immediately arrested on charges of murder and kidnapping.

Their trial in Australia in mid-1872 had far-reaching effects for it drew the attention of the world to the terrible crimes being committed in the name of South Seas islands recruiting.

Meanwhile, however, long before the Carl affair broke into the headlines, more tragedies were taking place.

By the time the Carl had reached Fiji in December 1871 and transferred 80 of her cargo to the schooner Peri, the plan of escape long maturing in the minds of the Malaitamen needed only one trivial incident to spark it into action.

Late one afternoon as the kidnapped islanders were quietly preparing their evening meal on deck, a European member of the Peri's crew became suddenly enraged at the spectacle of the natives' eating habits.

"You pigs," he screamed at them.

Next moment he rushed into the midst of the squatting groups, seized the natives' daily ration of rice cooking in the pots and threw it into the sea.

The angry islanders looked up to see themselves covered by the rifles of three other members of the crew.

That night one of the Malaitamen wormed his way through a chain-hole in the bows and clung to a rope hanging from the vessel's side.

He was followed by others until about a dozen were clinging to the rope.

The one of them climbed silently on deck and began helping himself to a pile of trade goods heaped in one corner. Before long every man had a weapon.

Just before the Peri reached its island destination the Malaitamen struck. Given no chance of defending themselves one white man and three Fijians were quickly killed and thrown overboard.

But the rest of the plan miscarried.

A fourth Fijian crew member, whom the islanders had intended should navigate the vessel to the Solomons, dived over the side and began swimming.

In the excitement of trying to follow his movements in the water the remaining two white men were allowed to take refuge in the cabin.

Desperately trying to defend themselves the two whites started a fire behind which they hoped to snatch one of the boats and escape. But there was no longer any holding back the maddened islanders.

Ignoring the flames they hacked away at the cabin walls until finally a wide hole appeared and the two men fled on deck to be hacked to pieces.

The fire was eventually brought under control but not before all the Peri's fresh water had been used up putting it out.

Most of the food was consumed the same night—in one furious drunken feast to celebrate their victory over the hated white men.

Later, when their heads cleared, the islanders considered the problem of how to get home. Beyond the knowledge that the Solomons lay somewhere to the west nobody had any idea what course to steer.

A longboat from HMAS Basilisk comes alongside the Peri in the Great Barrier Reef. Most of the natives aboard were near death.

Then head winds defeated their efforts to make westwards and the Peri was allowed to drift, sails set and helm lashed, wherever wind and current took her.

Several days later the already-gaunt natives were chewing boards hoping to extract some nourishment from the wood. That was when 25 Leli men came to a decision.

Cannibalism was taboo on their little islet but, in the circumstances, seeing that they might never reach land again they agreed that the taboo might well be lifted.

The rest of the castaways were too exhausted to resist.

One morning the Leli men clubbed to death a young girl and cooked the most succulent portions—breasts, thighs and the fleshy parts of the hand in a great iron pot on deck.

In the evening they devoured a second girl. And after that they ate two bodies every day, one at morning and one at evening.

Thirty men and women were killed and eaten while at least another 20 died of starvation. In the end only the Leli men remained.

Then the cannibalism ceased and the survivors sat down to watch one another die.

Finally on 5 February 1872, with only 13 of their number still barely alive, their schooner was carried through a narrow opening in Australia's Great Barrier Reef and sighted HMS Basilisk on her way north to survey the coast of New Guinea.

The few who had strength enough to stand braced themselves for one final effort.

As the Basilisk's boats headed over the water they fumbled desperately round the deck for weapons. If they were all going to be killed, they vowed, they would kill some of the whites first.

Soon after, however, they realised the seamen had come as friends.

Just 25 years were to pass before the story of the strange sequel to the rescue of the survivors of the Peri became known.

In 1897 a missionary in Fiji discovered that one of his flock was a Solomon Islander.

And it was from this native that the missionary learned how the Peri survivors, while being taken back to their island from Queensland, had become convinced the white crew intended eating them.

To escape this fate the islanders had escaped overboard one night and had taken refuge in Fiji.

Artist of Love and Crime

IN 1656 the lovely Mrs Thomas Ivie of London took out papers with the Lords Commissioners suing her absent husband for alimony. Mr Ivie retaliated with a statement accusing his wife of cruelty and unbridled extravagance.

During the resultant litigation Thomas Ivie published a pamphlet that most modern societies would ban on the grounds of obscenity.

The pamphlet began by outlining some of Mrs Ivie's financial extravagances. Then it detailed the lady's acts of immorality with a series of lovers including a father and son combination.

Many of his wife's bad habits, Ivie said in his little publication, were taught her by her aunt, a Mrs Williams, who owned a brothel "in a little blind alley".

There was a story that while the pamphlets were given away free, copies were later retailed among students of such literature at sums ranging up to two guineas.

But if Thomas Ivie was technically guilty of defamation none could accuse him of toying with the truth for every allegation was based on scandalous fact.

With that entree into the pages of London's history, the beauteous Theodosia Ivie went on to achieve added notoriety as one of England's most competent forgers.

Theodosia was born about 1631, the daughter of a struggling doctor named Stepkin whose one purpose in life, following the child's birth, was to marry her off to some man of means.

His great ally in this campaign was his daughter's beauty. And it was this asset alone (for the almost penniless medico could afford no dowry) that led to Theodosia's marriage to the son of Sir George Garrett.

A few years later Theodosia was a particularly lovely widow scanning the matrimonial horizon for a man just like the charming and wealthy Thomas Ivie who had recenly returned from India after losing his own wife.

The attraction was mutual, although for quite different reasons, and in 1649 Theodosia became Mrs Thomas Ivie.

164

Right from the moment they entered the matrimonial home in London, Ivie began wondering what he had let himself in for. He was wealthy but Theodosia's ability to spend far exceeded his ability to earn.

Nevertheless he was still too infatuated with his lovely acquisition to voice disapproval and went on meekly footing the bills that arrived by the sheaves.

He even tolerated her blatant infidelities in the matrimonial home. Ivie knew that when Sir William Killigrew was not making love to his wife the knight's son was.

Then there was young Snelling who was often to be seen sneaking from dark corners with the lovely Theodosia. And there were dozens more. Thomas Ivie didn't even get to know their names.

He blamed much of his wife's indiscretion on her aunt, the brothel owner Mrs Williams. Indeed he was convinced it was Mrs Williams who persuaded Theodosia to change her name to Clarke and arrange a tryst at Long Acre with Snelling.

Thomas Ivie, almost but not quite, reached the end of his amazing patience when word reached him that Theodosia was plotting with her brother to have him murdered.

To ensure her brother would be well out of the way if suspicion centred on him after the murder, Theodosia had already collected a passport and had arranged passage on a ship.

Although the murder plot was abandoned when Thomas Ivie found the passport, Theodosia soon had another plan which would free her of her unwanted husband and assure her of substantial alimony at the same time.

This plot got under way when Mrs Ivie took her servant, Jenny Gilbert, to a quack who had been paid in advance to examine the young servant, then announce that she was pregnant.

On returning to her house Theodosia let it be known that she had irrefutable evidence of an affair between her husband and her maid. At once Thomas Ivie took the girl off to three reputable doctors all of whom refuted the quack's diagnosis.

Mrs Ivie then tried another tack. She promised to give Jenny Gilbert a large sum if she would swear that her master had seduced her. When the girl refused, Theodosia denounced her to the Cromwellian authorities as a Royalist spy.

Without even the pretence of a trial the shocked girl was thrown into goal where her health declined rapidly.

Several weeks later the authorities realised they would have a corpse on their hands unless the girl was released. But by then it was too late and Jenny Gilbert died within weeks of winning her freedom.

Meanwhile the ever-forgiving Thomas Ivie was facing serious financial trouble. Theodosia had made such a hole in his capital that he decided to abandon the city house and move to his family estate at Malmsbury.

He begged Theodosia to come with him but the flighty beauty had no intention of burying herself in rustic surroundings with an unexciting man like her husband. So Thomas went alone.

And that was when Theodosia took action through the Lords Commissioners charging her husband with cruelty and financial neglect and demanding stiff alimony.

In reply Thomas Ivie sent the commissioners a statement in which he claimed that during the first eight months of the marriage his wife had spent the enormous sum of $1,600 on clothes and $6,000 on what she called "household expenses".

He also pointed out that instead of being penniless, Mrs Ivie had $2,500 worth of jewellery which he had told her to sell for her own benefit. In present currency this would be worth about $50,000.

After that Theodosia personally faced the commissioners accusing her husband of every boudoir indecency her imagination could conjure up. And the lies were presented with just the right amount of weeping.

Judge Jeffrey in action. Theodosia Ivie faced the fearsome 'hanging judge' on 4 June 1684 and lost her case.

The result was that Ivie was ordered to pay his wife $600 a year alimony and the outraged husband published his pamphlet detailing his wife's extravagances and over-enthusiastic love life.

In 1660 Theodosia, for some reason or other, contacted her husband and suggested they should resume married life. Ivie was still deeply in love with the worthless beauty and jumped at the offer.

At the Restoration when King Charles II returned to the throne from which Cromwell had thrown his father, he immediately rewarded those who had remained loyal to his cause.

And thus it was that Thomas Ivie was knighted and his lascivious wife became the Lady Theodosia.

Until Thomas Ivie's death some years later the couple lived happily together with their young daughter.

Nor did Theodosia have any real problems when Thomas died for he left her a comfortable income while she also had a property at Wapping left her by her father.

The Wapping estate had been originally owned by an ancestor, Stepkin, who had disposed of part of it before his death. That disposed part of the estate was now worth a fortune.

Theodosia determined to get her hands on it. And the obvious solution to this impasse was forgery.

But first she needed a forger and the best way of getting one was to utilise her arts of seduction.

At once Theodosia remembered the charming Mr Duffett, a brilliant penman, who she had seduced some years earlier under the very noses of his wife and his parents-in-law, Lord and Lady Salkeld.

Although Theodosia was now approaching 40, she was still amazingly beautiful and Duffett again succumbed to her advances and in repayment for her favors offered to do a little pen work for her.

At that time the land on which Lady Ivie had her eyes was owned by two men, Whichcott and Bateman, who had bought it from the deceased estate of Richard Glover who had bought if from her ancestor Stepkin.

Now Theodosia took a piece of parchment, gave it the appearance of

A contemporary photograph of Westminster Hall. It was here that Thomas Neale challenged Lady Ivie before the judge, Baron Jeffrey.

age by exposing it to the weather, and had Duffett prepare a yellowish ink that also gave the appearance of age.

When the penman had finished working on the document it stated that the land's original owner, Stepkin, had leased the parcel of land to Glover. No mention was made of a sale.

But when Duffett came to forging Stepkin's signature he could not get it just right.

Annoyed, Theodosia took up the pen and with a flourish copied her ancestor's signature. It was so perfect a court later awarded her the disputed land.

Yet still more of Stepkin's original estate remained in other hands. Lady Ivie refused to rest until she had all of it.

Another forgery, this time Theodosia's exclusive work, and the building specutator Thomas Neale found himself without any land with which to speculate.

Nevertheless Neale, convinced he had been the victim of a fraud, had the case re-opened in 1684.

According to the document Theodesia had originally submitted to the court, Stepkin had signed the lease to this land in the reign of Mary Tudor. It was dated December 1555.

The document gave Mary's titles as Queen of England and Spain. But as her husband Philip did not become King of Spain until January 1556, there was obviously something wrong with the document.

Neale took the matter to court and on June 4, 1684, the hearing opened in Westminster Hall before the domineering hanging judge, Baron Jeffrey.

The first witness was Mrs Duffett, wife of Theodosia's assistant forger of the Glover lease. She said she had actually seen the forgers at work and then detailed how the pair had aged the parchment and ink.

The upshot was that Judge Jeffrey returned the land to Neale and ordered that Lady Ivie be charged with forgery.

But Theodosia was lucky for at her trial the evidence of the chief witness against her, Mrs Duffett, was discredited on the grounds that she was inflamed by jealousy and had herself been caught in adultery following the seduction of her husband by Lady Ivie.

Apart from that Duffett himself could not be found so that the prosecution case had no weight. Lady Ivie was discharged.

Lady Theodosia Ivie died in 1695, leaving her daughter, by her husband Thomas, an estate in which she included Neale's land.

Even a court finding had failed to convince her that her forging ability was not perfect.

Mutiny on the "Lady Shore"

O N the last day of July in 1797 the ship Lady Shore, bound for Australia via Rio de Janeiro, was bowling along with a stiff breeze filling her sails about 400 miles off the Brazilian coast. Battened below her deck were 66 bedraggled hussies whose careers of prostitution and thievery had finally earned them free passage to the shores of Sydney Cove.

However it would have been very difficult to say which were the more discreditable specimens of humanity—the female convicts or the detachment of the NSW Corps travelling as their guards.

From the moment the redcoats reeled aboard in England, Captain Willcocks and the Lady Shore's officers had a grim premonition that they were in for trouble.

The soldiers consisted either of the sweepings of British military prisons or of deserters from the French Army who had been virtually shanghaied into the corps as an alternative to internment.

They were a drunken, riotous, undisciplined gang and, even before the Lady Shore left Portsmouth, Willcocks had been warned of a plot to seize the ship.

The Lady Shore had been at sea for seven weeks and Willcocks believed that perhaps his fears were unjustified when, just before daybreak on 1 August, the storm broke.

Aroused by the crash of musket shots the captain rushed from his cabin, to be bayoneted in the breast and throat as soon as he set foot on the deck.

Within half an hour the mutiny was over. Three men were dead or dying, a dozen more were wounded and the redcoats, with their fellow conspirators among the crew, had seized the Lady Shore.

A fortnight later came the dramatic sequel when 29 of the rebels' captives were cast adrift in an open boat to make their perilous way to the South American coast.

Though the occupants of the little vessel survived to tell their tale the mutineers were never brought to justice. The loss of the Lady Shore remains one of the few successful pirate coups in early Australian history.

It was January in 1797 when the Colonial Office sent a despatch to

Governor Hunter in Sydney informing him of the projected departure of the Lady Shore.

The ship, Hunter was told, would be carrying 66 female and two male convicts, a company of reinforcements for the NSW corps and a large supply of tools and agricultural implements for the half-starved settlement on Sydney Cove.

However in April, after many delays, the Lady Shore was still anchored off Gravesend in the Thames being fitted and provisioned for the long voyage.

There she took on the women who trooped aboard under the avid gaze of the sailors who well knew the reputation of female convict transports as little better than floating brothels.

At last, early in May, the Lady Shore dropped down the Channel to Portsmouth where Lieutenant William Minchin marched on board with his motley collection of redcoats.

Also at Portsmouth the Lady Shore received "Colonel" George Semple, one of her two male convicts and one of the strangest rogues ever sentenced to transportation to NSW.

An 18-gun sloop of the late eighteenth century, similar to the Lady Shore.

Veteran of the Russian and Dutch armies, soldier of fortune, con man, swindler and liar extraordinary, Semple had finally been nabbed by the law for the sordid offence of stealing a few cambric shirts from a London shop.

Captain James Willcocks, master of the Lady Shore, greeted Semple as befitted a gentleman—a courtesy that was to save many lives later during the bloody upheaval of the mutiny.

The month the Lady Shore lay in Portsmouth Harbour saw the outbreak of one violent dispute after another between the ship's officers and the soldiery.

It was soon obvious that timid, dithering young Mr Minchin had little control over the men whom John Black, the purser, described as "the greatest set of villains that ever entered a ship".

Nothing could prevent the redcoats breaking into the convict quarters, enjoying the rough favors of the women and making the ship hideous with their drunken brawls.

On one occasion the senior NCO, Sergeant Hughes, swaggered about the deck with a drawn sword threatening to "cut the limbs off" anyone who tried to check his comrades.

At Willcocks' insistence Minchin arrested the sergeant and put him in irons. Next day it seemed that the ruffians of the corps would explode in rebellion before the ship even put to sea.

The Chief Officer, John Lambert, was twice knocked to the deck by the enraged troops and then belaboured with a bundle of wet washing by the brawny wife of one of the Irish soldiers.

More sinister was the report by Semple that several of the French conscripts had approached him with a plot to seize the ship soon after she left port.

Having repented of deserting the Revolutionary armies the Frenchmen wanted to return to their native land and they suggested that Semple seize the chance to flee from British justice with them.

However, aware of Semple's talent for dramatic tales, Willcocks was dubious about the story. In any case he believed the foreigners too heavily outnumbered to start any trouble.

Thus on 8 June, with some foreboding, Captain Willcocks put to sea and steered south-west across the Atlantic on the long haul towards Rio de Janeiro, his first port of call.

The redcoats were quiet enough, provided they were assured of grog and access to the women, though ominous signs occasionally disturbed the ship's officer's peace of mind.

Three of the Frenchman—Delahaye, Dubois and Thierry—were observed in huddled consultation with some of the wilder members of the crew.

In the soldiers' quarters were about 100 extra muskets and a large store of ammunition destined for Sydney which had been taken from the hold in defiance of Willcock's orders.

Nevertheless the mutiny, when it came, took the officers and loyal seamen of the Lady Shore completely by surprise.

"Colonel" George Semple, one of the strangest rogues ever sentenced to transportation, acted as liaison officer between the Lady Shore's mutineers and their victims.

At 4.30 am on 1 August Chief Officer Lambert, who had the watch on deck, noticed shadowy figures gathering near the foc'sle.

He heard the mutter of voices and the sound of muskets being loaded. In the dim lantern light he saw the glint of bayonets.

Dashing into his cabin Lambert seized two pistols and emerged just as the mutineers launched their charge towards the ladders leading up to the quarterdeck and the ship's wheel.

Delahaye, the Frenchman, fell cursing with a pistol ball in his breast. Lambert's second shot stopped another redcoat with a shattered arm. Then he was overwhelmed.

Wounded in four places by musket fire or bayonet stabs Lambert managed to stagger into the purser's cabin for refuge, where Black had just been awakened by the uproar on deck.

Black slammed the door just as musket butts beat a tattoo on the timbers. Then, snatching up a pistol, he fired through the window that looked out on to the main deck in the ship's waist.

A howl of execration told him the ball had found a mark. In the momentary confusion Lambert determined to make a break for the hatchway leading down to the "great" cabin in the stern.

By now, however, the decks were swarming with mutineers from stem to stern. As Lambert, faint and covered with blood, reeled out of the cabin door he was shot through the head and killed instantly.

Meanwhile the fate of Captain Willcocks had already virtually decided the outcome of the mutiny.

Aroused by the first musket shots the captain had clambered up the companionway from the stern cabin only to find himself surrounded by the waiting redcoats.

A bayonet stabbed into his chest below the heart. Another gashed his throat. Mortally wounded Willcocks fell headlong back down the ladder into the cabin.

There, according to one story, Lieut Minchin, who had not lifted a finger to resist the mutineers, was busy concealing himself behind some casks.

"Sir, your men have seized my ship!" Willcocks gasped, with blood gurgling in his slashed throat. And in fact the Lady Shore was now completely in the hands of the mutineers.

The ship's guns were loaded and dragged into position with their muzzles pointing down the hatchways and against the doors and windows of the officers' cabins.

Semple offered to conduct the surrender negotiations to prevent a general massacre and a few minutes later the surviving officers yielded up their arms to the rebels.

Next morning the bodies of Willcocks, Lambert and Delahaye went overboard into the Atlantic and then the mutineers met in council on deck to choose their leader and make their plans.

The elected "captain" was the Frenchman Dubois and his proposal that they sail for the Spanish South American port of Montevideo was greeted with acclamation.

Since Spain was at war with Britain they would be safe there from British vengeance. And the convict women heartily agreed that they would rather ply their familiar trades in Montevideo than languish at Sydney Cove.

There remained the problem of disposing of the officers and the handful of loyal soldiers and seamen, and once more their lives trembled in the balance.

In fluent French, Semple harangued the chief rebels and never had the veteran swindler used his silver tongue to better effect.

On 15 August a fortnight after the mutiny, the longboat was swung out and 29 people—including Semple himself, Minchin's wife and several other women—were embarked in it.

With them they had three small kegs of water, four bags of bread, a few pieces of salt beef, five gallons of rum, a set of sails and a compass.

All they knew of their position was that they were about two days sail from the Brazilian coast and roughly in the latitude of Cape Frio, about 200 miles north of Rio de Janeiro.

But wind and weather were kind. Only 48 hours later the longboat steered through the great rollers crashing on the sandbars and entered the little Brazilian port of San Pedro.

Not a life had been lost on the voyage and the mutineers had an equally uneventful cruise to the haven of Montevideo.

Of the figures in the drama Minchin eventually reached NSW where, after his military career, he became a well-known settler and pioneer of the Minchinbury estate where vineyards flourish today.

"Colonel" Semple escaped the convict colony. But he ended up in prison in London again and drifted deeper into obscurity and degradation until he vanished from the records in the 1820s.

Historians have speculated about how many inhabitants of modern Uruguay include among their ancestors the English trollops who landed in Montevideo from the Lady Shore 170 years ago.

Counterfeit King
of the West

A DANDIFIED little man who looked like a travelling salesman rode into the booming mining centre of South Pass City in Wyoming late on the afternoon of 26 May 1872.

He tied up his horse outside a saloon called Happy Halligan's Whisky and Good Time Emporium and went in.

After several whiskies the newcomer's mind drifted to the promised "good time" represented by a blonde and buxom female entertainer who was bellowing out her version of the popular song Buffalo Girl.

Observing his interest another drinker at the bar told him he was wasting his time unless he had struck it rich and had "a poke full of nuggets."

The singer, he added, was Molly Morris 'the highest priced woman in Wyoming.' For one brief interlude of love she charged $100.

The newcomer smiled with relief. As long as the lady was for sale the price was of little consequence to him.

Although the visitor, Sam Yeager, was not a prospector with a bag of nuggets to fling around, he still had plenty of cash when a charmer like Molly Morris took his fancy.

And the reason for this was that Sam Yeager made his own money, a business he continued until a hangman's rope brought to a sudden end the career of the Wild West's most amazing counterfeiter.

Sam was born in Lawrence County, Ohio, in 1837 the son of a quack who brewed and peddled a dubious remedy labelled Dr Yeager's Wonderful Liniment for Man and Beast.

From his father Sam inherited a talent for fraud and soon developed into a cheap crook and petty swindler. Then at the age of 25 he switched to counterfeiting.

The enterprise proved successful until, with the nation returning to normal after the Civil War, Federal agents arrested Yeager for passing spurious coins.

He was convicted and sentenced to four years in the Federal prison near Wellsboro, Pennsylvania.

Released early in 1872 Sam Yeager decided to move to the frontier country of the West where law enforcement officers were few and a counterfeiter could easily make a fortune.

Quickly retrieving his counterfeiting equipment which had been left with

176

relatives at Covington in Kentucky, he headed west and arrived in Wyoming a couple of months later.

With his saddle bags heavy with counterfeit eagles (a $10 gold coin then in wide circulation) Yeager rode into South Pass City one evening and handed some of the coins over to the beauteous Molly Morris.

Completely infatuated with the saloon charmer Sam Yeager tarried in the town and spent the next three evenings, and many more spurious eagles, in her company.

By then however the girl's curiosity was roused and she asked her temporary lover where he got the money he threw around so freely.

Coyly Molly Morris suggested he must have a secret gold claim up in the mountains. Sam Yeager shook his head and told her that he made his own money—as much as he wanted.

While the girl listened incredulously the counterfeiter confided that he could comfortably make 500 spurious eagles in a day.

He sold these for $5 each to saloon-keepers who palmed them off on unsuspecting customers.

After that Yeager asked Molly Morris to marry him. But as she received such offers every day from free-spending prospectors, gamblers and outlaws she was not very impressed.

So in desperation Yeager offered to set her up in a mansion in the nearest big city of Denver. This was nearer the mark and Molly finally agreed to marry him when he had saved $100,000 in genuine money.

Early next morning an elated Yeager rode out of town confident that by selling his spurious eagles to saloon keepers he could make the $100,000 and claim his fiancee in a few months.

An hour later he set up camp in a lonely spot and from his bags produced a 10-mould die, a small charcoal stove and several ingots of copper. By noon he had poured 500 copper coins.

During the afternoon he plated them with a thin layer of an alloy of which nine parts were gold and one part was silver-copper, the same ratio used by the U.S. Mint for bona fide gold coins.

Late the next day Yeager arrived in the rugged frontier town of Split Rock, 60 miles east of South Pass City.

There he soon sold his 500 counterfeit eagles at half price to a money-hungry saloon-keeper known as Dirty Dugan.

After repeating the operation in the Wyoming towns of Saratoga, Hanna, Encampment and Horse Creek, Yeager returned to South Pass City for a night of love with Molly Morris.

Then after leaving his accumulated profits with her for safe keeping, he moved south into Colorado where business proved just as satisfactory until he reached the town of Virginia Dale on July 16, 1872.

There Clements Murray, the first saloon-keeper to whom Yeager put his proposition, proved to be an honest man.

He refused to buy the spurious coins and as soon as the counterfeiter left called the marshal, Elijah Gates.

Had Sam Yeager stuck to counterfeiting and shunned love his successful career might have lasted longer.

When Yeager was arrested by Gates as he was about to enter the Trail Saloon down the street, he asked the marshal if he could have a whisky before he was taken to the gaol. Gates agreed.

Over drinks bought by Yeager, Gates revealed his pay was $70 a month. His eyes widened when the counterfeiter offered him a partnership and an immediate profit of $2500.

When Gates accepted the proposition, Yeager quickly sold 1000 spurious eagles to the saloonkeeper at $5 each. Half of the profit of $5000 was handed to Gates.

Immediately the marshal pocketed the money he arrested Yeager for counterfeiting saying he would keep the $2500 as "witness's expenses" in the coming trial.

Pending the trial Yeager was visited in his prison cell by Stephen Potts, editor of the Virginia Dale Courier.

"It would be hard to conceive of a more dispirited miscreant than this little wrongdoer," the paper subsequently reported.

"He reposed miserably on his bunk pondering the wages of sin, interrupting this meditation only to curse Marshal Gates with the basest of expletives."

Yeager's trial began on July 19 in the lobby of the Hobbs Hostelry with the town's only lawyer, 33-year-old and wax-moustached Gilbert McCain, acting as judge.

It did not make any difference that McCain, who had been practising in the town for three years, had previously been disbarred in Dayton, Ohio, for embezzling from a client.

Soon after the proceedings began Marshal Gates laid several of Yeager's counterfeit eagles in front of the judge as evidence.

McCain stared incredulously at them for they were no ordinary counterfeits but the work of a craftsman.

At the first opportunity McCain blandly adjourned the court for one hour announcing he wished to interrogate the prisoner and find out who were his accomplices.

Everyone then thankfully trooped into the adjoining bar of the hotel while McCain took Yeager into a corner of the lobby.

Yeager confirmed that he made the spurious eagles himself and estimated that if he worked hard he could produce 1000 a day for a profit of $5000.

That was enough for the judge who proposed they become partners. Yeager agreed and was told not to worry and to leave everything to McCain.

The court resumed at the end of an hour. Soon after Sam Yeager was convicted and sentenced to 10 years by the judge.

Next morning Marshal Gates set out to escort Yeager to the Colorado State Penitentiary at Canon City.

An hour later the stillness of the lonely trail to Canon City was broken by the boom of a 10-gauge shotgun.

As Marshal Gates fell dead Gilbert McCain rode out from his hiding place and freed the leather thongs that bound Yeager's hands.

On the way to Yeager's camp McCain explained that any one of a dozen

Dodge City in 1878. It was typical of the towns visited by Yeager as he wandered the Wild West making and selling spurious money.

outlaws who had threatened to kill the marshal would be blamed for his death.

Returning quickly to his counterfeiting operations, Yeager was able to increase production simply because his partner took over the time-wasting task of selling the counterfeits.

Over the next couple of months Wyoming and Colorado were flooded with the beautifully manufactured counterfeit eagles.

"They were as handsome eagles as one would wish to see," banker Stephen B. Ruehling of the town of Yuma wrote later in his memoirs. "And they readily passed inspection until the plating began to wear off."

Every fortnight Yeager and McCain rode to South Pass City where Sam spent his time with Molly Morris who already had saved $70,000 of the $100,000 she demanded as a condition of marriage.

Yet despite that bank roll she still insisted that Yeager pay the regular fee for her favors. His one hope was that the charges would cease once they were married.

Meanwhile Gillbert McCain had also been impressed by Molly Morris's beauty and became a client of hers on his visits to town.

But he had doubts about her character and several times tried to point out to his partner that he was putting too much trust in South Pass City's leading courtesan.

On 28 September, 1872, the two men rode into the Colorado town of Sterling and, with a good stock of counterfeits, booked into an hotel.

But again Sam Yeager struck an honest saloon keeper. The outraged man drew a revolver and held him prisoner until U.S. Marshal Henry Larney arrived to take him into custody.

As Larney hauled the prisoner off to Sterling's gaol McCain, hearing what had happened, rode hurriedly out of town.

One night, while waiting for a circuit judge to arrive in town, Marshal Larney made the mistake of leaving the gaol in charge of a deputy Roy Shively.

Some hours later Yeager persuaded Shively to accept 50 genuine double eagles (worth $20 each) which he had concealed in a money belt under his shirt.

In return Shively left his saddled horse in a lane at the side of the gaol building and stood sufficiently close to the counterfeiter's cell to allow him to grab a revolver from his holster.

Taking the weapon Yeager supposedly forced Shively to unlock his cell door and then made his escape. Three days later he rode into South Pass City.

As Molly Morris was not downstairs in Happy Halligan's saloon he went straight up to her room.

He stopped outside the door and heard voices. It did not take him long to realise that his fiancee and his partner Gilbert McCain were inside. And he clearly heard McCain say to Molly: "Yeager is sure to get a sentence of 10 years."

Then Molly told McCain that she had never intended to marry "the little runt" but only to get his $100,000 and then elope with "a high class gentleman" like his partner.

Without waiting to hear more, the enraged Sam Yeager burst into the room. McCain and Molly Morris were in bed.

Before they could speak Yeager's revolver exploded twice. In that instant he became a double murderer.

A blood-thirsty lynch mob hanged Yeager within an hour from a crossbeam in Kelly's stable next door to the saloon.

Women were scarce in the Wild West and the killer of one as beautiful and as accommodating as Molly Morris could hardly have expected any other fate from the lonely males of South Pass City.

Sisters for a Royal Bed

ONE day early in 1738 Louis XV of France summoned one of his ministers and ordered the official to find him a mistress forthwith. For a moment the minister was shocked, for Louis, in an age of licentiousness, had been notoriously faithful to his queen.

Nevertheless being a well-disciplined minister the man hid his agitation and rushed off to select a woman who would best suit the King's tastes.

The candidate finally produced for Louis' inspection was Mme de Mailly, the possessor of a plain face, a superb figure and a witty tongue. She was also completely without morals.

Actually when the King first sighted Mme de Mailly she was posed to best advantage, lying stretched on a sofa and showing a beautiful leg with a garter tantalisingly unhooked.

And thus began the notorious careers of the five married daughters of the Baron de Nesle, all of whom were to become Louis's mistresses in chronological order according to their ages, from the oldest to the youngest.

The story of the history making sisters began late in 1737 when Louis suddenly became tired of the celibate marriage his Queen Marie, daughter of Stanislas, exiled King of Poland, was inflicting on him.

Just 34 years of age Marie had already borne her husband 10 children and had decided to retire from the marriage bed.

Every approach by the King was met by some excuse or other. She felt ill, Marie would claim, or it was some saint's day, and she could not leave her devotions to grant favours to her husband.

In the end the Queen did not even bother making excuses. She simply locked her boudoir door against Louis who hammered on it and, in the face of this final insult, roared: "Madame you will not get the chance to insult me again."

From that moment the once-faithful King set himself on the course that was to lead to the moral degradation not only of himself but of his entire court.

Actually there are many historians who believe that it was the debaucheries of Louis XV's court that sowed the seeds that sprouted into the revolution of 1789 and the execution of Louis XVI and his family.

Early in 1738 Louis XV decided to follow the example already set by many of his courtiers and take a mistress. The process was easy enough. He simply instructed his Government to get him one.

Mme de Mailly was selected chiefly because she was interested in love and not politics. She was also amusing and if her face was plain her figure compensated.

When Louis was led into Mme de Mailly's salon he was accompanied by seven courtiers including the Duke de Richelieu.

Later Richelieu wrote: "Mme de Mailly reclined on a sofa in an attitude of voluptuous abandon showing the most beautiful leg to be seen at court with the garter becomingly undone."

The sight caused the unsophisticated King to blush and retreat a little. At once his courtiers pushed him forward and Mme de Mailly "grabbed his arm in a grasp from which there was no escape".

A week later the King had forgotten those first embarrassing moments and had ordered the construction of a special suite for his mistress in the Versailles Palace.

And it was in this suite that he, Mme de Mailly "and several chosen companions of similar inclinations conducted nocturnal festivities in honor of Venus and Bacchus".

For two years Mme de Mailly was the apple of Louis' eye, an eye that never wandered towards the hordes of other courtesans who hovered in the background waiting for the moment when the King showed signs of boredom.

Mme de Mailly was the ideal mistress. She seemed genuinely in love with her handsome monarch and demanded nothing of him—neither riches nor honours. All she wanted was his love.

And when the King inevitably grew tired of her she left the palace as unobtrusively as she had come.

Meanwhile, a year before the partnership ended, Mme de Mailly had innocently introduced her royal lover to her younger sister Mme de Vintimille.

All Louis saw when he first met Mme de Vintimille was her sensuously inviting face. He had no way of knowing that it cloaked a hard, unscrupulous nature that was soon dedicated to the seduction of the King and the life of affluence and luxury that would follow.

Mme de Vintimille kept at her task for a year. Victory came when Louis, as kindly as he could, dismissed Mme de Mailly and escorted her younger sister into the love bower at Versailles.

What attracted Louis to Mme de Vintimille remains a mystery unless it was the aura of depravity that enfolded her for by now the King's own inclinations verged on the depraved.

The second royal mistress was taller than her lover, she was arrogant and bad mannered. Apart from that there were many who considered she was quite ugly.

A younger sister, Mme de Flavacourt, once said of her: "She has the

face of a grenadier, the neck of a crane and she smells like a monkey."

Nevertheless Louis became infatuated with Mme de Vintimille, enjoying her sparks of wit and tolerating her domineering bad tempers. Indeed the King probably loved her more than any of the long line of de Nesle sisters.

Yet there was one famous occasion when the courtesan nearly went too far.

One evening the King propositioned her only to be met by an impatient gesture signifying she was in no mood for dalliance. Louis's reaction astounded her. He flew into a fearful rage.

Realising her position was threatened, Mme de Vintimille threw herself to her knees, clasped her arms about the King's legs and with tears coursing down her cheeks begged for pardon.

Looking down at the woman the King snapped: "You need a cure like having your head cut off. And you have a pretty long neck at that."

About a year after this episode Mme de Vintimille gave birth to a son who, she hoped, would replace in the King's affections the beloved Duke de Anjou who had recently died.

But Mme de Vintimille was never able to know how Louis reacted to his

Mme de la Tournelle, later the Duchess de Chateauroux, second youngest of the five de Nesle sisters. She managed to draw most from the royal coffers.

illegitimate son, for less than a week after the birth of the Count de Luc, peritonitis killed her.

Louis was grief stricken and at once invited the next of the sisters, Mme de Flavacourt, to visit him in the palace love suite and console him.

Mme de Flavacourt was far more attractive than her two older sisters and was quite willing to accept Louis' suggestion that she should fill the vacant post of royal mistress. But there was a snag.

Her husband, unlike the spouses of Mme de Mailly and Mme de Vintimille, was unwilling to hand over his wife even to his country's King. And he made his attitude embarrassingly obvious.

Louis liked Mme de Flavacourt but not enough to become involved with an outraged husband. So, after enjoying her company for a few weeks, he sent her back to her family and again called on the services of the gentle, understanding Mme de Mailly.

The King retained Mme de Mailly for a few months then, seeking again the novelty of a new lover, replaced her with her sister, the 28-year-old Mme de la Tournelle.

The most attractive of the de Nesle sisters, Mme de la Tournelle was

185

tall, dignified and the possessor of a milk-white skin that dazzled her monarch. She was also without principles.

When first notified that Louis wished her to take up residence in his love bower at Versailles, Mme de la Tournelle accepted the offer on three conditions.

Her older sister must leave the palace and never return; she must be given her own residence and not be forced to meet her lover in secret and she must be created a duchess within a year of taking office.

By now Louis's whole existence was compelled by sensuous desires and he agreed to every condition.

Mme de Mailly was transferred to a cold, cheerless room in the Tuileries. Here she discarded the luxurious gowns Louis had given her and replaced them with peasant garments. She also sought consolation in her religion.

Once when she arrived late at a church service the priest interrupted the ceremony to allow her to take the pew reserved for her. At that a worshipper called: "What a hubbub for a public strumpet!"

Turning to the man Mme de Mailly said softly: "Since you know her faults, please pray for her."

In October 1743 Mme de la Tournelle was created Duchess de Chateauroux and was given an annuity of $180,000.

Having achieved position and income the duchess now turned to the task of reawakening in the indolent, pleasure-saturated King an interest in the affairs of his country.

His Prime Minister, Cardinal Fleury, was dead and his mistress insisted he should take over the reins of government as well as the command of his armies.

Succumbing to these demands Louis travelled to Metz with the duchess to take command of military operations during the War of Austrian Succession. But it proved to be an unfortunate journey for the ambitious Duchess de Chateauroux.

At Metz food poisoning forced Louis into bed. The pain was great and, fearing he might die, the dissolute monarch decided to confess his sins.

It is possible his absolution depended on his promise to rid himself of the cause of his sins—the Duchess de Chateauroux.

Anyway, when he had partly recovered, the courtesan was ordered to return to Paris and was told to keep clear of her lover in the future.

Nine days later Louis' health returned to normal. Feeling his old self again he handed the armies back to his generals and rushed post haste to Paris to reclaim his mistress.

He never did see her for the Duchess de Chateauroux's body was burning with a fever she had contracted at Metz. A few days later she died still refusing to have anything to do with the man who had so recently and cruelly dismissed her.

Now only one of the five de Nesle sisters remained—Mme de Lauraguais, the youngest and one of the most attractive of the notorious quintette.

Louis sent for her and she answered his summons. Mme de Lauraguais

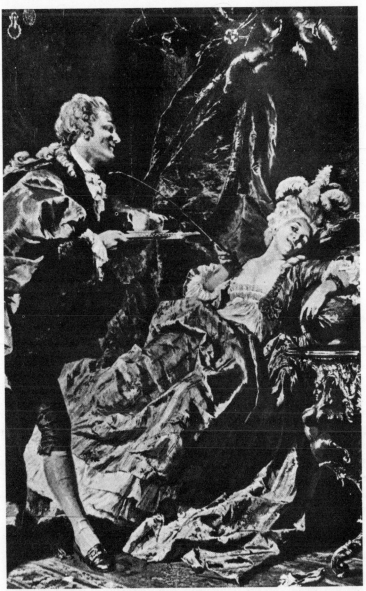

Louis XV of France with his most famous mistress, the Marquise de Pompadour. The lovely Pompadour came into the King's life only after he had finished with the de Nesle brood.

tried her best but she lacked the amorous enthusiasm that had won her sisters important roles in the life of Louis XV.

The king maintained her for about 10 months although his visits to her were never regular and practically stopped altogether in the last months of the relationship.

Now all the de Nesle sisters had been sampled by Louis of France. To console himself he turned to the lovely Antoinette Poisson, later to become known as the Marquise de Pompadour.

The Scandal of Reverend Beecher

ONE Sunday morning in March 1876, the famed clergyman, Henry Ward Beecher, was preaching to his flock in his fashionable Plymouth Church in Brooklyn and, as usual, was holding it enthralled despite the dullness of the subject matter.

The congregation was more accustomed to being lambasted on a theme that once was almost obsessive with the preacher. The theme was adultery.

But Beecher had not touched on the subject for some time. And the reason was that only a few months earlier a jury had acquitted him of committing that sin with Elizabeth Tilton, the wife of a parishioner.

Beecher was approaching an oratorical crescendo when suddenly a middle-aged man jumped up in his pew.

"I've been silent for too many years," the man thundered. "Long ago I received a deathbed confession from a certain lady of this church of adultery with Mr. Beecher. . . . "

The man who spoke was Henry Bowen, founder of the Plymouth Church. And the congregation knew that the only deathbed he had ever stood beside was that of his wife Lucy.

Yet despite this new accusation of adultery and the nationwide publicity that followed it, the Plymouth Church flock remained on the side of their preacher. Indeed they later officially expelled Bowen from their church.

After that second assault on his reputation, the Rev. Henry Ward Beecher continued happily along earning a salary larger, probably, than that attained by any other clergyman.

Nor did he seem upset by the ditty the children sang in the streets as they swung their skipping ropes and pranced up and down:
Preacher Beecher is my name,
I'll preach until I die,
I never kissed Ted Tilton's wife,
I never told a life.

The only difference the charges relating to the Sixth Commandment seemed to make to the Rev. Beecher's life was that until his death in 1887 he kept well clear of the more attractive female members of his flock.

188

The Rev. Henry Ward Beecher, central figure in a controversial trial.

The Rev Henry Ward Beecher first became news in the years before the Civil War when, during his mighty campaign against Negro slavery, he preached to his congregation with a mulatto girl beside him in the pulpit.

Placing his arm around the girl's shoulder, Beecher would cry: "Look at her. What is she worth? Who bids? This is a girl who knows the meaning of the Sixth Commandment.

"He who takes her will do more than profane her flesh. He will rape her immortal soul. We must act now to buy her from her bondage."

As a result of these appeals (usually with a different girl in the pulpit each time) the Plymouth Church's collection plates could not hold the money that poured into them.

At that stage of his meteoric career it was estimated that Beecher was

189

earning about £10,000 a year from his church alone. Added to that were his lecture fees.

Most of his sermons in those days seemed to deal with sex. And the one facet of the subject that seemed to interest him most was the Sixth Commandment.

He referred to it as "That vice which it has pleased God to be more full and explicit with than any other."

Having won a reputation as a hater of sins against purity, Beecher was able to get himself into situations with women that would have compromised a lesser man.

There was hardly a citizen in America who would even suggest that the famous clergyman, Henry Ward Beecher, was capable of leading any female astray.

Indeed when he was in Indianapolis in 1839, the mother of the lovely Betty Bates, who had a crush on the 26-year-old clergyman, was delighted to have Beecher chaperon her daughter on a trip to New England.

It was as a direct result of Beecher's growing reputation as a preacher and as a man with a deep spirit of reformation that the wealthy Henry Bowen, who had recently built the Plymouth Church at Brooklyn Heights, asked Beecher to take over the parish.

Immediately Beecher took the job, fashionable New Yorkers began flocking to the Plymouth Church. On a Sunday the pews blazed with jewellery, furs and some of the prettiest faces in the city.

Among the first to welcome Beecher to his new parish was Lucy, the young and beautiful wife of Henry Bowen. In no time she was visiting him regularly in his home to take a course of religious study.

And that was about the time Beecher began producing his string of mulatto girls and using them as examples of what was going on in the slave-ridden South.

One girl stood placidly alongside the great preacher as he raged: "I call on you to save her from licentiousness, adultery and concubinage worse even than goes on in a Turkish harem."

As a result of this spectacular approach to the problem of slavery, many New York socialites arrived at the church on Sundays to find their seats had been taken by newspaper reporters.

And even when the Civil War put an end to slavery it did not stop the Rev Beecher talking on his favorite subject.

One of his most popular lectures which he gave during nationwide tours was entitled, Strange Women. The moral was that young men should save themselves for the girl they intended to marry and the subject matter was close to the bone, according to some critics.

Then in 1862 Lucy Bowen died. A few months passed before the flock noticed that Bowen was keeping well clear of the man he had put into the pulpit. Indeed they had not even spoken to each other.

It did not seem to worry Beecher who was now financially on top of the world.

190

His children, by his wife Eunice who was often taken for his mother, were sent to the most expensive schools while he gave his daughter a wedding that must have cost a fortune.

But if Bowen no longer spoke to him, the clergyman had another friend, Theodore Tilton, who had married a pretty choir girl, Elizabeth.

The couple often visited the clergyman while Elizabeth sometimes dropped in alone to pay her respects when she was passing his house.

When Harriet Beecher Stowe's book, Uncle Tom's Cabin was first published in 1851, the clergyman decided to emulate his sister by writing a book himself. The result was Norwood, which he sold on the understanding that it be dramatised for the Broadway theatre.

He was immediately subjected to severe criticism, for at that time most churchgoers regarded the Broadway theatres as dens of iniquity.

Then startling rumours began circulating about the Rev. Beecher's moral life. It was said he was carrying on with Elizabeth Tilton.

The rumours reached a climax late in 1874 when Tilton gave notice of an action claiming 100,000 dollars damages against Beecher for alienating his wife's affections by committing adultery with her.

Many saw the action as revenge by Tilton who earlier had been dismissed from his job as editor of a religious newspaper when Beecher had used his influence against him.

When the case came before the court in January 1875, Tilton testified that one night in 1870 his wife Elizabeth had broken down and had admitted to him that she had committed adultery with Beecher.

Elizabeth had told him, Tilton said, that she had resisted the clergyman's advances until he had assured her that love and every expression of love was basically good.

Tilton said he forgave his wife and stood by her for four years until she suddenly abandoned him and his children.

Some letters his wife had left behind, Tilton told the court, showed she had continued carrying on with Beecher during those four years.

When Henry Ward Beecher took the witness stand the court was packed with women who had come to admire the man they believed was incapable of doing any wrong.

The clergyman soon had the court laughing by sniffing in a clownish manner at a bunch of violets. His fans in the huge room almost burst their sides when he asked the judge if he had taken up the collection.

Then he staggered the entire nation by refusing to swear an oath with his hand on a Bible.

Yet despite his refusal to take a formal oath Beecher admitted kissing Elizabeth Tilton when her husband and children were not present. But he did deny adultery.

Beecher gave a poor account of himself under cross-examination and continually answered questions by saying he could not remember.

During the trial that lasted five months, several New York newspapers began condemning Beecher as a "hypocrite". Others simply suggested his

When Harriet Beecher Stowe wrote Uncle Tom's Cabin her brother, Henry Ward Beecher, tried to emulate her success by producing his own novel, Norwood.

answers to questions were not helping his case.

Then towards the trial's end, Beecher's lawyer, William Evarts, changed tactics.

He began harping on the theme that if the nation's best-known clergyman was found guilty of adultery it would give the sin respectability in the eyes of sophisticated adults.

And in the eyes of the young, like Sunday school children, it would utterly destroy their trusting innocence in men they should look up to.

After being locked up for eight days the jury could not agree. No new trial was instigated and Beecher returned to his church to be completely exonerated of any blame by a special advisory council of his flock.

The publicity that surrounded the sordid case did not affect Beecher's standing in New York. In fact, the sale of pews so increased that the sum raised by their auction skyrocketed by 12,000 dollars that year.

Then a few months after the court hearing's end, Henry Bowen rose to his feet in the middle of a sermon and accused Beecher of having seduced his wife Lucy.

After saying that Lucy had confessed to the sin on her deathbed, Bowen went on: "He had given her a key to his study where they met secretly for many years.

"But one day she saw another lady of this church leave his study. She also had a key of her own."

Bowen tried to go on but his voice was drowned out by the congregation's abuse and hisses. He turned and almost ran from the building.

After that the Rev. Henry Ward Beecher went on to even greater fame lecturing all over America and even visiting England where he was received with tremendous enthusiasm.

Later he became an ardent supporter of women's suffrage and fought the cause fearlessly despite ridicule and bitter opposition.

Early in 1887 he suffered several apoplexy attacks and died in Brooklyn on 8 March.

He was accorded one of the biggest funerals in New York's history to that time.

THE LADY OF THE CAMELLIAS

Marie Duplessis was little more than an exclusive harlot but, as the mistress of Alexandre Dumas, she inspired him as the immortal Dame aux Camelias.

La Dame aux Camelias

ONE day in 1847 a coffin, recently disinterred from a humble grave, was carried to an imposing vault in a Paris cemetery. Around the coffin stood a small group of men including the famed author, Alexandre Dumas the Younger.

Tears coursing down his cheeks, Dumas broke the silence with a horrifying request. Would the undertaker, he asked, open the coffin that he might once again look on the adorable countenance of Marie Duplessis.

Realising putrefaction must be in an advanced state, most of the group moved out of the vault leaving only the undertaker and Alexandre Dumas with the corpse of the tragic woman who had proved completely unworthy of the love of the idealistic Dumas.

But at last the body was exposed and the great author gazed on all that was left of the chief inspiration of his immortal novel, La Dame aux Camelias.

The once-beautiful face was unrecognisable. But the long black hair remained as lustrous as ever. Seemingly unrevolted, Dumas gazed long at the foul relic then quietly and alone left the cemetery.

Marie Duplessis, dubbed courtesan by historians, but more truly an exclusive harlot, began the career that was to bring unhappiness to many of the great of Europe, when, in 1824, she was born in a dwelling attached to a draper's store in the French village of Nonant near Caen.

When her mother died, Marie was reared by her drunken father who spent more time drinking with his cronies than attending to the welfare of his daughter and his drapery business.

In 1836 when Marie was 12, her father discovered she was no longer a virgin.

But instead of lamenting his daughter's loss of innocence he decided to capitalise on it by hiring her as a mistress-housekeeper to an acquaintance who was then in his 70s.

The arrangement worked well and gave Plessis (his daughter later added the "du" to her name) a regular income. At least it did until Plessis discovered his old friend was sub-letting his daughter to friends as ancient as himself.

Plessis took Marie out of service and with her set off for Paris where he

195

hoped to apprentice the child to a brothel-keeper.

Plessis was never sober from the moment he reached Paris. The result was that he never got round to signing the necessary papers. In the end he simply abandoned his daughter.

Marie now became one of the city's thousands of abandoned children. Her clothes no more than rags, she slept where she could and existed on scraps stolen from garbage cans.

Finally it was her pretty face beneath the grime that covered it most of the time, that allowed her to get an underpaid job as a messenger for a corset manufacturer.

Taking advantage of her lessons in frugal living, Marie was able with the passing of time, to save enough to buy a hat and a dress.

With her pretty face now complemented by flattering clothes, Marie Duplessis was able to graduate into the grisette class; underpaid working girls who, in exchange for board and lodgings, became the house-keepers and mistresses of students.

Finally she accepted the offer of a restauranteur of some means to become his mistress on the promise he would set her up in her own establishment.

Inundated by gifts of fine clothes and expensive jewellery by the restaurant keeper, Marie was able to move into more exclusive circles. It was then she met the young and wealthy Count Ferdinand de Monguija.

The infatuated count provided his exciting new find with a luxurious apartment, taught her to read and write and even gave her lessons in elocution and social graces.

When she had learned enough of these refinements, Marie accepted the offer of the 22-year-old Duc de Guiche to move into his even more luxurious residence.

Marie's decision to abandon the lovelorn de Monguija was made in unusual circumstances.

She had just left the notorious dance haunt, the Prado, one evening when the Duc walked up to her in the street, literally lifted her into his arms, and carried her off to his magnificent mansion a few blocks away.

By the following morning Marie Duplessis had made up her mind that the Duc offered more luxury and security than her current lover. So she had her baggage brought over from de Monguija's apartment.

Bewitched by his acquisition, the Duc de Guiche put his great wealth at Marie's disposal. She dressed in clothes that were envied even in court circles and went abroad in carriages complete with footmen.

It was inevitable that Marie Duplesssis should tire of the Duc. But when she left him she transferred her affections, not to a single man, but to a club-full of them.

The club was the exclusive Paris Jockey Club, an international brotherhood, that insisted on a spirit of camaraderie among members.

Each new lover kept Marie for a week or two then handed her on to a fellow club member.

With gifts of clothing, jewellery and money being lavished on her as she passed through the Paris Jockey Club, Marie finished her tour enjoying luxury more befitting a princess than a Parisian demi-mondaine.

Revelling in the notoriety that surrounded her, Marie Duplessis nightly attended the theatre always accompanied by at least two of the city's well-known rakes.

Sitting in her box with pearls in her hair and always a bouquet of camellias

One of Marie's most tempestuous liaisons was with the composer Franz Liszt.

FRANTIŠEK LISZT

in her hand, Marie gloried in the stares of the audience.

Yet Marie Duplessis never enjoyed good health. Indeed the germ of tuberculosis had been sown when, as a child, she haunted the streets of Paris.

Nevertheless it was this disease, slowly spreading throughout her system, that gave her the ethereal beauty and the almost transparent, camellia-white complexion, that distinguished her from other women.

Then in the midst of the gay life, Marie, deciding she needed a holiday, set off for a tour of the German spas.

Giving her favors freely as she progressed from one place to the other, Marie saw to it that her holiday was highly profitable. And when she returned home her retinue had grown by one—the wealthy Russian octogenerian, Count Stackelberg.

Immediately Marie reached Paris, her ancient lover set her up in a magnificent mansion, loaded her with gifts and, in return for an occasional kind smile, allowed his mistress to continue entertaining younger men.

It was at the opera that Alexandre Dumas the Younger, the illegitimate son of the famed author, first set eyes on the radiantly beautiful Marie Duplessis.

When Dumas saw her in her box with Stackelberg he assumed the old man was her grandfather. On learning the truth he was disillusioned. But it did nothing to dampen the 18-year-old youth's desire to win her as his mistress.

Soon Dumas contrived to win an invitation to one of Marie's famous soirees.

Despite his attentions, the beautiful courtesan scarcely noticed the pale young man. But because his eyes never left her he was the only one to notice when Marie Duplessis drew herself apart from a group of people and quietly entered her boudoir.

Dumas followed her in. She was sitting in a chair coughing violently. She held a handkerchief to her mouth. It was stained with blood.

Dumas threw himself to his knees and begged that he be allowed to take her away to some retreat where her health could be restored.

It was then Marie noticed the look of adoration in the eyes of Alexandre Dumas. His devotion and youth charmed her. Next morning when he left her boudoir he had her promise to leave Paris with him.

Accepting Marie Duplessis for what she was—a delicate, beautiful harlot—Dumas showered her with gifts bought with the substantial allowance his father made him.

For three months they lived in idyllic happiness in a country villa. Then she began taking other lovers. Dumas tolerated it for a time before exploding with jealousy.

But he could not persuade his beautiful mistress to give herself to him alone. She told him frankly she must return to Paris before she lost contact with the wealthy lovers who offered her security.

Immediately the couple returned to the capital Dumas learned that

198

substantial investments made by his father had failed. The older Dumas was bankrupt and the allowance to his son was stopped. Young Alexandre Dumas walked out of the life of Marie Duplessis.

But his departure caused Marie no concern for now she had a new lover, the famed pianist and composer Franz Liszt.

This alliance, after a few tempestuous months, came to an end when Liszt took the post of music master in the German Grand Duchy of Weimar. He had to leave Marie behind, for even he dared not arrive in Weimar with a woman of Mlle. Duplessis' reputation.

In 1846, when Marie was 22, the amazing vitality she had managed to summon despite the deadly disease that was in her, collapsed almost overnight.

The muscles and flesh withered and the skin, drawn like parchment over the bones, became transparent. The eyes sank into their sockets and the teeth protruded until her face assumed the likeness of a death mask.

First her lovers, including Count Stackelberg, left her, unable to look upon the ghastly apparition. Her friends soon followed them.

Unable to earn an income she found herself penniless. She told her servants she could no longer pay them, yet they elected to stay with her until her inevitable death.

Then one night she somehow dragged herself from her bed and went to the opera. She again wore the camellias but there ended the similarity between La Dame aux Camelias and the living skeleton sitting in one of the theatre's boxes.

A few days later, hearing of her impending death, Count Stackelberg hurried to her side while one of her last lovers, Viscount de Perregaux, hired all kinds of dabblers in medicine to aid her.

For days she hung on to the hand of a servant as though the constant contact would stop her slipping from the world.

Then one evening early in 1847 she sat up, screamed three times, and fell back on to the bed. They put a mirror to her mouth but it showed no vapour mist. Marie Duplessis was 23.

Told of the death of La Dame aux Camelias, Alexandre Dumas hurried to Paris but arrived many days after she had been buried in the poorer section of Montmartre cemetery.

Jointly Dumas and de Perregaux obtained permission to have the body removed to a fine vault in a more exclusive section.

And when the coffin was opened the decay on the once beautiful features of Marie Duplessis did not seem to unduly affect Alexandre Dumas. It was the sight of the lustrous hair that always remained in his memory.

A year after Marie Duplessis's death, Dumas produced his first novel, La Dame aux Camelias. It became a best seller and for years had all Europe in tears.

Later the operatic composer, Verdi, put the story to music and called it La Traviata. It seems, one historian has said, that Marie Duplessis did not deserve such immortality.

Jack Tom or The King of Jerusalem

ON the last Sunday in March, 1832, an excited crowd collected outside the Rose Inn in the ancient city of Canterbury. Their tattered smocks branded most of them as poorly-paid rural workers wandering south-east England in search of casual employment.

But among them was a sprinkling of small shopkeepers and such local craftsmen as stonemasons and carpenters from the cathedral. A few women hung on the outskirts of the throng.

The motley crowd had gathered to hear an election speech by one of the strangest candidates who ever tried to win a seat in the House of Commons.

The candidate described himself as Sir William Percy Honeywood Courtenay, King of Jerusalem, Earl of Devon, Knight of Malta and former king of the gipsies.

Actually, he was Jack Tom, the son of a Cornish inn-keeper.

As befitted a man who claimed so many distinctions, the black-bearded 32-year-old Sir William cut a picturesque figure.

Beneath a flowing cloak he wore a bizarre eastern costume of crimson velvet adorned with gold epaulettes. Hanging from his belt was a Turkish scimitar glittering with gems of apparently great value.

His oration was as unconventional as his appearance. He began his address by shouting: "Down with the tyrants!"

This popular sentiment aroused such enthusiasm that it was some time before Sir William could outline his policy which appealed forcibly to the poverty-stricken peasantry.

He stood for the abolition of all rates, tithes, taxes and customs dues, the sacking of public officials, the extinction of companies and corporations and the establishment of the Millennium.

Without bothering to explain how all this was to be accomplished, he wound up with a ringing "Vote for Courtenay!" and made a dramatic exit into the inn.

At that time the franchise was so restricted that Canterbury could muster only about 8000 qualified electors and few of them were to be found in the crowd which cheered Courtenay.

Yet so strong was Courtenay's personality, that he all but unseated the sitting member.

Having thanked the 3000-odd who had voted for him, he announced that he intended to visit Arabia and left Canterbury as mysteriously as he had arrived.

Jack Tom's brief political career began on a note of farce. It ended in tragedy.

Six years after the Canterbury elections, he was killed in a bloody affray which strewed Bossenden Wood with the bodies of his deluded followers.

John Nichols Tom was born in the Cornish village of St. Columb Major in 1799.

Modern psychologists consider that he developed delusions of grandeur at an early age but the simple villagers saw him only as an unusually bright boy with a passion for learned books and outlandish clothes.

Young Jack became top scholar at the local school where his knowledge of history staggered the village dominie and the local vicar.

Jack's angle on history, however, was unorthodox.

While his schoolfellows hero-worshipped such notable outlaws as Dick Turpin, Robin Hood and Claude Duval, Jack Tom was interested only in political reformers, the more violent the better.

In particular he admired William Longbeard, a rash democrat who lived in the reign of King Richard Coeur-de-Lion.

Appointing himself the "savior and apostle of the poor", Longbeard led an army of peasants to London to protest against the polltax. He finished on the gallows.

Seven hundred years later his ideas and even his appearance were to inspire the son of a Cornish publican.

Jack Tom's school record won him a job in a solicitor's office. But at 21 he abandoned the law and took over a small inn at Wadesbridge.

A keen business man, he made the tiny hostelry pay so well that he was given a position as traveller for an important firm of wine and spirit merchants.

His charm, good appearance and ready tongue not only made him a fine salesman but gained him an attractive wife with enough money to set him up on his own account.

At 27 he invested his wife's capital in a malthouse in Truro, the county seat of Cornwall.

As a maltster and hop merchant he was highly succesful. Then he began mixing politics and business and organised a small society whose aims were to "reform abuses and nationalise the land."

Apart from Tom, who was in deadly earnest, the members of the group were all pure theorists. Yet they were dabbling in theories that, in 1830, were regarded as dangerously subversive.

Their leader, moreover, developed a flair for flamboyant public speaking. Becoming intoxicated by his own oratory, Tom declared that the Millennium was at hand and that he was the man destined to usher it in.

In 1831 he announced that he was finished with the drudgery of commerce. Henceforward he would devote himself to the welfare of the human race.

Lady Hester Stanhope believed in the Millennium but not in Sir William Courtenay.

This statement was dismissed as so much hot air until he sold his prosperous malthouse, pocketed the proceeds and disappeared from Truro leaving his wife penniless.

Arrived in London Tom renamed himself the Honorable Percy Sydney and took modest lodgings in the suburb of Pentonville.

Having instructed his landlady never to interrupt him while he was thinking, he spent the first few weeks either lying in bed or pacing up and down his room with occasional breaks for meals.

One result of these prolonged cogitations was the sprouting of his beard, a rare facial distinction in those clean-shaven days.

As soon as the beard had passed the stubble stage, its owner called himself "Baron Moses Rothschild."

Then he took up a collection among the Jewish citizens of the East End allegedly on behalf of their brethren who were being persecuted by the Turks.

After still another change of name, he received a good price for an imaginary boarding school in the north of England.

Then the Millennium's advance agent packed his guineas in oyster barrels and left his lodgings without paying his rent.

Fitting himself out with an exotice wardrobe he went to Canterbury.

Sir William Courtenay, as he now styled himself, created a sensation in the historic city.

Although some sceptics doubted his triple claim to be King of Jerusalem, Knight of Malta and Earl of Devon, the more gullible accepted the extravagant stories of his travels.

Sir William's beard, his oyster barrels of gold, his lofty bearing and the mystery with which he surrounded himself made him a favourite with the ladies.

And his alleged friendship with half the potentates of Europe gained him entree to some of the most exclusive houses in Canterbury.

Also, his habit of tipping in guineas made him so popular with the underprivileged that his decision to stand for the House of Commons received great public support.

Although he was not elected his committee was well satisfied with his performance at the polls. A shade more luck would have sent him to Westminster.

Twelve months later Tom turned up again calling himself 'Lord Courtenay, Prince of Arabia.'

Among those he tried to impress was the celebrated Lady Hester Stanhope, daughter of the Earl of Stanhope and niece of William Pitt, the former Prime minister.

Learning that Lady Hester believed in the approach of the Millennium, Courtenay dressed himself in his oriental robes and sought an interview with her.

But Lady Hester was not convinced of his sincerity. She sent a servant to interview Courtenay and when the man reported unfavorably she refused to see him.

Announcing that he had just returned from another visit to the Holy Land he started a weekly political newspaper in which he proclaimed the imminence of the Millennium.

Cheering admirers mobbed him in the streets while once an enthusiastic crowd took the horses from his coach and pulled it round Canterbury to the strains of Rule, Britannia.

But now his newspaper, The Lion, was rapidly eating up his capital.

The dream in which he lived began to fade when a waiter from whom he was forced to borrow £11 had the self-styled Knight of Malta arrested for debt.

Courtenay's upper-class partisans dropped off at once but the proletariat rallied strongly to his support.

The populace of Canterbury was so inflamed by his arrest that two companies of infantry had to be called out to prevent a riot.

The debt was paid by a friend, but more trouble loomed ahead. Being opposed to customs duties Courtenay volunteered to give evidence on behalf of some brandy smugglers who had been caught red-handed.

Jack Tom or the King of Jerusalem in one of his bizarre costumes. Although he claimed to be the true Messiah there was method in his madness.

In the witness box his vivid imagination got the better of him.

He committed such flagrant perjury that to the fury of the turbulent crowd which tried to storm the court he was sentenced to seven years' transportation to Van Diemens Land.

By now, however, the authorities realised that his mind was unhinged. Instead of being shipped off to Tasmania he was sent to the County Asylum.

A model patient, he showed so few signs of mental disorder that the Home Secretary, Lord John Russell, ordered his release and had him placed in the care of a farmer at Boughton.

Tom's behavior remained rational until 1838. Then, suddenly asserting that he was the reincarnation of the Messiah, he fled.

Raising a pitiful little army of about 100 illiterate peasants and workless farmlaborers, he told them that he was the reincarnated Redeemer and that the hour had come to strip the rich of their ill-gotten gains.

Convinced by his fiery oratory that they, too, were invincible and invulnerable, his forlorn followers shouldered ancient muskets, pitch-forks, hoes and clubs and marched on Canterbury.

At once three special constables were sworn in and sent to arrest the Messiah.

Being only amateur policemen the blundering constables made a wild rush at him.

Courtenay, whose mental aberration had reached a dangerous stage, shot one of them. The others fled.

Marching on, the advance guard of the Millennium camped that night at Bossenden Wood. Next morning, 31 May 1838, they found the way barred by a detachment of infantry.

Believing themselves proof against any mortal weapons, the hungry peasants faced the redcoats without flinching.

At that a humane young officer who believed he could make Courtenay see reason rode out to meet him. The gesture cost the officer his life. The "Peasants' Messiah" shot him dead.

This was the signal for a volley from the soldiers. Courtenay and several of his supporters fell mortally wounded. With a wild yell of rage the rest charged the troops, only to be met by a line of bayonets.

The battle was over in a few minutes. Bewildered at finding that their invulnerability was an illusion, the peasants fled leaving nine dead and many wounded.

A man of many fantastic aliases, John Nichol Tom died at the age of 39.

Yet his tragic career was not without some beneficial repercussions.

Appalled at the state of the peasantry the Government took the first steps towards organising a system of rural education.

Also the establishment of county constabularies ensured that the law would no longer be enforced by soldiers or untrained special police.

Shrine of Devilry

A NY evening about the year 1760, villagers along the quiet reaches of the Thames, 40 miles from London, might have seen a procession of boats pulling towards the ivy-clad buildings of Medmenham Abbey. Torch-lights in the abbey garden gleamed on marble statues of naked goddesses, and on the scarlet and black robes of a group of men waiting to welcome the boats. Inside the abbey, under ceilings "glittering with unspeakable frescoes", a great banquet was prepared for the "monks" of Medmenham and their guests, the most beautiful and wanton courtesans of London. The hosts were members of the Hellfire Club, the band of rakes whose orgies of lust and blasphemy made Medmenham a sink of iniquity even to free-living Georgian England.

Arch-priest of Medmenham's bizarre rituals was the "black baronet", Sir Francis Dashwood. His colleagues in the Hellfire Club included a prime minister, an Admiralty lord, and some of the most celebrated politicians, noblemen and wits of the age.

They were, said one contemporary, "learned in luxury, sedulous and patient seducers, veritable troubadours of obscenity", and they organised vice on the most flamboyant scale since the days of Imperial Rome.

Francis Dashwood was born in 1708, and was only 16 when he inherited his father's huge fortune and the estate of West Wycombe Park, on the Thames in Buckinghamshire.

By 1742 he had bought a seat in Parliament, and was a favoured crony of Bubb Dodington, Lord Sandwich, and other Tory friends of the Prince of Wales in opposition to old King George II.

Three years later, to the astonishment of his friends, Dashwood wed the widowed Sarah, Lady Ellis, a "poor, forlorn Presbyterian prude" who soon vanished into neglected obscurity.

Dashwood was already notorious among London rakes, a haunter of the fashionable Covent Garden brothels, gambler, and "three-bottle" wine bibber, when the Hellfire Club originated in 1746.

It began with informal meetings attended by Dashwood, Dodington and Lord Sandwich, with their Doxies, dice and bottles, at the George and

The "black baronet" Sir Francis Dashwood. He dedicated Medmenham Abbey to Satan.

Vulture tavern off Cornhill.

Though the Hellfire was destined to become the most infamous of them all, many other clubs with similar aims and membership flourished on the seamy side of 18th century London society.

There was the Society for the Propagation of Sicilian Amorology, the Sunday Night Club, which mixed black magic and prostitutes; the World Club, with obscene epigrams engraved on its wine glasses.

Lord Wharton had founded a club that dined on Holy Ghost Pie, haunch of mutton described as the Devil's Loins, and Breast of Venus, a dish of two chickens garnished with cherries.

Dashwood's society, however, soon outstripped the others in fame, and it had swollen to 40 members when the George and Vulture was destroyed by fire in 1748, forcing them to seek a new home.

When it was decided to shift to more discreet headquarters outside London, Dashwood remembered the ancient abbey of Medmenham that had been mouldering to ruin for centuries on the banks of the Thames not far from his own estate.

Francis Duffield, the abbey's owner, was persuaded to lease the building to the leaders of the Hellfire Club, the "twelve apostles", and Dashwood was given charge of the rebuilding and "decorations".

For three years the work went on. Gangs of workmen were hired in London and sent home each night, to prevent them talking to the local inhabitants about the curious orders they were given.

When at last the club members moved in, they were delighted and astonished by Dashwood's "ingenious fancies", by the luxury of the gardens, the rebuilt cloisters, chapel and dining hall.

Lewd painted parodies of religious scenes covered walls and ceilings. Statues designed to "raise amorous fire" stood in every niche, surrounded by sumptuous hangings of blue, silver and crimson.

Off the main hall were cells for "private devotions", equipped with comfortable sofas. Over the main entrance was cut the words "Fay ce que voudras" ("Do what you will"), the motto of Rabelais' Abbey of Theleme.

Adjoining the hall was the chapel, with its altar carved in the form of a nude woman. Here the Black Mass was celebrated amid paintings of famous Roman prostitutes.

The biggest collection of pornography in England filled the shelves of the abbey library. Most of the volumes had the names of hymnals and prayer books stamped on their covers.

Ivy-clad Medmenham Abbey, headquarters of the most evil cult England has known.

Even the garden sloping down to the river was laid out in the form of a female body.

Dashwood was solemnly installed as abbot of the "Order of St. Francis", and the titles of steward, high treasurer, and other offices were parcelled out among his chief colleagues.

It was a strange gang that assembled amid the obscene paraphernalia of Medmenham Abbey, ranging from evil of the deepest dye to lunatic eccentricity.

Most vicious of them all was the lean, saturnine figure of Lord Sandwich, First Lord of the Admirality, inveterate "gambler and harlot keeper", who "was followed eyerywhere by the smell of brimstone."

Sandwich kept a baboon as his "private chaplain", and locked the villagers out of the church on his estate while he preached ribald sermons to a congregation of cats.

Much of the Medmenham ritual was evolved by Paul Whitehead, an elderly Tory pamphleteer of noisome reputation, who also wrote the blasphemous "psalms" chanted by members to the music of flutes.

One of the richest "monks" was Thomas Potter, son of an Archbishop of

Canterbury, who squandered £100,000 on a succession of orgies and black magic ceremonies before he died mad at the age of 40.

George Selwyn, who haunted public executions disguised as a washer-woman, Lord Stanhope, son of the elegant Earl of Chesterfield and Robert Vansittart, an Oxford professor, were among the other members.

Several years after moving to Medmenham, the Hellfire Club acquired three more famous recruits—Lord Bute (soon to be George III's prime minister), the radical politician John Wilkes, and the poet and renegade parson Charles Churchill.

The "monks" tried to keep their proceedings hidden from prying eyes, but by about 1760, London was ringing with stories of the depravity enclosed within the old abbey walls.

Concealment became impossible when Dashwood and Lord Sandwich began shipping boatloads of the most notorious London harlots to share the revels as "nuns" and "little sisters".

Main sources of supply were the establishments of Mother Stanhope and Charlotte Hayes ("Santa Carlotta"), who boasted that they kept "the largest and most beautiful stock of girls in London".

They also provided more experienced "discreet vestals" for Medmenham, ranging from Fanny Murray and Betty Roach (the fashionable mistresses of Dashwood and Sandwich) to Betty Weyms—a handsome, one-eyed trollop from the Rose Tavern.

The sensual revels of Medmenham reached their peak in the early 1760s when, almost every week, the Hellfire members and their "nuns" gathered for their unholy rites and orgies of feasting and debauchery.

The "monks", however, had little in common but their license. Soon after the accession of George III and the return of the Tories to power, they were split by bitter personal and political quarrels.

John Wilkes hastened the break-up of the club when, in the dim light during a celebration of the Black Mass, he released a monkey dressed as a devil.

Sandwich fell on his knees, screaming with terror as the monkey jumped on his back. He already hated Wilkes as an enemy of the Tories, and he soon found means of avenging the humiliation.

In Parliament, he read a copy of Wilkes' Essay on Woman, an obscene, privately-printed parody of Pope's famous Essay on Man. Wilkes was ex-pelled from the House, threatened with arrest, and fled to France.

Then, when Lord Bute became prime minister, he made the incredible blunder of appointing his fellow Hellfire member, Francis Dashwood, as Chancellor of the Exchequer.

Dashwood's first budget speech was greeted with hoots of laughter. After two years as the most fantastically incompetent chancellor that Britain ever had, he was driven from office by public contempt.

Bute's own fall soon followed. Meanwhile, Dashwood had retired to West Wycombe to reorganise the scattered and diminished band of "monks".

Sightseers were prowling round the notorious abbey, so Dashwood decided to enlarge and fit out the honeycomb of caves beneath his estate as the new headquarters of the fraternity of "St. Francis".

A banqueting hall 50 feet high was hacked out of the rock, with winding, torchlit corridors leading to an inner "temple" and a series of small, richly-appointed cells for the "devotions" of the "monks" and their female companions.

Here, on a smaller scale, the orgies were resumed under the superintendence of Dashwood and his latest mistress, the actress Frances Barry, whom he had stolen from a rich London draper.

Some famous visitors attended the subterranean revels, notably Benjamin Franklin, the spokesman for the rebellious American colonists, whom Dashwood entertained at West Wycombe in 1772.

Another visitor initiated into the dark mysteries was Joseph Banks, just returned from his round-world voyage with Captain Cook, and soon to be chief advocate of the settlement of Botany Bay.

By 1775, however, many of the original Medmenham debauchees had vanished. Churchill had drunk himself into an exile's grave in France. Madness had killed Potter, and Whitehead had died a penitent after burning a great mass of his obscene writings.

Wilkes and the "lascivious bullfrog" Dodington were entirely devoted to political careers. Others had grown respectable with age, and were anxious to forget the unholy splendours of Medmenham Abbey.

Dashwood himself lingered on in decaying health until 1781, mumbling incantations and swearing he was haunted by Whitehead's ghost, while the furnishings rotted away in the damp, deserted caves.

When he died on 11 December 1781, and was buried in the magnificent tomb he built beside the village church, the scandals of the "monks" of Medmenham had become nothing more than a memory.

Voodoo Queen's Eerie Cult

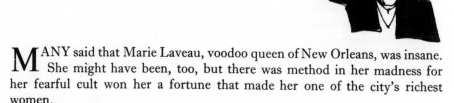

MANY said that Marie Laveau, voodoo queen of New Orleans, was insane. She might have been, too, but there was method in her madness for her fearful cult won her a fortune that made her one of the city's richest women.

Marie Laveau, a beautiful quarter-cast Negro, could sate the desires of all those interested in voodoo mysticism.

She had love philtres for spurned women, rejuvenation concoctions and rites for ageing men, sure-fire curses for enemies, charms to ward off evil and even protection from the law for wrong-doers.

And all she needed for this magic was a temple, dried frogs, human hair clippings and nail parings, animals' teeth, bats and lizards, skulls and a jar or two of blood—human if possible.

Yet despite her psychological charlatanism the voodoo queen, now known to history as "the last American witch." wielded enormous power among the hordes of Negro and white voodoo cultists in 19th century New Orleans.

And her following never diminished despite whispered rumors that she not only offered chickens to her deity on the altars of the "sepulchres" that dotted the city, but at times resorted to human sacrifice.

Nevertheless it all paid good dividends, for at her death in 1881 at the age of 87 she owned valuable New Orleans property including mansions and dozens of smaller houses she rented at inflated fees.

Marie Laveau was born in a ramshackle New Orleans cottage in 1794, the daughter of a rich out-of-town planter and a good-looking half-caste Negro he maintained to entertain him during his city visits.

The girls' mother had, since her own childhood, been steeped in voodooism, the frenzied superstitious cult that had been brought to America by the early African slaves.

Marie grew into an unusually attractive young woman whose destiny would normally have been a position as a paid mistress of some white planter.

Actually she did attend the quadroon dances which the whites used as a market place to select casual or even permanent lovers.

But the contacts she made came to nothing, for her father quickly broke up the liaisons and finally married her off to another quadroon, a carpenter named Jacques Paris.

212

The trouble was that Jacques was more enlightened than most of his race and ridiculed the voodoo cult. This attitude so aroused Marie that the pair quarrelled violently and cotinually.

The marriage finally broke up when the reigning voodoo queen, Marie Saloppe, who was growing old, selected the lovely Marie Laveau to succeed her when she retired to enjoy the wealth she had accumulated.

But until such time as she took over the cult, Marie Laveau had to have some form of income. She chose hairdressing but spent all her free time with Marie Saloppe learning her trade as queen elect of the Lake Pontchartrain voodoo temple.

As a hairdresser young Marie had access to the homes of the wealthy whites, many of whom had absorbed the superstitious nature of the negroes and, being bored, were ready for any entertaining diversion.

Among those intrigued by Marie Laveau's stories of the amazing effects of voodoo curses and charms was the wealthy Mme Forshey, the wife of a planter.

One day Mme Forshey told her attractive hairdresser that her husband had forbidden her to visit their out-of-town plantation. The woman said she knew the reason—her husband was having an affair with the young daughter of a Creole.

At that Marie Laveau saw her chance. She told her client she could have her husband back for a fee of $100.

Mme Forshey at once handed the money over and agreed to fall in with the young voodooist's scheme.

Taking an apple, Marie Laveau muttered incantations over it then ordered her client's maid to conceal it on Mme Forshey's plantation, explaining that as the apple shrivelled so would the planter's love for the girl.

Weeks passed and Marie Laveau again visited Mme Forshey.

The delighted woman told her that her husband's mistress had disappeared from the district and at M. Forshey's request she was already preparing to move back to the plantation.

After that the voodooist's fame quickly spread among New Orleans' white population. Her income soared and she was able to abandon the hairdressing business.

The next client to add to her reputation as a mystic was the wealthy merchant, Aristide Broutin, whose son was shortly to be tried for murder.

Broutin told Marie Laveau that if she could use her power to influence the jury in his son's favor, he would make her a gift of a fine city residence.

As far as Marie Laveau was concerned the solution to Broutin's problem was simple—she set out to visit the Negro who was the sole witness to the killing.

For an hour the raging cultist hurled curses at the fear-stricken Negro assuring him of all kinds of dire consequences if he did not retract his story.

And to make sure the inevitable acquittal would be attributed to her, Marie Laveau was in court performing strange voodoo rites when the Negro witness recanted his earlier statement and the prisoner was discharged.

The old city of New Orleans scene of public voodoo ceremonies that paled before the rites cult followers practised in the privacy of their temples.

As the demand for her services grew Marie Laveau went into the voodoo manufacturing business turning out love philtres by the dozen lots and selling all kinds of charms and curses.

It was about this time that Marie Laveau heard of the death of her husband Jacques Paris and promptly formed an illicit union with a ship's captain, Christophe Glapion, who was about 20 years older than his mistress.

One of Glapion's first tasks as consort of the famous voodooist was to march out into the New Orleans swamps and snare a black snake Marie needed as one of her voodoo rites' props.

The snake, surrounded by the usual paraphernalia of the skulls of humans and animals and jars of blood, deeply impressed the clients who were now packing into her home each night to attend her bizarre ceremonies.

It was inevitable that Marie Laveau's growing popularity should arouse the anger of the reigning voodoo queen, Marie Saloppe.

When Marie Laveau heard that her rival was heaping ritual curses on her she decided to bring the Saloppe reign to a sudden end.

One night when Marie Saloppe was holding a voodoo meeting at her Lake Pontchartrain temple, Marie Laveau set out from her house and, followed by Glapion carrying the caged sacred snake, headed for the Saloppe headquarters.

When Marie Laveau entered the temple the cultists were dancing insanely to the beat of drums. Then someone noticed the new arrival. The drum beating ceased, the dancers froze.

Then the two rival voodoo queens opened up on each other screeching ritualistic curses and occasionally reverting to more earthy insults.

In the end it was Marie Laveau who won the shouting match. Marie Saloppe ran out of breath and, leaving the temple in the hands of the new voodoo queen, turned, and with a few followers, left the building.

After that Marie Laveau celebrated her victory by killing the sacrificial chickens for the first time and smearing her followers with their blood.

The new voodoo queen never looked back after that. Her following became enormous and the dollars poured in like a flood. She was no spendthrift and invested every cent carefully.

As time passed Marie produced 15 children to Glapion. Eight died (some during the yellow fever and cholera epidemics) but she remained unaffected and by 1854 when she was 60 still looked years younger.

Marie Laveau with her mansions, her rows of tenements and her great tracts of land around New Orleans was accepted as one of the richest—white or colored, male or female—citizens in the deep South.

Each Sunday thousands of her followers packed into the city's Congo Square where their queen presided over ceremonial voodoo dancing.

But while this voodoo dancing in the city square served only to amuse the whites, what went on at the Lake Pontchartrain temple would have set their hair standing on end.

At these ceremonies hundreds of half-insane Negroes, supplemented by a small number of whites who paid huge fees for the privilege of attending, carried out obscene rites centred around the figures of attractive quadroons.

Marie Laveau reached the pinnacle of her voodoo power when she first offered the sacrificial chicken and smeared her followers with its blood.

Then there were the white women who paid hundreds of dollars so that the voodoo queeen might infuse them with the power to attract lovers.

Once, when police raided one of Marie Laveau's sepulchres, the officers found almost a score of these white women. Most were near naked and were taking part in a strange ceremony with Negro men.

Although such scandals invariably set up a public demand for the suppression of the cult, officials dared not intervene for fear of the reaction the voodoo queen's rage would cause in her followers.

For instance, in the case of the white women found in the sepulchre with the Negroes, the authorities accepted the excuse that they were simply being treated for rheumatism.

Although Marie Laveau had nothing to worry about from the authorities, her position as monarch of New Orleans voodooism was once seriously challenged by a man, the huge, tattooed Negro known as Dr John.

Claiming he could read minds and assuring voodooists of the extraordinary powers of his charms he soon built up a substantial business selling pebbles and shells which, he claimed, would ward off all evil.

As time passed Dr John's following and income increased so that he was able to build his own temple not far from Marie Laveau's headquarters on Lake Pontchartrain.

Dr John lived happily with 15 of his more attractive female followers until the evening in 1865 when Marie Laveau found his body in her temple. He had been stabbed repeatedly.

At once the voodoo queen was arrested and, despite statements by some of her followers that they had sighted the dead body before their queen's arrival, she was placed on trial.

But before the hearing could begin one of Marie Laveau's daughters, Marie Glapion, took the sacred snake and a heavy piece of wood and marched off to Dr John's temple.

There she threatened two of the dead voodooist's followers with all kinds of curses as well as a good beating with the piece of wood unless they told police they had stabbed Dr John in a fit of jealousy and had dragged the body to the Laveau temple.

The threats worked and Marie Leveau was released. At once she announced Marie Glapion would be her successor as voodoo queen and went into retirement.

For the rest of her life until her death in 1881, Marie Laveau spent her time enjoying her great wealth and taking food parcels to the prisoners in the city's gaols.

Marie Glapion did not have the mesmeric personality of her mother and it was her reign that saw the beginning of the end of mass voodoo worship in America's deep South.

The Noble Art of Seduction

GRANDMA HORTENSE, Duchess Mazarin, was not everyone's idea of a grandmother. At 36 she was disconcertingly beautiful and wherever she travelled she was followed by a cavalcade of dewy-eyed lovers.

Even her nephew, the youthful Chevalier de Soissons, was madly in love with her and in a fit of jealousy killed a rival for his amorous aunt's affections.

At the time of the Duchess's notorious careeer one of her admirers described the lovely grandmother as: "Tall, dark, with a well-rounded figure."

"Her hair is curly jet black, her mouth exquisitely shaped, her eyes have the sweetness of blue, the briskness of grey and above all the fire of black."

There were even well-founded rumors that the startling grandmother's salon was nothing more than a school at which students received expert instructions from the principal "in the noble art of seduction".

The Duchess Mazarin was born Hortense Mancini in Italy in 1647 and was one of the seven beautiful nieces of Cardinal Jules Mazarin, France's chief minister during the era of the Grand Monarch, Louis XIV.

Over the years all the Mancini girls were brought to France by their uncle who planned to set them up in marriages which would consolidate his influence at the King's court.

But of all the girls Hortense was most loved by her uncle, a kindly man despite his power obsession.

After several years at an exclusive convent with her sister, Marie, Hortense was let loose on Paris's aristocratic society to immediately infatuate the Duc de la Meilleraye. Marie did even better, being wooed by the youthful Louis XIV.

But the liaison between Louis and the youthful Marie did not please Cardinal Mazarin, who was already planning to marry the monarch off to the Infanta Maria Theresa of Spain.

So to bring the affair to a sudden end he packed both Marie and Hortense off to La Rochelle where the flood of letters that followed them proved that neither had been over-faithful to their established lovers.

Although the Cardinal was aware that Hortense was not really in love

with the strait-laced Duc de la Meilleraye, he believed the nobleman would prove a worthy custodian of the Cardinals' vast fortune Hortense would inherit on his death.

Thus taking the name of the Duc and Duchesse Mazarin the 15-year-old Hortense and the 29-year-old Duc were married in the chapel of the Mazarin Palace on 28 February 1661.

Less than two weeks after the union, Cardinal Mazarin died, leaving an estate valued at about 40-million livres in the custody of the already wealthy Duc Mazarin.

Although Hortense was prepared to tolerate the loveless match with the Duc, she had not bargained for the extraordinary trials she was to suffer as his wife.

She soon discovered that her husband was not only a religious fanatic but was obsessed by jealousy and suspicion. For one thing he believed she had willingly allowed Louis to seduce her and even accused her of an incestuous relationship with her own brother, the Duc de Nevers.

The Duc's jealousy reached a peak when he found a love letter Hortense

The Palace of Versailles.

had written to the handsome Chevalier de Rohan. The date showed the letter had been written after the marriage.

Following the discovery of the letter Hortense's life became a misery. The Duc refused to allow her out of his sight, and even when he travelled to Alsace and Brittany as Governor of these two provinces, she was forced to accompany him.

Apart from that the domestic staff was bribed to spy on her, while, as an added safeguard against possible unfaithfulness, the Duc saw to it that his wife was almost-perennially pregnant.

But Mazarin's jealousy was not the only trial Hortense had to endure for his religious fanaticism carried him to equally ridiculous extremes.

For instance he later wanted to knock out his daughters' front teeth so that designing gallants would find them unattractive. He also took to roaming the streets warning citizens of the terrible consequences of immorality.

Then one day, carried away by his insane fervor, he decided to destroy all the art treasures left him by Cardinal Mazarin and which he considered offended his sense of purity.

For a start he mutilated several works of historic artists like Titian and Correggio. Then, armed with an axe, he went berserk in the Palace Mazarin.

He spent the entire day destroying everything that offended him. Then he rested and continued on through the night.

Next day, Saturday, he enlisted the domestic staff to help him. The destruction ended at midnight when Mazarin announced it was sinful to work on the Sabbath.

Meanwhile Hortense's lascivious tendencies had been kept firmly in check by her husband's supervision and by the series of pregnancies. Yet it was inevitable she should break the chains and in 1668 she announced she intended leaving the castle and living her own life.

Hortense, although well aware of her husband's eccentricities, was scarcely prepared for his reaction to this announcement. Flying into a rage he had her imprisoned in the Convent of Chelles, then administered by his aunt.

Quickly the abbess and Hortense became firm friends, a relationship that so displeased Mazarin he had his wife transferred to the stricter Convent de Les Felles de St Marie.

Hortense didn't like the place and made such a nuisance of herself that the nuns were happy to send her back to Chelles where she and the abbess continued their interrupted friendship.

Nevertheless the Duc and the Duchess were finally reconciled after Mazarin agreed to Hortense's demand that they should share separate apartments in the family palace.

The arrangement might have worked had not Mazarin convinced himself that his wife was nightly entertaining a string of young noblemen in her apartment.

In the end his jealousy became so outrageous that Hortense decided to flee to the home of her sister Marie in Italy.

During the journey Hortense travelled disguised as a chevalier and was escorted by a man named Courbeville, an employee of the Chevalier de Rohan.

Freed of the shackles of her half-mad husband and at last in a position to seek the kind of love she had been denied, Hortense at once appointed Courbeville her temporary lover and delighted in his company all the way to Italy.

The journey was so long and pleasant that when Hortense finally arrived at her sister's home in Colonna she was pregnant either to Courbeville or some other handsome young man she had met along the way.

After the birth of the child Hortense moved on to Rome where she took up residence with another cardinal uncle, Mancini, who wasted no time forcing the young woman's distraught husband to allocate her a yearly pension of 24,000 livres.

Although the Duchess accepted numerous lovers none could satisfy her. She dreamed of the perfect partner but who he was and where he was she did not know.

Nevertheless she was determined to find him and, with her sister Marie,

The Duchess Mazarin.

set off on a man-hunting expedition back across Italy and over the border into France.

Infuriated by stories of his wife's escapades, the Duc Mazarin ordered a company of his soldiers to find his erring Duchess and arrest her.

They never did succeed in finding her although once she was forced to hide in a fish pond as they rode past.

In the end she accepted sanctuary in the house of an earlier admirer, the Duc de Savoy. Although Savoy visited her apartments regularly she also allowed herself to become the lover of a young gallant Cesar Vicard.

Three years after this idyll began the Duc de Savoy died. He was scarcely in the grave when his widow ordered the unwelcome guest from the palace.

After that Hortense again adopted the disguise of a wandering chevalier and, escorted by a small bodyguard, continued her love quest. She had still not found her dream man when, in 1675, she set sail for England.

Many stories concern the reason for the famed Duchess's decision to visit England. One says she had been invited over by political opponents of Charles II's current mistress, the French Duchess of Portsmouth, to lure the King away from her influence.

Another claims she was simply invited by the Duchess of York, wife of the future James II, brother of Charles.

At any rate when the Duke of York set eyes on Hortense for the first time he immediately put a furnished mansion at her disposal.

And it did not take long for Charles himself to become infatuated by the beautiful 29-year-old Duchess Mazarin. His night-long visits to her culminated in his decision to appoint her his official mistress.

Charles enjoyed the lovely Frenchwoman's company but he was less pleased by her habit of carrying on a series of other liaisons at the same time.

He completely lost patience when he discovered Hortense was regularly entertaining the Prince de Monaco.

Hortense Mazarin was not concerned when Charles returned to the arms of the Duchess of Portsmouth and stopped her allowance, for there were dozens of other wealthy and noble suitors willing to take the King's place.

The Portuguese Ambassador, for instance, followed her about like a lap dog while even her infatuated nephew, the Chevalier de Soissons, killed her Swedish lover, Baron Baner, in a fit of jealousy.

Scarcely anything in London rivalled the entertainments at her mansion. There, often for days on end, guests revelled in an orgy of gambling, drinking and love-making.

In one night alone Hortense won $10,000 from Charles's mistress, the actress Nell Gwynne, at the gambling tables. And apart from that the Duchess gave personal lessons to the young beauties who flocked to her salon in "the noble art of seduction".

Meanwhile the Duc Mazarin continued making efforts to have his wife return to him. At times Hortense replied to his requests saying she would return under certain conditions. But the Duc insisted she should come back on his terms.

Mazarin even begged Louis to have her extradited but the King washed his hands of the whole business. Nor did Mazarin's decision to stop her annuity have any effect on her for there were too many noblemen in England willing to finance her.

In a final desperate effort the Duc Mazarin went to the courts asking for complete ownership of his wife's property. He won the case and Hortense made her decision to spend the rest of her days in England.

Hortense, Duchess Mazarin, died in 1699, still a beauty despite her 53 years. Indeed her admirer and philosopher, Charles de St Denis, Seigneur de St Evremond, wrote: "She would needs die the greatest beauty in the world."

At her death the Duc Mazarin at last won possession of the elusive wife he had loved in his own strange way.

The body was first taken to Paris and then, as of old, with him on his journeys to Alsace and Brittany.

A year after death it was buried in the church of Notre Dame at Liesse. Later it was re-interred in the tomb of Hortense's uncle, Cardinal Mazarin, in Paris.

A Mire of Passion and Cruelty

I N May 1616, Frances Howard, Countess of Somerset, and "the wickedest woman in England", appeared with her husband in Westminster Hall to answer a charge of cold-blooded murder by poison. Despite the ravages of sickness and imprisonment and the austere woollen robe and plain white ruff of her dress, the young countess was still a figure of almost ethereal beauty.

Red-gold hair fell in masses from beneath her black velvet cap. Dark, long-lashed eyes set off the peaches-and-cream complexion that had once enraptured the court of King James 1.

Confessions extorted by torture from their accomplices had already proved beyond doubt the guilt of Frances Howard, and to a lesser degree her husband, in the macabre death of Sir Thomas Overbury.

The full story sent a shudder of horror through England. Never had a court of law listened to such a monstrous catalogue of crimes—of illicit passion, sorcery and fiendish cruelty—as that on which Frances Howard and her paramor were arraigned.

Royal intervention saved the guilty couple from the headsman's axe, for Somerset had once been "sweet Robin Carr", the pampered favorite of the doting King James I.

But their fate was little better than living death. Condemned to share exile and disgrace, they lingered on for years, their love turned to bitter hatred and haunted by nightmare memories.

The seeds of tragedy were sown in 1606 when Frances Howard, then a pretty and innocent child of 13, was wed to Robert Devereux, Earl of Essex, the 15-year-old son of Queen Elizabeth's favorite.

The marriage was purely a dynastic alliance arranged by the girl's parents, the Earl and Countess of Suffolk. Essex was immediately packed off to Europe to finish his education, and Frances was taken to King James's court by her mother.

The Countess of Suffolk was a notorious wanton and it was soon apparent that her rapidly-budding daughter was only too eager to follow in her footsteps.

Frances was barely 16 when she was reputed to be the mistress of the King's son, Prince Henry. Two years later she was involved in a more open and dangerous liaison with the rising royal favourite, the 22-year-old Robin Carr, Lord Rochester.

Carr, a slender, fair-haired youth with charming manners and effeminate good looks, had begun life as a humble page to the Earl of Dunbar in Scotland.

In Edinburgh he met Thomas Overbury, an English lawyer, man of fashion and poet, who persuaded him to come to London to seek his fortune after the Scottish James I succeeded Elizabeth in 1603.

Overbury's friendship was valuable, but Carr's career was really launched one day three years later, when he was thrown from his horse in the tilt-yard and broke his arm.

King James witnessed the accident. Next day the royal surgeons were fussing round the injured youth, and soon the King himself visited "sweet Robin's" bedside to present him with jewels and give him lessons in Latin.

By 1610 Carr, now Lord Rochester, was James's personal secretary. He was also the owner of great estates, including the confiscated property of the disgraced Sir Walter Raleigh.

By then, Frances Howard's infatuation for Carr was the common talk of the court. Round the brainless and conceited favourite began a web of intrigue that started as grotesque comedy but quickly darkened into tragedy.

Overbury made no secret of his hatred for Frances. He hoped to profit from Carr's elevation and feared that the intrigue would end in the favourite's ruin and disgrace.

Overbury pleaded with his friend to spurn "that filthy woman". The only result was that Carr repeated all his insults to Frances, and deepened her resolve to get rid of the "meddling lawyer".

Then the Earl of Essex returned from abroad to claim his rights as a husband, and Frances found another stumbling block in the path of her passion.

Essex was a stolid, sanctimonious young man, with no trace of his father's headlong spirit that had once captivated Queen Bess. The thought that she was legally tied to such a block drove Frances to insane fury.

Through trusted servants she began making inquiries in the evil London underworld of charlatans, poisoners and magicians. Her money soon procured the creatures she needed.

One was a physician's widow and sorceress, Mrs Turner. Another was an apothecary named Franklin, a compounder of love philtres and deadly poisons guaranteed to "consume all the flesh from the bones".

With their aid, Frances set out to murder her dull husband. She served him poisoned wine laced with nutmeg. She made him "fair tarts and jellies" sugared with posionous crystals.

When Essex fell sick but obstinately refused to die, Frances turned to black magic. Mrs. Turner made small wax images of the earl which Frances pierced with pins and melted over a brazier, muttering prayers that her

Frances Carr, Countess of Somerset (née Howard) (1593[?]–1632)
by an unknown artist

Frances Carr, Countess of Somerset, formerly the wife of the Earl of Essex.

husband's flesh might likewise waste away.

All was in vain. Essex seemed proof against both potions and sorcery. Meanwhile, with frantic impatience, Frances noted signs that Carr's affections might be waning.

Abandoning attempts to kill her husband, she turned her plots against her most relentless enemy—the jeering, flaunting Sir Thomas Overbury, who openly swore he would break up the affair between Carr and the "harlot Howard".

At Frances' urging, Carr asked his royal master to send Overbury on some diplomatic mission abroad. Overbury, though offered the choice of France, Spain or Russia, refused to quit London.

On 22 April 1613, Sir Thomas Overbury was sent to the Tower to abide there until the King's displeasure cooled. But Frances Howard was determined that he should never emerge alive from its grim stone walls.

How much Carr knew of his mistress's diabolical scheme is dubious. Later, when each of the pair was trying to blacken the character of the other as much as possible, Frances swore that he was a willing accomplice.

Whatever the truth, there can be little doubt that Frances was the chief planner and instigator of the monstrous cruelty that hounded Overbury to his death.

The first step was to win the connivance of the Lieutenant of the Tower, Sir Gervase Helwyse. Then a sinister ruffian named Weston was appointed Overbury's gaoler and personal attendant.

Overbury was completely unsuspecting. He still regarded Carr as his friend and, as the weeks passed without the King relenting, he begged the favourite to use his powerful influence to free him.

Carr promised to do his best. In the meantime, he said, Frances was full of remorse for her enmity and had ordered her own cooks to prepare delicacies for the unhappy prisoner.

The "cooks" were Mrs. Turner and apothecary Franklin. Since Overbury's death had to appear the result of natural sickness, they had to work subtly—feeding him poison in small, tasteless doses.

Day after day, Weston the gaoler carried into Overbury's cell goblets of choice wine, plates of spiced cakes, tarts and custards, slices of roast sucking pig, and other morsels to tempt his palate.

Powdered arsenic was mixed with salt, cantharides with the pepper, and a variety of other "cunning infernal poisons" were mingled in the wine and dusted over the fruit in the tarts.

By the end of June 1613, Overbury was emaciated, feeble and racked by constant fits of pain and vomiting. But he still clung to life and believed his sickness was due to his unhealthy prison.

However, he no longer had any illusions about Carr's friendship. Bitterly he swore to ruin the favourite, upbraiding him as "the most odious man alive, with no more affection than a colt in the park".

The doses of poison were increased. But Overbury was now so tortured in mind and body that he scarcely touched the food. A few months later came the last hideous act in the drama.

On 15 September an apothecary's apprentice entered the cell to treat Overbury with an enema—which Franklin had filled with a corrosive acid so strong that drops of it blistered the skin.

Within three hours, death had mercifully ended Overbury's agony. On Helwyse's order, the corpse was hastily stripped and tossed into a grave in the moat of the Tower.

Just 10 days later Frances won a second triumph. A court of judges and divines decreed that her marriage with the Earl of Essex was null and void on the ground of the earl's impotence.

The verdict was the climax of a long, sordid inquiry that dragged on while Overbury was rotting in the Tower.

A "committee of noble matrons" upheld Frances's plea that she had never lived with Essex as his wife, though strange rumors persisted that a veiled maid-in-waiting had been substituted for Frances when the matrons investigated her claims to chastity.

On 26 December 1613, Frances Howard was wed to Robin Carr, who had been created Earl of Somerset by King James so that his rank should be equal to his bride's.

The marriage ceremony was the most sumptuous Whitehall Palace had ever seen. The King gave the couple £10,000, and the courtiers vied with each other in raining costly presents on the all-powerful favourite and his radiant bride.

Two short years sufficed to bring retribution, hastened by Carr's growing arrogance and the emergence of handsome young George Villiers, future Duke of Buckingham, as the King's new idol.

By July 1615, rumors that Carr and his wife had been implicated in Overbury's death were so strong that Helwyse decided to save his neck by fully confessing his share in the plot.

King James, horrified and incredulous, ordered Chief Justice Coke to begin an inquiry. Weston, Franklin and the harridan Mrs. Turner were seized, lodged in the Tower and "put to the question".

On 7 November Frances Howard's three wretched instruments dangled from Tyburn gallows. By then Carr was in the Tower, but Frances, expecting the birth of a child, was allowed to live under guard in her house.

It was May of the next year before the pair appeared in Westminster Hall to hear rough-tongued Chief Justice Coke sentence them to death for "savage murder upon Sir Thomas Overbury".

King James, weeping sentimentally over the fate of his former favourite, commuted the sentences to life imprisonment. In 1624, not long before his death, he freed them both from the Tower.

A condition of the pardon was that they never appear again in London. For eight more years Frances and her ill-starred lover existed in bitter isolation and mutual hatred until she died in 1632.

Robin Carr, Earl of Somerset, lingered on in obscurity until 1645.

York Minster. One of the finest examples of English medieval building. It was considered by Jonathan Martin to be 'the abode of Satan.

The Mad Incendiarist of York

ON the night of 1 February 1829, a wild-eyed, shabbily dressed little man ran busily about inside the cathedral of York Minster, the light of his candle gleaming eerily on the great medieval columns, the ancient tombs and soaring stained glass windows.

He tore down the rich hangings of the archbishop's throne, collected bibles, hymn books, cushions and any other inflammable material he could find and heaped them against the wooden stalls of the choir.

Occasionally he paused to fall on his knees and pray. Mysterious voices and visions stirred in his demented brain urging him not to falter in the task which God had assigned him.

Then, having set alight to the pile of material and watched it begin to burn briskly, Jonathan Martin slipped quietly into the street and left the cathedral to its fate.

All next day York Minster burned causing a havoc that brought a great part of its roof crashing down and left 130 feet of its length a gutted, smouldering shell of ruin.

The mad incendiarist had done his work well. And the horrified citizens and cathedral dignitaries could not say they had not been warned.

For weeks beforehand Jonathan Martin, the notorious wandering preacher, prophet and pamphleteer, had been telling them that the abode of Satan would "come rattling down in smoke and flames."

Once he had been locked up in a lunatic asylum for threatening to murder a bishop. Wherever he went he left a trail of riot, disturbance and religious fanaticism.

To Martin the burning of York Minster, one of the noblest masterpieces of English medieval building, was simply the grand crowning achievement of his whole life's labors.

The famous arsonist was born at Hexham, Northumberland, in 1782, the son of an impoverished former soldier who had set up as a fencing master.

Young Jonathan was apprenticed to a local tanner. A lonely, melancholy and deeply pious youth, he was regarded as somewhat simple-witted by his family and workmates.

In 1804 on a sudden impulse he set out to walk to London. Already he was troubled by strange dreams that God had "marked him among the righteous" for some special purpose.

No sooner had he reached London than he fell into the hands of the press gang which was scouring the cheap lodging houses to enlist recruits for the Royal Navy.

In his simplicity Martin thought he was signing on for a voyage in a merchant ship in which he hoped to do good work by spreading religious light among the rough sailors.

Instead he found himself aboard the 74-gun battle-ship Hercules and for the next six years served as a conscript at sea during the naval campaigns of the Napoleonic Wars.

He harangued his comrades about God's wrath and told them of his visions. They thought him mad and were glad to see the last of him when he was finally paid off in 1810.

About a year later Martin arrived at Norton, in Yorkshire, where he resumed his trade as a tanner, married a local girl and for a while settled down peacefully in the small market town.

He joined the Wesleyan Methodists and became a figure of notable piety. But soon his dreams returned, more terrible and overwhelming than ever.

He denounced himself as an atrocious sinner. He said his dead mother had appeared in a vision and told him he would end on the gallows if he did not take up his appointed task.

His chief obsession was the Church of England and its parsons who disgraced their cloth by attending theatres and balls, drinking and fox-hunting with the rural squires.

He took to disrupting Anglican services. Once he had to be dragged from the pulpit by the leg as he tried to harangue the congregation about the iniquities of their vicar.

Eventually the scandalised Wesleyans expelled him from their church. Soon he lost his job as well and Jonathan Martin set out on the wanderings that lasted the rest of his life.

With his long-suffering wife and infant child he tramped from place to place, picking up temporary work and often forced to beg the price of bread and lodgings.

His younger brother, now established as a popular painter of huge biblical canvases in London, sent him a few shillings to prevent the disgrace of him actually starving in a ditch.

Sometimes charitable Methodists took the family in and Martin repaid them by preaching in their chapels or in the market places until his vituperations ended in riots and showers of rubbish.

In 1818 he chanced to be in Stockton when he heard that the visiting Bishop of Oxford, Edward Legge, was to hold a confirmation service on behalf of the Bishop of Durham.

Martin had frequently roared that all bishops deserved to die as servants of the anti-Christ. And now, according to his crazy mind, a victim had been delivered into his hands.

The incendiarist Jonathan Martin gave dignitaries plenty of warning that he intended destroying the 'abode of Satan.'

From a fellow lodger he contrived to borrow an ancient, rusty horse-pistol. Asked why he wanted it he simply replied: "Why, to shoot the bishop with, of course."

All night he wrestled with prayers and visions with the loaded pistol under his pillow. Next morning was the day of the service. But Bishop Legge was not destined for sacrifice.

The magistrates had already been informed. Martin was dragged from his bed and taken to the town gaol where a doctor pronounced him an obvious madman and unfit to stand trial.

From Stockton he was moved to a lunatic asylum at West Auckland, a filthy, squalid hole where Martin vainly tried to drown the howls of the other inmates by singing psalms.

Before long Methodist sympathisers got him transferred to slightly cleaner quarters in the Gateshead asylum where he languished for the next three years.

Despite his religious ravings, his ceaseless prodution of weird writings and drawings and his fits of black melancholy Jonathan Martin proved a model prisoner.

It was not until his faithful wife visited him in the spring of 1821 and told him she was dying of cancer that he determined to escape from confinement.

One night he managed to break his rusty fetters, knock a hole in the plaster ceiling of his room and remove enough tiles to reach the roof of the asylum building.

From there he dropped to the top of the surrounding wall. Before daybreak he was miles away across the countryside towards the village where his wife lay on her deathbed.

Before she breathed her last he had to flee again. He was hiding under an assumed name in Darlington when in September 1821 he heard that her sufferings had ended.

By now some of his former Methodist friends had brought their influence to bear and the authorities made no further attempt to recapture the runaway from Gateshead asylum.

For the time being Jonathan Martin seemed harmless enough and in the next few years he became famous as a wandering preacher and pamphleteer all over the north of England.

In 1825 he persuaded a Darlington printer to publish his Life, which he hawked around the countryside riding on a skinny donkey and clad in an old sealskin coat and velveteen breeches.

The Life was a shoddy, poorly-printed booklet of 56 pages but its bizarre contents made it highly popular and Martin disposed of 14,000 copies to his credulous customers.

The Anglican church remained his chief enemy and the book was stuffed with horrifying prophecies of the damnation awaiting its "blind bishops and hypocritical priests."

Sometimes the avenging angel was Martin himself. But he had also had visionary interviews with a mysterious Son of Bonaparte who was to "arise with a great army from the sea."

According to the visions the pious Frenchmen were to conquer England in a tremendous battle, burn London to the ground and massacre everyone who did not turn to the Lord.

It was Christmas Eve in 1828 when the prophet arrived in York to make a final plea to the ecclesiastical dignitaries of the ancient cathedral city of the north of England.

He wrote them letters demanding that they abandon their worldly ways before the wrath of God brought the walls and towers of York Minister tumbling down on their heads.

When this brought no response he distributed pamphlets denouncing

The towers and west front at York Minister which escaped damage during the fire of 1829.

bishops and clerics as "serpents and vipers of hell, wine-bibbers and beef-eaters whose eyes stand out with fatness."

He was beset by visions of the cathedral "wrapt in smoke and flames." On 1 February, 1829, he decided that the Lord could wait no longer.

That afternoon, having spent his last pennies on a candle and a bowl of soup, he went to York Minster and concealed himself behind one of the tomb monuments after the evensong service ended.

About midnight he lit the fire. Before daybreak he had gone from York on a borrowed horse and was riding northward planning to spread the glad tidings throughout the countryside.

Not until 7.30 am on 2 February did dense smoke rolling from the cathedral's windows warn the citizens of York that their great church was in peril.

When fire-fighters burst in they found an appalling sight, for already the whole eastern end was a mass of flames where the choir stalls, throne and altar screen were blazing furiously.

An hour later the roof began to collapse, raining molten lead and massive charred timbers down to complete the havoc. By afternoon one-third of the minster was a smouldering shell.

No one doubted the identity of the lunatic incendiary. At once the hue and cry after Jonathan Martin began, with mounted dragoons from the York barracks leading the hunt.

Martin, meanwhile, had made little attempt to cover his tracks. Four days later he was found in a cottage near Hexham reading the bible to the villager who was sheltering him.

On 31 March he was tried for arson at the York Assizes and the jury took only seven minutes to decide that he was not guilty on the grounds of insanity.

Jonathan Martin went back to a lunatic asylum, this time the famous 'Bedlam' hospital in London. And there he stayed, sinking into deeper madness, until death released him on 27 May 1833.

"Bold, Brown and Beautiful"

EARLY in the year 1648, an 18-year-old girl named Lucy Walter arrived in the Dutch city of The Hague to join the flood of royalists who had fled from Cromwell's England.

Lucy arrived penniless and friendless, but, being also "bold, brown and beautiful", she did not languish in that condition for long. Within a few months, she was the mistress of the exiled young King Charles II.

In April 1649, she became mother of the king's illegitimate son, the wastrel Duke of Monmouth.

Only ten years later, after a short life of scandals and amorous adventures, Lucy Walter was dead. Moralists who afterwards tried to unearth her career for the benefit of posterity could not even discover where she was buried.

The merry monarch Charles II was to have many more paramours after his restoration to the English throne, but none endured a life as turbulent or a fate as tragic as his first love, Lucy Walter.

Daughter of a Welsh squire, William Walter, Lucy was born at Boch Castle in Pembrokeshire in 1630.

Walter fought for the royalist cause in the Civil War. In 1644, Boch Castle was captured and destroyed by a Parliamentary army, but Lucy and her mother escaped to London, to live in poverty during the final victory of Cromwell and overthrow of Charles I.

When Lucy first launched on her precocious career as a courtesan is uncertain. Puritan London might have seemed an unpromising field for her talents, but Lucy soon found no lack of "protectors".

Early in 1648, Algernon Sidney, son of the Earl of Leicester and an officer in Cromwell's army, acquired her from a fellow officer for 50 gold pieces, a modest sum in the light of Lucy's later celebrity.

To Sidney's chagrin, his regiment was transferred to Ireland before he could enjoy the bargain. But he suggested to Lucy that she might try her fortune in Holland, where the cavalier exiles would no doubt be more appreciative of her qualities than the burghers of London.

In addition, Sidney's brother, Colonel Robert Sidney, was living at The Hague and could be expected to shelter her. It transpired that the colonel

Charles II took Lucy Walter as his mistress only to cast her aside when stories of her depravity disgusted him.

did more than shelter her, for he immediately made Lucy his mistress.

Lucy's brazen charms caused something of a furore at The Hague. Lord Clarendon, chamberlain of the exiled royalist court, slightingly called her: "This private Welshwoman of no good fame, but handsome."

The diarist Evelyn, however, found her "bold, brown and beautiful". Another courtier said she "had not much wit, but much of the sort of cunning that her profession usually have".

A few months later, Lucy could afford to ignore all their contempt or hostility. She made a conquest of Prince Charles Stuart himself, soon to be recognised by the royalists as King Charles II, after his father was beheaded in London in January 1949.

Charles was then 18, the same age as Lucy. He was a handsome, selfish and sensual youth, who, for most of the past year, had been sailing with a few ships off the English coast in half-hearted attempts to rescue his father from Cromwell's clutches.

In the middle of 1648, Charles gave up his futile cruising and returned to The Hague. He met Lucy Walter, was fascinated by her, and, to the dismay of Clarendon, determined to acquire her as his mistress.

Colonel Sidney proved no obstacle, handing her over to the prince with the ungallant remark: "Let who will have her. She's already well sped!"

Lucy, who for some reason had adopted the name of Mrs. Barlow, was transferred to a lodging in Rotterdam. There, on 9 April 1649, her son Monmouth, was born.

Her lover, now recognised as King Charles II by the royalists, at once admitted the child's parentage, though many of his courtiers busily spread the rumor that Robert Sidney was the real father.

Charles' brother, the Duke of York, asserted that the child "was as like to the wart on his nose". But York, as a possible heir to the throne, had strong reasons for denying the royal blood of Lucy's offspring.

Charles' infatuation continued throughout 1649. He took Lucy to Paris when he went to plead for the aid of Louis XIV in recovering his throne. Despite the poverty of his little court, he lavished on her money and jewels.

The end came in 1650, when Charles set out for Scotland in the desperate hope of reconquering England with a Scottish army, only to meet crushing defeat at the battle of Worcester a year later.

In October 1651, after being hunted through half the length of England, Charles reached the Channel and escaped back to Holland. He was greeted by almost incredible news about the behavior of his mistress, Lucy Walter.

Charles listened with furious disgust as Clarendon and the courtiers poured stories of Lucy's depravity and wanton infidelities into his ear.

Only four months earlier, she had had a child by Colonel Henry Bennett, the future Earl of Arlington. Her "profligate loose-living" had so scandalised the honest citizens of Antwerp and the Hague, that they threatened to drive her out of their towns.

Charles flatly refused to see her again, though, according to the Duke of York, "she tried all her little arts and tried vainly to persuade the king that she would forthwith quit her scandalous life".

Driven to desperation, Lucy then asserted that she and Charles had been secretly married at Liege in 1649, in the presence of a "low groom" named Edward Progers who was notorious as the king's confidant in his amorous intrigues.

Lucy's claims gained little belief at the time. But they were revived years after her death, when Charles was king and the Whigs were trying to exclude the Catholic Duke of York from succession to the throne.

Then, every scrap of evidence was raked together to prove that the marriage had taken place, and their child, the Duke of Monmouth, was rightful heir. Nobody, however, seriously credited Lucy's story.

Rejected by Charles and treated with insolent contempt by his courtiers,

Lucy Walter with a portrait of her son.

Lucy found shelter in Rotterdam with John Harvey, a nephew of the famous physician who discovered the circulation of the blood.

Charles allowed her to retain his child, though he sent agents to spy on her movements and they gradually built up a damning dossier about her procession of lovers and her generally dissolute life.

In 1655, Lucy moved to The Hague as mistress of Tom Howard, brother of the Earl of Suffolk. In February of the following year, Colonel O'Neale warned Charles that her licentious conduct was bringing all the royalist exiles into grave disrepute.

Lucy's maid Ann Hill, said the colonel, had offered to disclose all the sordid details of her private life, but had been terrified into silence when Lucy stabbed her in the ear with a bodkin.

Only consideration for King Charles prevented the authorities of The Hague from having Lucy "banished the town, as an infamous person, and by the sound of drum".

The prospect of having his cast-off mistress drummed through the streets amid mobs of jeering Dutchmen was too much for Charles. He sent Lord Clarendon to get Lucy out of Holland as quickly as possible.

Clarendon offered her a yearly pension of 5,000 livres (about £400), payable through an Antwerp merchant bank, if she returned to England and kept her mouth shut about her association with Charles.

On condition of being allowed to take her seven years-old son with her, Lucy agreed. Charles himself relented enough to visit her before she sailed, and gave her a pearl necklace worth £1,500 as a parting gift.

Early in June, 1656, Lucy and her lover, Tom Howard, stepped ashore from an Antwerp brig in London and took obscure lodgings above a barber's shop in the Strand.

Lucy posed as the widow of a Dutch sea captain. But Cromwell's secret agents in Holland knew all about her liaison with Charles, and, to the Puritan dictator, she was potentially a dangerous royalist spy.

Only a fortnight later, Lucy was arrested and carried off to the Tower of London for questioning that lasted for almost a month.

Calling herself "Lady Walter", Lucy admitted proudly that she had been a royal mistress, but swore that Charles was not the father of her son. No shred of evidence could be found that she was a spy.

Lavinia Fenton.

Actress to Aristocrat

ONE September day in 1751 a big luxuriously-appointed coach with an English ducal crest emblazoned on the door panels rolled up to the best inn in the French spa resort of Aix-en-Provence.

The annual appearance of my lord the Duke of Bolton, with his mistress, parson, valet, cook, maid and two huge mastiffs, was something of an event in the pleasant little town.

For at least 10 years the duke had been coming to drink the waters. The dogs and servants sometimes changed, but the mistress and parson never.

However, with her delicately rouged and powdered little face, Lavinia Fenton looked very much the same as when she had been the most bewitching actress on the London stage.

And the parson was no longer a mystery to the society of the various European cities and spas around which the Bolton entourage perambulated year after year.

At first it had been thought that my lord was a very pious man and took the clergyman with him to provide spiritual consolation on his travels.

"No, damme, no!" the duke growled. "I keep him by me that he may marry me to Miss Fenton the instant I hear news that my infernal wife is dead!"

On 21 September 1751, when the party once more arrived at the Inn of the Golden Pheasant in Aix, the duke found a bulky missive from London awaiting him.

That evening, with the parson stammering through the ceremony in the candle-lit inn parlor, Lavinia Fenton, illegitimate daughter of a coffee house wench, actress and amourous adventuress, became Her Grace the Duchess of Bolton.

The story of Lavinia Fenton was a striking illustration of the rewards of fidelity, patience and good sense.

Lavinia was the toast of London when she snared the infatuated Duke of Bolton not only into running away with her but also into promising to wed her.

Having done so she was prepared to wait more than 20 years to become his duchess, rigidly faithful to her protector and abandoning all the pleasures of love she had tasted so often before.

There was no hint of this coming magnificence when Lavinia first saw the light of day in the back room of a cheap London coffee house in 1708.

Her mother was a maid in the house and her probable father was a naval officer named Beswick who went back to sea a few weeks before the child was born.

Lt Beswick left the mother a few guineas and instructions that the infant was to be named Porteous, if a boy, and Lavinia if a girl.

He also urged his mistress to "retire into the country and resist any more temptations". Having bequeathed this excellent advice he sailed away and was killed in the wars.

Far from seeking rural seclusion Lavinia's mother used the money to set up her own coffee house at Charing Cross and soon married one of her admirers, a tradesman named John Fenton.

Lavinia was given her step-father's name and she spent her earliest years until the age of 13 at the coffee house.

By then she was already a budding beauty with a well-formed figure, coquettish dark eyes and a gift for singing and dancing that delighted the fashionable gentlemen who frequented the house.

Mrs Fenton was not averse to her daughter's precocious conquests but, believing she needed a little more polish, packed her off to a select boarding school.

The experiment in teaching Lavinia Fenton ladylike manners was not

Lavinia Fenton in "The Beggars Opera"

245

successful. Within two years she was back at the coffee shop after rocking the school to its sedate foundations.

The climax had come when she was caught one night entertaining a young lawyer behind the garden rose bushes. Next day she packed her trunk and departed.

The beaux of Charing Cross welcomed her back with open arms and Mrs Fenton now decided that her daughter had better find a husband as soon as possible to keep her out of more mischief.

Lavina, however, had other ideas. The fine gentlemen might not be prepared to marry her but she knew how to extort a handsome return for her favours.

Rarely was the sharp-witted girl deceived in her calculations though she could be just as warm-heartedly generous as grasping when the occasion arose.

Once when she was not quite 16 she went off for a month in the country with a Portuguese nobleman who wooed her ardently with promises of jewels, money and a mansion full of servants.

The next time she heard of the foreign charmer he was in the Fleet debtors' prison, disowned by the Portuguese Embassy and likely to languish in his cell indefinitely.

Hastening to visit him Lavina was deeply touched by his miserable plight as he flung himself at her feet and begged for forgiveness.

Selling all the jewels, gowns and gewgaws given her by other admirers Lavinia raised enough cash to pay his debts and put him on board a ship for Portugal.

It did not take her long to recoup these charitable losses, despite several more mishaps in her amorous career.

The most galling was when a handsome young suitor who had posed as the heir to a rich line-draper turned out to be a mere apprentice in the draper's shop.

Not only that but he had the insolence to ravish Lavinia when they were strolling one evening in Hyde Park before she made the discovery.

The momentous hour in Lavina Fenton's career came in 1726 when she was 18 years old and faced nothing better than the precarious life of a superior kind of harlot.

For years she had been entertaining the coffee house patrons by mimicking the famous actresses of the day and singing the latest airs from the Italian opera house.

Among her listeners one summer evening in 1726 was a friend of the managers of a dilapidated, near-bankrupt little theatre in the Haymarket.

A few days later, armed with a letter of introduction, Lavinia arrived at the theatre to join the swarm of second-rate and unemployed actors who hung about the door hoping for a temporary engagement.

Intrigued by her pretty face and assured grace, the managers at once agreed to give her a trial in the old melodrama, The Orphan.

In tragedy Lavinia was a flop. But the story was very different five weeks later when she appeared as the lively innkeeper's daughter in Farquhar's comic masterpiece, The Beaux Stratagem.

With all London singing her praises it was obvious that the dazzling new star would soon move on from the scruffy purlieus of the Haymarket.

In 1727 Lavinia signed a 15/- a week contract with John Rich of the theatre in Lincolns Inn Fields, an event that was to be a turning point in the lives of both of them.

Rough, crafty, hard-dealing John Rich was facing a crisis of dwindling audiences in the teeth of intense competition from the famous house in Drury Lane.

Late in 1727 he determined to take a gamble on a bundle of tattered manuscript that poet John Gay had been hawking unsuccessfully round the London theatres for months.

It was a play with songs and music called The Beggar's Opera. And Rich and his fellow managers had never read anything like it before.

Instead of the customary ladies and gentlemen the cast was made up of highwaymen, thieves, cut-throats, gaolers and their flaunting, bedraggled doxies.

And besides uproariously parodying all the polite conventions of Italian opera, the play was stuffed with deadly satire against Prime Minister Walpole and his government.

Nevertheless Rich decided to take the plunge. The result was one of the most astonishing successes in theatrical history.

The Beggar's Opera opened on 29 January 1728, and continued for 62 performances—a run absolutely unprecedented on the London stage up to that time.

Rich had hand-picked his company. But it was Lavinia Fenton as Polly Peachum, the bold highwayman's mistress, who filled the house with the most rapturous thunders of applause night after night.

There were Lavinia Fenton bonnets, fans and gloves. Books of verses were published about her, her highly mythical "life" was written and print shops could not keep pace with the demand for her engravings.

Meanwhile, planted night after night in his box throughout the whole season, sat Charles Paulet, third Duke of Bolton, gazing in rapt devotion at the gambols of Polly Peachum.

His infatuation became the talk of London. The wits wagered whether he would one night leap on to the stage and cut highwayman Macheath's throat out of jealousy.

For years the 45-year-old duke had lived apart from his cold, strait-laced duchess but never before had scandal suggested that he sought amusement elsewhere.

Then in June 1728 came the final sensation when London society was staggered to learn that the Duke of Bolton and pretty, witty Polly Peachum had run away together.

The theatre never saw Lavinia Fenton again—though, according to one cynical observer, she "gave the most remarkable performance of her life in the role of a ducal mistress".

Modest, unassuming and completely faithful despite her passionate nature Lavinia continued to live happily with her lord and the most vicious gossips could find nothing to say against her.

Bolton bought her a London house and an estate in Yorkshire but the couple spent much of each year travelling Europe in a style befitting one of Britain's proudest peers.

Lavinia's belated elevation to the rank of duchess made little difference to their mode of existence and in any case their life as a legally married couple was brief.

When the duke died in August 1754 his title went to his brother but almost all his vast estates were divided beween Lavinia and their children born out of wedlock.

The bereaved Lavinia was then 46 but she was still a ripe beauty ready for any amorous encounter that offered.

Dr Thomas Kelly, a dashing Irish surgeon at Tunbridge Wells, was reputed to be among those fortunate enough to comfort the duchess in her years of widowhood.

It was among these final whiffs of scandal that Lavinia Fenton, Duchess of Bolton, died at Greenwich on 24 January 1760.

The interior of the old Haymarket theatre in London at about the time Lavinia Fenton made her stage debut.

"A Harpy in Borrowed Plumes"

WHENVEVER learned historians dig into the seamy netherworld of London life in the second half of the 17th century they continually encounter the name of a certain notorious woman known simply as Mother Cresswell.

However the lady never sullies the pages of school history textbooks and for a very good reason. For Mother Cresswell was probably the most infamous "madam" of her own or any other era.

Almost every contemporary reference breathes the hatred and disgust sober citizens felt for the outrageous Mother Cresswell and her evil trade in feminine flesh.

"A foul harpy in borrowed plumes without a rival in her wickedness", was how one chronicler described her. "An adept in every diabolical art of seduction", said another.

Yet in the gaudy and unashamedly licentious age of Restoration England there were few more colorful characters than Mother Cresswell.

She was the friend of wits and poets, she was protected by some of the most powerful courtiers, her lavish bordello was the scene of political intrigues that affected the history of England.

And she died as all the moralists prophesied she would—a raddled, penniless old crone within the squalid walls of the Bridewell prison for women.

The Bridewell authorities had little sympathy for the dying Mother Cresswell. They had housed too many of her victims who has been dragged off the streets of London in the last stages of disease and despair.

Once the Bridewell inmates had been fresh and innocent young country girls, until Mother Cresswell's spies ferreted them out and lured them into her clutches in the bright lights of London.

How many helpless girls were ruined by her ruthless traffic was never known though, according to one account, more than 200 passed through her establishments in town and in the nearby countryside.

Mother Cresswell (her Christian name is not recorded) was born about 1625 and was probably a country girl herself who came to London after the end of the Civil War between King and Parliament.

She was a notable beauty, a "buxom, bouncing lass", and even during Cromwell's Puritan regime she had no difficulty in finding protectors among rich and influential citizens.

When Charles II was restored to his throne in 1660 she was still in her 30s but already a wealthy woman with a house in town, another in the suburb of Clerkenwell and a third in the country just outside London.

It was soon apparent that the Restoration was going to usher in an age of blatant immorality after the rigors of Puritan rule. And Mother Cresswell was ready for the change.

"With the bloom of beauty fading from her cheek" she could not rely on finding lovers among the gay young courtiers, wits and rakehells whose swaggerings dominated the social world under the Merry Monarch.

However if Mother Cresswell could no longer personally provide female charms she was determined to supply them plentifully by proxy.

She began by converting her big Clerkenwell house into a luxuriously-appointed brothel, filling it by recruiting young servants, tavern maids and other girls seeking a soft and easy livelihood.

Before long business was so brisk that she turned her country residence into another establishment, a snug rural retreat catering for a richer and superior class of patrons.

Despite these attractions Mother Cresswell had many rivals in her trade, for Restoration London was the heyday of the madams.

Never before had they flaunted their wares so shamelessly and never before had they wielded such power or achieved such spectacular notoriety in the world of rank and fashion.

They covered every social grade of vice; from the exclusive Madam Bennett (Mother Cresswell's most dangerous rival) to a foul hag known as Old Mother Damnable who operated in an alley appropriately named Dog-and-Bitch Yard.

It was in Madam Bennett's salon near Covent Garden that the profligate Earl of Rochester held a mock "court" and recited his obscene poems to the delight of the aristocrats and trollops who thronged around him.

It was to Madam Bennett that William Wycherly, the wit and dramatist, dedicated his play, The Plain Dealer, railing her ironically as "the great and noble patroness of rejected and bashful men".

He also praised her tireless industry in "keeping so busy that others may lie down". She extinguished lust with lust, said Wycherly, "like burning down houses to stop the progress of a fire".

However Mesdames Cresswell and Bennett were not the only procuresses catering for the roving courtiers of Charles II and the rich young heirs of city merchant houses.

In the Strand was the particularly handsome brothel run by Madam Beaulie, a gorgeously-gowned Frenchwoman who specialised in looking after foreign diplomats and other distinguished visitors to England.

Her most exalted customer was a French duke who came to London in an attempt to negotiate a marriage between the Dauphin and King Charles's niece, Princess Mary.

The wedding plan fell through, but the duke was in no hurry to quit the delights of Madam Beaulie's house, where a fresh girl was provided for his entertainments each day.

Faced with competition like this the resourceful Mother Cresswell decided that she must cast her net wider in search of attractive bait.

The supply of London girls of suitable age and charms was not unlimited. But all over rural England was an almost inexhaustible stock, if only it could be herded to London.

By the 1670s Mother Cresswell's agents were busily at work all over the

peaceful English countryside looking for candidates to adorn their employer's establishments.

They visited country fairs, market places, taverns and any locality where they were likely to find pretty and rosy-cheeked girls who were discontented with their rough rural swains.

Those gullible enough to fall for the smooth talk of Mother Cresswell's spies were packed off to London by coach, with the promise of a job in a "splendid household" at the end of the journey.

Some fled when they learnt the reality of their employment and either starved in the London streets or tried to beg their way back to the country.

But most of them stayed, dazzled by their fine dresses, their fine lovers

Mother Cresswell escaped the fate of most of London's madams. Here one of her contemporaries, Mrs. Cellier, is pillioned and mocked by onlookers.

William Bedloe, one of the group exploiting Charles II's fear of "popery", arranged meetings with his associates in Mother Cresswell's Clerkenwell brothel.

and the prospects of easy money—until their charms faded and Mother Cresswell ruthlessly bundled them out.

The luckier ones were handed down to the cheaper brothels. The rest drifted on to the streets, to be periodically rounded up and flogged as vagrants and eventually to die in Bridewell or in some slum rat-hole where they had crept for shelter.

Not all of Mother Cresswell's country recruits were forwarded by her industrious agents.

Her hirelings were posted at all the London inns where coaches arrived from the provinces to watch for girls coming to the big city in search of jobs or to look for friends and relatives.

"By these and other devilish arts", said one contemporary annalist, "the celebrated procuress snared into their ruin as many young women as might make Satan himself envious."

However Mother Cresswell's downfall began when she rashly involved herself in the political and religious intrigues that kept Britain in turmoil during the last years of Charles II.

Despite her noisome reputation she had always been careful to keep up a pretence of sober piety and respectability.

She dressed modestly, attended church regularly, where she prayed "in loud vehement tones", and frequently lectured her young ladies on the need for attending to their devotions.

Though she entertained the most blasphemous and foul-mouthed wits of the day it was recorded that Mother Cresswell herself was never guilty of a single coarse expression or unseemly gesture.

Her misfortune was to become the friend and confidant of several of the most disreputable scoundrels who infested the seamier side of London's political world.

The royal stallion, Charles II, had sired numerous bastards but he had no legitimate children and it seemed inevitable that his brother, the Duke of York, would succeed him on the throne.

However the Duke was a Catholic and many of the English nobles and statesmen were determined to find some means of debarring him and maintaining the Protestant succession.

Out of the turmoil of factions emerged a handful of desperate adventurers determined to exploit the "No Popery" agitation for their own greedy ends.

The infamous Titus Oates, a renegade Anglican priest and then a renegade Jesuit, was the leading figure in concocting fantastic stories of Catholic plots to murder Charles and put his brother on the throne.

William Bedloe, a former gaolbird and confidence trickster, was another of the group. In 1678 the government granted him £500 for information on the entirely mythical "Popish Plots".

And it was in Mother Cresswell's brothel in Clerkenwell that Bedloe and many of his associates met to spin their schemes and fabricate their crazy stories.

For two years Bedloe was one of the lords of the famous procuress's harem while Mother Cresswell zealously aided him by gathering information through her tribe of agents.

Then in 1680 Bedloe's reign abruptly ended. Having rioted away all the official reward money he fled to Bristol where he died, beggared and generally despised, a few months later.

Titus Oates and his cronies in Mother Cresswell's house contrived to keep the flames of religious fanaticism roaring for a few more years until the stories of the "plots" utterly collapsed.

In 1684 Oates was arrested, flogged almost to death and languished in prison until William and Mary came to the throne after the exile of James II in 1688.

Meanwhile Mother Cresswell's golden days were over. As her business dwindled she sank into poverty and disrepute. The fine houses were sold to meet her debts and soon she was penniless.

About 1690 the gates of Bridewell prison closed on the shabby, whining and sanctimonious hag who had been the Queen of Vice in the glittering days of Restoration London.

As she lay dying she bequeathed 10 guineas to the prison chaplain provided that he "spoke nothing but well of her in the funeral sermon".

As she was lowered into her grave the ingenious parson won his fee by declaring briefly that "her name was Cresswell, she lived in Clerkenwell and she died in Bridewell".

The Profits of Promiscuity

THE English-born Mlle Cora Pearl kept one of the most intriguing "little black books" in Paris. It contained the names of 1003 men who had been her lovers at different times during her promiscuous career.

Actually there were more, but the famed courtesan never found time to record for posterity the identity of these men who played minor roles in her career.

Cora Pearl made the first entry in her book when she was 15 and the last 25 years later. This meant her average love affair lasted, at the most, nine days.

Contemporaries usually referred to the notorious harlot as "that woman without a heart". And they were probably right for, as far as is known, real love had nothing to do with Cora Pearl's amorous pursuits.

Indeed at the height of her notoriety and affluence she was asking and getting the modern equivalent of $600 for 12 hours of her valuable time.

Cora Pearl, the courtesan whose conquests included the sensuous Emperor Louis Napoleon, was not really beautiful. Her chief attractions were her vivaciousness and a strange magnetism that surpassed all beauty.

Born Emma Elizabeth Crouch in Plymouth, Devon, in February 1842, the future demi-mondaine was the daughter of William Crouch, a song-writer who composed the deathless ballad, Kathleen Mavourneen.

When Emma was seven her father became involved with a mistress and, deserting his family, migrated with the woman to America.

Mrs Crouch, who had mothered 16 children, was saved from destitution by the advent of a man of means who offered to provide for her family on condition she became his de facto wife. Filled with gratitude the woman accepted.

Soon after her mother's protector moved into the house, Emma was sent to a school at Boulogne in France. And there she developed into an attractive girl bubbling with the joy of life, trained in social graces and filled with an irresistible charm.

Emma Crouch was 13 when she finished her education and was let loose on a nation bent on recapturing the luxurious, sensual glamor of the Louis

257

XIV era.

Louis Napoleon himself had set the new standards to be observed by abandoning the arms of his Empress and accepting instead the embraces of a series of notorious courtesans.

Taking their lead from the Emperor, members of the nobility were soon trying to outdo each other in their acquisition of beautiful, expensive and uninhibited mistresses.

Overnight Paris became the mecca of attractive, young women intent on acquiring as quickly as possible a rich protector.

Further, this influx of some of the world's most beautiful women brought a stream of Europe's greats rushing to the city—men like the wealthy Turk, Khalil-Bey, the Duke of Hamillton, Lord Granville and even the Prince of Wales.

Emma Crouch was still a child when she first found herself mesmerised by Paris's new epoch of social decadence.

Although she wished to remain in the capital she obeyed an instruction from her mother that she should return to England and move in with her

258

The wedding of Prince Jerome Bonaparte. Never one to allow marriage to interfere with his extra-marital affairs, he spent a fortune on the worthless but fascinating Cora Pearl.

grandmother, Mrs Watts, who lived near Covent Garden.

Insisting that Emma should continue her education, Mrs Watts personally conducted classes in reading, arithmetic, languages and sewing.

Then came the Sunday morning that was to change Emma Crouch from a nonentity to a figure that will endure in the unsavory pages of France's history.

Just 15 years of age then, Emma was returning from church when a man, old enough to be her father, invited her to his home "for tea and cakes".

The cakes were provided but the tea was stiffly laced with gin. Next morning she awoke, Emma later said in her memoirs, to find herself in bed with the gentleman beside her.

When Emma told her seducer that she could never now return to her grandmother, the man gave her $20 and suggested in no uncertain terms that she get as far away from his house as possible.

That evening Emma rented a room and cried herself to sleep. Next day she began looking for work with some theatrical company.

Unable to get a position she was on the verge of despair when William

Buckle, the owner of a Covent Garden dance hall, offered her a position as his mistress. Emma accepted the post and later even accompanied him to Paris as his wife.

But Buckle's possession of his attractive young mistress was short-lived for when he was ready to return to London, Emma refused to go with him.

Changing her name to Cora Pearl, the embryo courtesan soon found a sailor who was willing to support her.

When his money was gone Cora transferred her affections to M. Delamarche who showered the fascinating English girl with luxuries until he too was on the verge of bankruptcy.

Week by week Cora Pearl continued clawing her way up the social ladder. At 18 she caught the eye of an ancient duke. Soon afterwards she transferred her services to the wealthy Prince Achille Murat.

Her first really important client was the Prince of Orange, son of King Charles III of the Netherlands.

The Prince, who might have later married England's Princess Alice had not Queen Victoria brushed him aside, established Cora in a luxurious apartment, bought her a carriage and showered her with jewellery.

But Cora did not allow the Prince's adulation to stop her pursuing her career for she also entered into brief liaisons with the Russian princes Narishkine and Demidoff as well as the French dukes Montebello and de Rivola.

There were also well-founded stories that Louis Napoleon himself had savoured the delights of the fascinating young Englishwoman.

Cora also found time to mulct fortunes from the Emperor's cousin Prince Jerome Napoleon as well as his handsome half-brother the Duc de Mornay.

Actually Prince Jerome Napoleon, who was then fat and ageing, made Coral Pearl a monthly allowance of about $2,000 and set her up in a magnificent mansion known as the Little Tuileries.

Having moved into her new establishment, Cora crammed it with a mass of expensive bric-a-brac, all monuments to her bad taste.

Yet the visitors who crowded her soirees were not interested in Mlle Pearl's ideas of beauty in art. They were there simply to savour the magnificent food and feast their eyes on the scandalously-displayed figure of their notorious hostess.

During "the season" when Cora travelled in royal style to vacationing places like Baden-Baden and Vichy, her usual crowd of admirers and lovers followed her.

On one of these holidays she entertained so lavishly that in a fortnight the food bill alone came to almost $10,000.

As Cora's notoriety grew so her conduct became more outrageous.

There was the time, for instance, when an admirer at one of her soirees suggested that her skin was so pink-white that it must be painted on.

To disprove the man's contention the courtesan unblushingly stripped before all the guests.

Another time when the Duc de Gramont Caderousse presented her with

The notorious English-born courtesan, Cora Pearl.

a silver bath tub, she invited a crowd to watch her bathe unclothed in the tub that had been filled with champagne.

Yet even if guests were not always treated to such exotic entertainment, they were sure to be treated to a fiery display of their hostess's coarse and bawdy repartee.

Meanwhile, the sensualist, Jerome Bonaparte, continued footing most of the bills for his mistress's wild extravagancies. Nor did he complain when Cora announced she would like to capitalise further on her fame by appearing on the stage.

Producers were delighted to have the crowd-catching Cora Pearl play the part of Cupid in Offenbach's Orpheus in the Underworld during the 1867 Paris Exhibition.

And their trust in her appeal was fully justified for on the opening night a house packed to the rafters was happy to pay up to $100 for a seat.

Cora Pearl tried to keep faith with her public by appearing on stage with wings, a bow and arrow and practically nothing else.

The audience whistled and stamped its feet, falling silent only when Cora prepared to utter her first line. Then the words came out: "I am Cupid. . . ."

The voice was coarse and nasal. It grated on the ears. Cheers turned to cat-calls. Cora Pearl's stage career was over although this was to have no ill-effects on her more notorious occupation.

Day after day a succession of lovers continued to enjoy the Englishwoman's favors while Jerome Bonaparte, with limited access to her boudoir, spent most of his time checking on his rapidly-sinking fortune.

When the Franco-Prussian War broke out in 1870 bringing Emperor Louis Napoleon's regime to an end, Cora persuaded Prince Jerome to take her to England.

Cora had not been long in residence in the exclusive Grosvenor Hotel when the manager, accepting the advice of more respectable guests, ordered her to take her patronage elsewhere.

Boiling with anger, Cora returned to Paris, turned her mansion into a hospital, and somehow endured the horrors of the city's siege by the Prussians.

Immediately 30 years of life had passed her by, Cura Pearl's promiscuity quickly began catching up with her. Her face became lined, her hair grew coarse. Lovers became fewer. Jerome Napoleon drifted off.

In 1871 Cora met Mr Alexandre Duval, the son of a butcher and cafe owner and heir to a vast fortune.

Duval was insane with infatuation and began inundating his new mistress with luxuries even she had never known.

Nothing was good enough for Cora Pearl. One string of pearls which he gave to his paramour cost him the modern equivalent of $300,000.

As far as Cora was concerned it was wonderful while it lasted. But it lasted for only two years. The mesmerised Duval was then bankrupt.

When Cora ordered her now penniless lover to leave her house, Duval waited until the door had slammed in his face and then shot himself.

Although Duval survived the wound, Cora Pearl's career was over.

When the mother of the would-be-suicide complained to the authorities that the wanton Englishwoman had been responsible for her son's financial and social disgrace, an order was issued banishing the courtesan from France.

After being ejected from one Continental capital after another, Cora gravitated to London. Later, hoping the authorities had forgotten her, she returned to Paris.

Piece by piece she sold her jewellery to keep herself from penury. But in the late 1870s she faced the inevitable. She was penniless.

She tried to make a living as a common prostitute but clients were few. Early in 1886 cancer began tearing agonisingly at her body.

In July that year, Cora Pearl died alone in a garret in the Rue de Bassano. She was 44.

The body of the now-forgotten English courtesan would have been buried in a pauper's grave had not a man, who had promised to publish her memoirs, donated a small plot in the St. Ouen cemetery.

And a kindly garret neighbor made a present of the nightdress in which the body was clothed.

The Countess of Montijo had only one real vice but it was sufficiently disgraceful to shock all Spain.

Democratic in Bed

ONLY in the realm of love could the Countess of Montijo be called democratic. Otherwise she was boorishly snobbish, ambitious and distastefully ostentatious. In affairs of the heart alone she raised no barriers.

If a man caught her eye, social rank or financial affluence meant nothing. Palace flunkies, lowly army officers or bullfighters, they were all the same to the amorous countess. And to prove her tastes were entirely without bounds she occasionally inveigled more prominent members of society like noblemen or heads of state.

Some historians excuse the Countess of Montijo's promiscuity on the grounds that her husband, a cold, distant nobleman, showed little interest in her, or any other woman for that matter.

Nevertheless he did give her sufficient attention to allow her to produce two daughters, one to become the wife of the powerful Duke of Alba, the other to take a place in history as Eugenie, Empress of France.

The daughter of a Scottish wine merchant whose parents fled from their homeland after the 1745 Jacobite rising, Maria Kirkpatrick, later the Countess of Montijo, was born in Spain in 1800.

Although Maria's father came from lowly stock, she always boasted that her French mother was descended from an ancient royal line.

With the passing of time Kirkpatrick's wine business in Malaga prospered. And his new affluence brought him new friends who flocked to his luxurious residence to taste his fine wines and feast their eyes on his beautiful daughter.

The wealthiest, if the ugliest of these visiors, was Cipriano de Guzman y Palafox y Porto Carrero y Peneneranda, Count of Teba and brother of the immensely wealthy Count of Montijo.

Maria Kirkpatrick was not concerned about ugliness. But wealth intrigued her. On 15 December 1817, the wine merchant's daughter became the Countess of Teba.

The union of a merchant's daughter and the scion of the great ducal house of Montijo caused an outburst of rage in royal and noble circles.

King Ferdinand was appeased a little when he learned that the bride's mother was of royal stock. But the old Count of Montijo refused to accept the alliance.

Being a bachelor his chief fear was that on his death his title and estates would pass to his younger brother and the Scottish coquette he had married. The thought appalled him.

To obviate this terrible possibility the Count of Montijo lost no time dragging a bride to the altar. Then, realising he was incapable of siring a child, he made arrangements to take possession of the child of a woman who had just become pregnant.

His plan was to announce his own wife's pregnancy then, nine months later, sneak the new-born child into his wife's bed.

Maria saw through the plot immediately the pregnancy of the new Countess of Montijo was announced. She won an audience with Ferdinand and asked that her husband be allowed to exercise the family rights and be present when the countess's child was born.

Quickly old Montijo announced that his wife had made a mistake. She was not pregnant after all.

In 1825 the Count of Teba lost favour with Ferdinand and was sent to Granada to take command of a regiment. He and Maria were still there in May 1826, when a fearful earthquake rocked the city.

Fearing she would be crushed to death in her shaking house, Maria fled into the garden. And there, as the old Moorish buildings of Granada crumbled about her, the Countess of Teba gave birth to her second daughter, the future Empress of France.

But meanwhile Maria and the count had grown apart. Politics had become Cipriano's new love while he detested the social life that attracted his pleasure-mad wife.

Finally when the count's political intriguing sent him fleeing to the sanctuary of France, Maria was left alone to seek solace in the arms of more passionate men.

Taking her two daughters with her to Madrid, the countess at once ventured on an orgy of love-making that was not to end until age had withered every physical attraction she possessed.

Any army officer that caught her eye was at once escorted to her bed-chamber. Flunkies too, enjoyed her favors. And there was a time when she developed an obsession for bullfighters.

Yet it was not until her husband received King Ferdinand's pardon and returned to Spain in 1830 that Maria was able to mix real love with her favorite pastime.

While in Paris the Count of Teba had become friendly with a young author, Prosper Merimee. And when the King told Cipriano he could return to his homeland, the Count decided to take Merimee with him.

Cipriano was not concerned that the author and his wife fell in love almost at their first meeting. He simply retired from the domestic scene allowing the pair to carry on an affair that scandalised Madrid.

Maria would scarcely move unless Merimee was by her side. And the young author, in turn, remained dazzled by the social position and beauty of his mistress.

It is said that Maria was the first to recount to Merimee the legend of the gipsy girl Carmen. Intrigued by the story the young Frenchman wrote the famous book that won him a place in literary history.

In 1844 following the death of Ferdinand and the civil wars that rocked Spain, the old Count of Montijo died. Cipriano was now Count of Montijo and owner of the palaces and estates that went with the title.

Maria revelled in the sumptuous luxury of the Montijo palaces and began squandering money. She even began spicing Merimee's love with the attentions of more casual lovers.

Then in July 1834 the civil war erupted anew. Blood flowed in the streets of Madrid and the Countess of Montijo, fearful for her life, fled to Paris.

There, when she was joined by Merimee, she set herself up in an establishment that rivalled anything in Paris. Her salon became the talk of the city and was continually filled with the great and near great.

It was at these soirees that Maria selected the lovers who would visit her privately. She still retained Merimee as her chief attraction but brushed aside his protestations that she should remain completely faithful to him.

It was only a matter of time before all Paris was talking about the insatiable appetites of the wealthy and beautiful countess from Madrid. Newspapers jibed at her while King Louis Philippe dubbed her "the Spanish cocotte".

Then in 1839 Maria received word that her husband was dying. She hurried home to attend the funeral and sign papers relating to the $50,000 annual income and the two palaces she was to receive from the estate.

Moving into the huge Carabanchel castle, Maria organised a never-ending series of fetes and balls that kept its scores of bedchambers continually filled with guests.

She even took to galloping through the streets of Madrid dressed in Arabian robes and accompanied by her latest lover.

During these amazing outings her treasurer would bring up the rear throwing handfuls of gold coins to the incredulous peasants who lined the route.

She even built a private theatre on the estate and brought Merimee from Paris to write plays and design scenery.

At that time, having tired apparently of lowly lovers, Maria began cultivating men of culture and wealth. Among the first of this new batch to savor her favors was the English Ambassador in Madrid, Lord Clarendon.

He was succeeded by the military dictator, General Narvaez, who had led Queen Isabella's army against the Carlist rebels.

When Clarendon was displaced he boiled with jealousy and called the general "an ugly, fat little man with a vile expression of countenance".

But her new lover's ugliness did not worry the Countess of Montijo for she realised he was the most influential man in Spain and could win her access to the royal court.

Later, when Maria had been appointed Lady-of-Honour to Queen Isabella she saw her eldest daughter married to the Duke of Alba who was

The Express Eugenie of France was a strait-laced woman. She inherited none of her mother's scandalous traits.

descended from King James II of England and his mistress Arabella Churchill.

But soon it became apparent to Isabella that her Lady-of-Honour lacked the basic morality required for this exalted position.

There were stories, for instance, of days-long entertainments at Carabanchel which were little more than orgies. The Queen was also given details of her Lady-of-Honour's participation in these debaucheries.

Then when it became known that one of Maria's servants, after being invited to her bedchamber, had stolen some of her jewels while she slept, Isabella dismissed the countess from her court.

In 1847 Maria and her 21-year-old daughter Eugenie fled towards Paris. Maria stayed a few days at Toulouse to take a few casual lovers, then continued on towards the city in her ornate coach.

For the next three years Maria and Eugenie wandered Europe living for brief periods in luxurious houses in London, Vienna and Brussels.

And even when the countess celebrated her 50th birthday she was still faced with the problem of selecting the lover of the day from the retinue of suitors who followed her progress.

Meanwhile in December 1848, Louis Napoleon, nephew of Bonaparte, was elected President of the new French Republic. In 1851 he took steps to have himself elected Emperor.

When Maria and Eugenie returned to Paris early in 1852, Louis Napoleon sent for Maria. He had met Eugenie in London in 1848, he recalled, and had never forgotten the young woman's beauty.

Louis Napoleon suggested to Maria that her daughter might become his mistress. But the countess flew into a rage and announced her daughter would have nothing to do with him under such terms.

Thus when Louis Napoleon became Emperor in November 1852 he announced he would marry the daughter of the Countess of Montijo.

Despite opposition from his advisers who objected to this union with the daughter of "the Spanish harlot", Eugenie became Empress of France on 30 January 1853.

But now instead of having great influence as the mother of the Empress, Maria found herself practically banned from the court. She tolerated this embarrassing situation for a few months then returned to her homeland.

As the mother of the Empress of France the Spanish royal court brought her back into its folds. But the ageing countess knew she had been re-admitted simply for diplomatic reasons.

She withstood the antagonism of the courtiers for only a short time before retiring finally and permanently to Carabanchel.

She was still there, an old withered woman, when news arrived that her daughter had fled to exile in England following France's defeat in the Franco-Prussian war.

Maria Kirkpatrick, the wine merchant's over-amorous daughter, died on 23 November 1879.

It is believed it was the interest shown by Britain's Prime Minister Herbert Henry Asquith in the goings-on at the Abode of Love that caused police to place guards on its gates.

Reverend Prince's "Abode of Love"

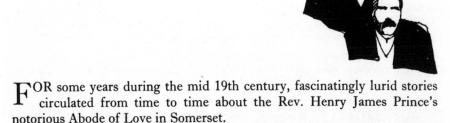

FOR some years during the mid 19th century, fascinatingly lurid stories circulated from time to time about the Rev. Henry James Prince's notorious Abode of Love in Somerset.

Invariably these rumors suggested that the abode did not cater (as Prince suggested) simply for spiritual love, but provided opportunities to sample an emotion of a more sensual form.

Indeed, it was said, the Abode of Love with its high surrounding walls that ensured complete privacy, was nothing more than a retreat where the disciples of the prophet, Henry Prince, indulged themselves in various forms of orgiastic delights.

As a promoter of the neoprophet racket, the Rev. Prince was not unique. Hundreds of others before and after him have relieved followers of their money by convincing them they possessed divine attributes.

What made Prince different was that he was able to dupe the staid English —a race normally impervious to the claims of false prophets.

Prince's ingredients for success were few and simple: a knowledge of the Bible, a gift of oratory, a touch of insanity and the offer to appease carnal desires.

With this formula he relieved wealthy clients of their fortunes, sowed the germs of insanity in the minds of his more unstable followers and brought the wrath of all England on his head.

The story of Henry James Prince, the self-styled reincarnation of the prophet Elijah, and Lord of the Agapemone (Abode of Love), began in 1811 when he was born in Wales to educated middle-class parents.

Entering a Church of England theological college in his youth, he showed unusual academic ability even if he did win a reputation as a religious radical.

Ordained in 1840 he was immediately sent as curate to the Rev. Samuel Starkey, rector of Charlynch parish in Somerset.

From the start, the Rev. Henry Prince was a hit with the parishioners. A blazing orator, he could keep the congregation on the edge of its seats for an hour or two while he lambasted them with verbal fireworks.

And as his oratorical fame spread, more people packed into the Charlynch

271

church to hear the brilliant young curate.

Yet the clergyman's extraordinary popularity raised no emotion of jealousy in the Rev. Starkey. Indeed he became one of his curate's greatest admirers.

But as time passed it became obvious to those unaffected by the young curate's emotional appeal, that he was slowly convincing himself he had supernatural powers.

Nor did the Rev. Starkey seem shocked when his curate finally told him he had absorbed the spirit of God. In fact when Starkey was suddenly "cured" of a mysterious illness, he attributed his recovery to a Prince miracle and became his curate's devoted disciple.

Finally came the day when it was found the Charlynch church would not hold the numbers wanting to hear the amazing Rev. Henry Prince. So the curate decided to extend his activities to other parishes.

This intrusion immediately had the other parishes up in arms. And the pastors protested so strongly to the Bishop of Bath and Wells that Prince's licence to preach was cancelled.

After that Henry Prince tried other methods of getting his message across. But each time he ended up at loggerheads with the hierarchy of the Church of England. In the end he decided to form his own religion.

For a start the community of the new religion was small—it consisted only of Prince and his ever-devoted disciple, the Rev. Samuel Starkey.

Working in the Charlynch district where they were already known, Prince and Starkey began a revival mission that had thousands pouring into their meetings.

Now Prince was so convinced he held the congregations completely under his domination that he felt safe in announcing that he and Starkey were the two Witnesses foretold in the Book of Revelation.

Although such a claim would have set most Engishmen rocking with laughter, the people of Charlynch swallowed the claim in its entirety.

Indeed they trembled in their seats when Prince thundered that he had "power over waters to turn them into blood and smite the earth with all plagues".

By now the Prince meetings had developed largely into frenzied revivalist gatherings with the "saved" suddenly jumping into the air or throwing themselves writhing to the floor.

Many ran right up to Brother Prince and, as an offering, emptied their pockets at his feet.

But this was only a start for the ritual caught on and soon wealthy disciples were pressing all kinds of valuable gifts on the prophet.

The Rev. Mr. Starkey gave Brother Prince a large gift of money, Mrs. Starkey came in with an annuity of £80, while Mr. Maber and his four sisters pooled their surplus capital and handed their divine master £10,000.

By 1849, Henry Prince was a wealthy man. And he could see even greater wealth in the offing.

To set this new money-making plan into motion, Prince and Starkey organised a massive appeal for funds to build their Agapemone or Abode of Love.

When the donations began rolling in, the pair bought 20 acres near the town of Bridgwater, surrounded it with high stone walls and in the centre built the luxuriously-appointed Abode of Love.

Finally the stables were erected and filled with blood horses and the gardens landscaped. Then the pair went hunting for people who would bring love (and money) to the abode.

The profitable new business got under way with the arrival of 60 disciples who, after handing over their worldly possessions to Prince and Starkey, settled in to enjoy the delights of the haven in which they would know neither grief, sickness nor death.

Within months of the establishment of the Abode of Love, strange stories concerning the goings-on inside were circulating all over England.

Most of these rumours suggested drunken orgies and sexual licence in the Agapemone. The wives of disciples, it was said, became communal property and were passed on from one member to another.

Substance was given to the stories concerning wife exchanging when Prince published a pamphlet quoting from the Scriptures in an attempt to justify the practice of free love.

Within seven years of the establishment of the Abode of Love, the excesses being practised behind the high stone walls so incensed the local citizens that a public meeting of protest was held at Bridgwater.

One speaker suggested the inhabitants of the Agapemone should be run out of the district while another said he had proof that in four years, at least 14 disciples had been so disgusted by what was going on in the Abode of Love that they had escaped over the walls.

Then in 1860 Prince and his Abode of Love again became front page news.

In that year Mr. Ralph Nottidge sued Prince in the Chancery Court for the return of £5,725 which his sister, Louisa, had given the clergyman as a gift.

Nottidge said he had first met Prince when he was a Church of England curate. He had been charmed by the young man but his sisters Louisa, Agnes, Clare and Harriet Nottidge had become almost insanely infatuated.

In 1845, Nottidge told the court, Louisa, who was then 41, had taken a house near the Abode of Love. But fearing for her sanity, he had persuaded her to return home.

Soon after, his sister was examined by a panel of doctors who came to the conclusion the woman really believed Prince was divine. Louisa was also convinced, the doctors decided, that Prince could make her immortal.

On the doctors' recommendation, Louisa was sent to a mental home and kept there until, with her physical health deteriorating, it was thought best to return her to her family.

According to Nottidge's story to the court, on the day Louisa was released from the mental home she was met by Brother Thompson from the Abode of Love and escorted to London.

There she signed over £5,725 to Prince and moved permanently into the Agapemone.

Continuing his extraordinary evidence, Nottidge said that at the dedication of a chapel some years earlier, Prince had asked two of his other sisters, Agnes and Harriet, to give glory to God by marrying two of the brothers in the Abode of Love. The women agreed.

Although Prince warned the women the marriages must be spiritual and no children (who would be heirs to their mothers' estates) must be born, Agnes forgot the terms of the marriage promise.

Thus immediately she became pregnant, Prince, realising the child would

be entitled to her estate, expelled her from the Abode of Love. Nevertheless the prophet still managed to relieve Agnes, Harriet and Clare, who married a Brother Cobbe, of £18,000.

At the end of the Chancery hearing, the court brought down a verdict ordering Prince to refund £5,725 to the estate of Louisa Nottidge who had since died in the Agapemone.

After paying over this sum, as well as court costs which were considerable, Henry Prince retired into the Abode of Love and spent the last 29 years of his life there.

In 1874 a wealthy London merchant signed over a huge fortune to Prince,

Bridgewater, Somerset, where citizens organised a meeting to protest against the existence of the scandalous Abode of Love.

then moved into the Abode of Love where he served the prophet as butler.

The butler's money infused the cult with new life. And when members of another bizarre religious group joined the Agapemonites, it became possible to set up branches in other parts of England including London. A mission was even sent to Norway.

In London an eccentric Church of England clergyman, the Rev. T. H. Smyth-Piggott, opened a £6,000 chapel called The Ark of the Covenant on behalf of the cultists.

After that, little was heard of the sect until, following old Henry Prince's death in the Abode of Love, Smyth-Piggott announced he was not only Prince's successor but was the new Messiah.

Smyth-Piggott tolerated months of standing on public platforms and being pelted with rotten fruit and eggs before retiring to a house in Upper Clapton with a harem of female disciples.

Later, when it seemed the public would storm Smyth-Piggott's private Abode of Love in Upper Clapton, he moved into the old Agapemone where, despite advancing age, he still managed to build a reputation for immorality.

In 1908 the Bishop of Bath and Wells took action against Smyth-Piggott under the Clergy Discipline Act and won a judgment stopping him from preaching outside the walls of the Abode of Love.

The Prime Minister, Herbert Henry Asquith, then took a personal interest in the matter.

As a result a police guard was placed outside the Agapemone, thus making Smyth-Piggott a virtual prisoner.

As passing time reduced the sinning potential of the intimates of the Abode of Love, it became known simply as a retreat for strange but harmless old men.

It was the end of a weird, and out-of-character, period of English history.

Fidelity's Fortune

OLD Thomas Coutts, banker to King George III, was distinctly out of place among the usual batch of stage-door-johnnies when he shuffled around to the rear of the Cheltenham theatre and asked the doorkeeper to take him to Miss Harriot Mellon's dressing room.

Recognising the famous banker, despite the ragged clothes he wore as a deterrent to beggars, the doorkeeper at once led the stooped and wrinkled millionarie up to the room occupied by the show's star.

Harriot Mellon, although almost half a century younger than her new admirer, was delighted by the call. Indeed she was so delighted that a week later she consented to become the old man's mistress.

And that was how Harriot Mellon, she of the "tall, fine figure, raven locks, ivory teeth, peach-like cheeks and coral lips", began the notorious career that was to make her one of England's richest women.

Old Thomas Coutts's death 17 years after that first meeting netted Harriot $4 million. And that did not take into account the $500,000 she had salted away from her pocket money allowance.

That mighty fortune allowed the one-time actress to buy something she had always wanted—a young husband.

The husband she selected was the Duke of St Albans, an impoverished nobleman almost young enough to be her grandson. It was an amazing switch for an amazing woman.

The story of the wanton who rose from poverty to fabulous wealth began in London on 11 November 1777, when she was born illegitimately to Sarah, an Irish shopgirl, and Matthew Mellon, an officer in the Madras Infantry.

Harriot was born when Mellon died while on his way to India to rejoin his regiment. Left without support, Sarah joined a company of strolling players and with her baby travelled throughout England and Scotland.

Sarah was 22 when she married the 18-year-old Thomas Entwisle, a musician in the company.

Why Entwisle ever married the strong-willed Irishwoman remains a mystery for he was so cowed by his wife that he even allowed her to beat

Harriot Mellon, mistress and second wife of banker Thomas Coutts.

him with a stick when she was displeased.

In 1794 the 17-year-old Harriot, something of an actress herself, performed a minor role in a play that was watched by the famous playwright and manager of Drury Lane Theatre, Richard Brinsley Sheridan.

Sheridan praised the pretty actress's performance and regretted it almost immediately for after that Sarah pestered him constantly to give her daughter a chance at Drury Lane.

Although Harriot in time achieved success at the famous theatre she never really rivalled her great contemporaries like Mrs Sarah Siddons, Mrs Dora Jordan or Elizabeth Farren.

In 1805 Harriot Mellon was chosen to star in a production at Cheltenham. Among the audience on the opening night was the decrepit old banker and Lord Provost of Edinburgh, Thomas Coutts.

An eccentric who walked abroad dressed in rags so that beggars might not pester him, Coutts completely forgot about his marriage vows when he first set his eyes on the lovely star of the show.

Immediately the last curtain had fallen Coutts made his way back stage and was soon introducing himself gallantly to the girl who was almost 50 years younger than himself.

After that Thomas Coutts, founder of the great banking house of Coutts and Co and father of three titled daughters, set to work making a complete fool of himself.

In time all London knew that old Coutts had settled the enormous sum of $800 a year on his protege. It also knew that he had provided her with an establishment and paid for every piece of jewellery and stitch of expensive clothing she wore.

Coutts's daughters, Lady Burdett, the Countess of Guildford, and the Marchioness of Bute, came to accept their father's favourite and even called for him at Harriot's establishment in little Russell Street after his regular visits.

The chief reason for this solicitude by Coutts's daughters was that they did not want to anger him by an open display of displeasure that might endanger their inheritances.

Perhaps their attitutes would have been different had they known that already the old millionaire had promised to marry his mistress immediately his wife died.

Apart from the Russell Street establishment Harriot Mellon was set up in a Highgate mansion. Both were luxuriously furnished by the love-lorn ageing banker.

With her pocket money Harriot also bought her mother and step-father a fine house at Cheltenham and provided them with an income that kept both in luxury.

To make sure her daughter's beneficences continued Sarah Entwisle spent much of her time in London instructing her daughter in the best methods of holding old Coutts's affection.

When Harriot waited on the old man like a servant it was done at her mother's insistence. Mrs Entwisle even made her daughter patch his clothes and darn his socks.

With mature logic Sarah Entwisle constantly pointed out to her daughter that her ancient benefactor was at a stage of life when comfort was more important than passion.

Nevertheless, Sarah added, Harriot could remain sympathetic only if her own desire for affection was satisfied. Therefore, the older woman advised, she should establish secret liaisons with younger lovers.

Harriot followed her mother's advice in general but forgot to remain discreet.

Thus one day a story reached Sarah that her daughter was showing an interest in a handsome young Belgian Army officer, Colonel Raguet. This interest, Mrs Entwisle was told, was certainly not platonic.

Ablaze with anger Sarah called for her carriage and sped through the night to her daughter's mansion in time to catch Harriot having breakfast with the colonel.

In the face of Mrs Entwisle's rage the colonel grabbed his belongings and fled the house.

Turning now to her daughter Sarah shouted: "I'll kill him. His very name proves he's nothing but a beggar. Mr Raggy indeed! He's just a

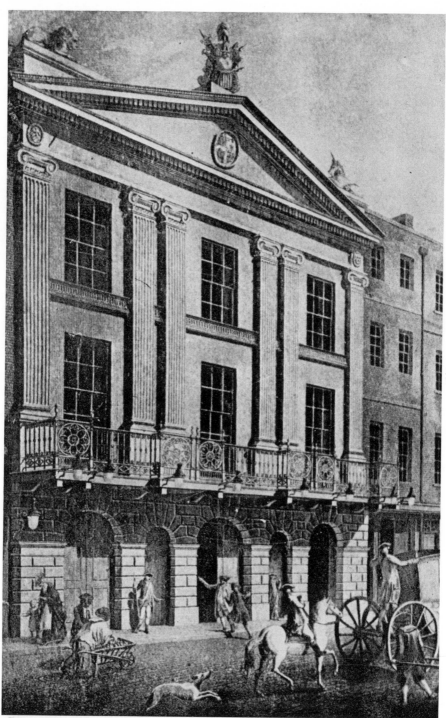

Drury Lane Theatre where Harriot Mellon achieved some success although she never rivalled her great contemporaries like Sarah Siddons and Dorothy Jordan.

Harriot Mellon, from a picture by Romney.

deceiving, fortune-hunting foreigner.

"If you don't get rid of him I'll be the death of both of you."

Fortunately details of the affair did not leak out until some time after Thomas Coutts's death in 1822.

As Harriot's show of affluence became increasingly scandalous, Coutts found himself the butt of biting jokes in his own circles. He denied having anything more than a passing interest in the beautiful Harriot Mellon but none believed him.

Finally, in an attempt to prove he was not responsible for her wealth, he arranged for Harriot to win $20,000 in a non-existent lottery.

To give weight to the story Harriot paid a down-and-out actor a small sum to announce that he had personally sold her the winning ticket.

From the actor's point of view it was a successful ruse, for he spent the next few years blackmailing the old banker's mistress.

Nevertheless the lottery story had no effect on the gossip. Indeed it was not long after this episode that the cartoonist, George Cruikshank, lampooned the couple by showing them holding hands under a canopy.

From the old man's pockets peeped sheaves of drafts on Coutts's bank drawn in favor of "Mellon."

On 4 January 1815, Thomas Coutts's wife, who had been insane for some years, died. Old Coutts, then 80, shed a tear at the funeral and a fortnight later, marched off to St Pancras church where he married the 38-year-old Harriot Mellon.

A week later Coutts's daughter, the Countess of Guildford, reluctantly moved out of her father's great mansion in Stratton Street leaving Mrs Coutts to move in as the new mistress.

The result of this was that Coutts's daughters refused to accept the new Mrs Coutts as their stepmother, which was understandable as all were older than the intruder.

Thomas Coutts reacted to this insult to his wife by removing his daughters' names from his will and nominating Harriot as his sole heir.

In time the banker had his wife presented at court and gave her unlimited money to entertain in a manner that had all London gasping.

The Coutts's guests ranged from the four royal brothers, the Dukes of York, Clarence, Kent and Sussex, to the sisters of Entwisle who were all grossly fat and smoked clay pipes.

On 2 March 1822, Thomas Coutts died after seven years of married bliss. Harriot was now one of, if not the, richest woman in England with assets valued at more than $4 million.

One of her first tasks as a widow was to arrange for regular payments to be made to Coutts's three daughters. At the time of Harriot's death the daughters had received nearly $1-million from her.

Living alone in almost regal splendor Harriot began dabbling in the occult. She developed wild superstitions, studied witchcraft and the supernatural and paid enormous sums to charlatans to interpret her dreams.

She became so frightened of ghosts that two maids were detailed to keep watch by her bed each night to scare them off.

Harriot was 50 when the youthful and impecunious Duke of St Albans began showing an unseemly interest in the woman who was old enough to be his mother or even grandmother.

Apparently intrigued by the thought of having a young husband for a change, Harriot led him off to the altar on 16 June 1827. For a wedding gift the Duke gave his wife a kiss. She gave him $60,000.

But if Harriot spent the money left her by Coutts lavishly she never forgot the memory of her benefactor.

And to prove this devotion she drove off once a week to Coutts's Bank (of which she was the chief shareholder) and, as the staff looked on, kissed the desk her husband once used.

Harriot died in 1837 leaving an annuity of $20,000 to the Duke. The rest of her estate (more than $2-million) went to Lady Sophia Burdett, one of Thomas Coutts's granddaughters.

It was a last gesture of defiance to the three noblewomen who had refused to call her "mother".

Love and Business with Charles II

ENGLAND had seen few house parties quite like that staged one evening in 1671 by the Countess of Arlington at her Euston family seat.

Although the guest of honor was England's licentious monarch, Charles II, most attention was directed to the beautiful 22-year-old Frenchwoman, Louise de Keroualle.

All England knew that the chief purpose of that evening's entertainment was to arrange the seduction of Louise by Charles whose previous advances had been repulsed by the strong-willed young woman.

The plan of seduction got under way when the Countess of Arlington announced that a mock wedding had been arranged to amuse the guests. The King himself, she said, had agreed to play the part of the groom. All present would be pleased if Mlle. de Keroualle would act the role of his bride.

The "wedding" concluded with Charles retiring to a bed chamber and the protesting Louise being pushed in after him by her hostess.

But the union that evening did more than give Louise a son by England's king and skyrocket her to a position of great affluence as chief of Charles's well-stocked harem.

It also allowed King Louis XIV of France to win England's support in a war that loomed against Holland.

Despite his scandalous dissipation and extravagance, the people of England forgave Charles most of his peccadilloes.

But one fault they could not swallow—the monarch's passion for Louise de Keroualle, cunning, cold and rapacious despite the doll-like beauty that mesmerised England's king.

Created Duchess of Portsmouth by the bewitched Charles, Louise, the paid agent of King Louis of France, later saw her illegitimate son raised to the peerage as Duke of Richmond.

Charles first met Louise de Keroualle, the 21-year-old daughter of an impoverished Breton noble, when she was maid-of-honour to his sister, the Duchess of Orleans, sister-in-law to the French king.

The encounter took place when the Duchess travelled to London with her suite hoping to arrange a treaty between her brother and her brother-in-law.

At that time war was looming in Europe and Louise sought the help (or at least the friendly neutrality) of England should Louis be involved in a war with Holland.

After listening to the case presented by his sister, Charles finally signed the Treaty of Dover.

But it was not friendship towards France that won Charles's support. Rather was it the three-million francs a year bribe the treaty offered for English participation in the war against Holland.

If Charles made no direct overtures to his sister's beautiful maid-of-honour, he saw to it that Louise left laden with gifts of jewellery when the party returned to Paris.

Among those who noted the effect Louise had on Charles was the French Ambassador, M. Colbert. He made a note that she might be useful later.

Soon after the Duchess of Orleans returned home with the Treaty of Dover, she fell ill and died suddenly. It was rumored she had been poisoned by her husband.

When this story reached Charles he flew into a rage and accused the French of being a race of murderers. He wanted to declare war on France. Even the three-million francs no longer interested him.

Stricken with fear, King Louis sent instructions to M. Colbert that Charles must be calmed and persuaded to stand by the treaty.

Now Colbert remembered the Duchess of Orlean's beautiful maid-of-honour. If she could demonstrate the lovable nature of the French to Charles, the English king might still stand by the treaty.

Immediately Colbert put the proposition to King Louis, the French monarch issued instructions that the young Breton be brought before him.

Louise promptly agreed to the King's plan, chiefly because the death of her mistress had left her penniless. Now she would receive an assured income from the French king. There was also the possibility of rich pickings at the English court.

At that time Paris was being visited by the Duke of Buckingham who harboured a burning hatred for his cousin, Lady Castlemaine, then Charles's favourite mistress.

When asked if he would present Louise at the English court, Buckingham readily agreed mainly because his great ambition was to see his cousin supplanted in his king's affections.

Soon after Buckingham had agreed to aid the plan, he left Paris with Louise for Dieppe. There the English nobleman decided to go on a fishing trip.

He installed Louise in an inn, told her he would send the royal yacht for her when he reached home, then set off on the fishing jaunt.

Ten days later M. Colbert was frantic. Louise de Keroualle seemed to have disappeared.

284

Louise de Keroualle failed in her attempts to wean Charles II from one of his favorite mistresses, Nell Gwynne.

Then Buckingham remembered: "Dammit!" he cried, "I knew I'd forgotten something."

At once the royal yacht put to sea and the fuming Louise was picked up.

Charles had no illusions about the reason the beautiful Louise had been sent to his court. Indeed all England knew she came as King Louis's agent to mend the rift between the two countries.

Now that the grief of his sister's death had passed, Charles's thoughts again turned to the annual three-million francs. And he decided to mend the breach immediately he could do so without loss of prestige.

Meanwhile if the lovely Louise wanted to offer herself as a bonus he had no intentions of rejecting the attractive gift.

Then Charles received a shock. His early advances were resisted by the desirable young Frenchwoman. Yet her coyness did not dampen his ardour. It simply whetted it.

But if England's king found the delay irritating, M. Colbert, harassed by demands for action from King Louis, was on the verge of a nervous collapse.

In desperation, Colbert approached the Countess of Arlington and persuaded her to invite Charles and Louise to a house party at her Euston family seat.

Confident the atmosphere at the party would bring Louise's defences

crashing down, Colbert wrote to King Louis: "I expect her to do her duty at last. I have impressed on her what is at stake."

To assist in Louise's seduction, Colbert arranged with the Countess to stage a mock wedding. Charles agreed to act as groom. Louise was cajoled into taking the bride's role.

At that time it was the custom to stage ribald celebrations at genuine weddings. These celebrations culminated in the retirement of the couple to the nuptial bed chamber.

Following the mock wedding that evening the celebrations followed the usual, almost lascivious, course. But when the time came for the couple to retire to the bed chamber, Louise resisted and shouted her protests.

So the Countess propelled her through the door in Charles's wake.

Charles II toasts the Duke of Buckingham. The women include the Duchesses of Portsmouth & Cleveland.

In March 1672, with Louise preparing to bear Charles's son, England declared war on Holland in support of France and Charles received the first instalment of his three-million francs.

Louise also received recognition from the grateful King Louis with the gift of an estate at Aubigny and the title of duchess.

And soon Lady Castlemaine had been supplanted as the King's favorite mistress by Louise de Kerouaille.

With Queen Catherine desperately ill, Louise even began dreaming that one day she might be Queen of England.

Then when Catherine showed signs of recovery, Charles soothed his mistress's grief by creating her Duchess of Portsmouth with an annual allowance of £10,000. Her son was later given the title of Duke of Richmond.

But if Louise had removed Lady Castlemaine from Charles's affections she was not so successful when she tried to tear her lover away from the actress Nell Gwynne.

Nell enjoyed the battles with Louise and delighted in intercepting Charles on his way to visit Louise and taking him to her own apartment.

In January 1676 the citizens of England, who held Louise in contempt, rejoiced at the news that the Frenchwoman might be discarded.

The reason for this hope was the arrival in England of the beautiful Italian Hortense Mancini, Duchess of Mazarin.

True to form Charles was captivated by the new arrival and set Hortense up in a Chelsea mansion. A year later he tired of the Italian and returned to Louise.

The chief reason for Louise's unpopularity was her monumental avarice.

Her allowance was officially £10,000 a year but this was not enough for her and she was always taking huge sums from other funds.

In 1677 alone her total income was £27,300 while in 1681 it was estimated she had accumulated capital of more than £136,000.

Louise de Keroualle saw the end of her days of glory one February morning in 1685 when word was brought to her that Charles was dying. Realising her very life would be in danger without the King's protection she began packing.

Then immediately she heard that Charles had died she dashed for a waiting coach and set out for the coast to board a ship for France.

Louise's carriage was almost at Dover when a squad of cavalry overtook it. Wasting no time an officer rifled Louise's luggage and took from it several pieces of the crown jewels.

Brought back to London, Louise protested that the gems had been given to her by Charles.

Nevertheless, not wishing to incur the enmity of Louis XIV, Charles's successor, his brother James, took no action against the notorious Frenchwoman.

In August 1685, Louise returned to France with most of the capital she had accrued during her reign as chief mistress of the King of England.

She retired to her estate at Aubigny and lived there quietly until her death in 1734. She was 85.

Pea Green's Jealousy

I N May, 1814 Miss Maria Foote made her first stage appearance at London's Covent Garden. It was a triumph with the audience standing to its feet at the performance's end and cheering the lovely 17-year-old until the theatre shook.

Next day one enraptured critic described her as "a pure and innocent beauty, the most delicate hand-maiden of our comedy, the loveliest of sufferers in our tragedies".

Having thus won overnight fame the beautiful Maria went on a titled-husband safari with no holds barred. One lover followed another as she sought the man of her dreams.

The result was that 10 years later the "pure and innocent beauty" had become the subject of foul pamphlets that besmirched her moral character and accused her of all kinds of sordid relationships.

Most of the accusations were true and for that reason her reputation remained in tatters for years to come.

Yet this notoriety did not stop her achieving her childhood ambition—the acquisition of a noble husband; and when she died at the age of 70 her contemporaries remembered the Countess of Harrington only as a woman of charming graciousness and dignity.

Maria Foote, the actress in search of a title, was born at Plymouth on 24 July 1797, the daughter of a spendthrift who had been an army officer but was then manager of a travelling theatre.

At 13 the child possessed such precocious beauty and charm that at the end of each stage performance under her father's management she stayed in her dressing room until Captain Foote had chased the stage-door-johnnies from outside the theatre.

By 1814 the girl had gravitated to London consumed by the desire to first make her mark in the theatre, then use her fame and other obvious assets to catch a nobleman in marriage.

A year after her triumph at Covent Garden and when her name was on the lips of every London theatregoer she travelled to Cheltenham where she met Colonel William Berkeley, central figure in a long and sensational lawsuit.

When Maria learned that the colonel would probably inherit the earldom of his dead father despite a claim by his younger brother Thomas that he was illegitimate, the young actress at once smelt a title.

Maria Foote went into the affair enthusiastically and within days of her first meeting with Colonel Berkeley they had become lovers. Now all she had to do was await settlement of the title dispute and lead Berkeley to the altar.

But it didn't turn out that way, for although the case had been going on for several years when Maria and Berkeley became lovers, it was destined to continue on for many more years before the ageing colonel abandoned his claim.

Meanwhile, passionately in love with the fascinating actress, Berkeley organised a benefit performance for her in Cheltenham and insisted on playing one of the leading roles himself.

After that Berkeley installed Maria in a villa on the Thames at Richmond and spent his time between the arms of his youthful lover and the London lawyers who were looking after his title claim interests.

Maria bore the colonel two children. She continually broached the matter of marriage but seemed to accept his excuse that a wedding was out of the question until the earldom was his.

By 1821 when Maria Foote was 24 it was obvious to her that she would never be the Countess of Berkeley. Already the House of Lords had decreed that William had been born illegitimately and had awarded the title to Thomas.

But Thomas regarded the finding as a slight on his mother's honor and had refused the title. So the case had gone back to the Lords for more years of wrangling.

The loss of the title was only one reason why Maria decided to abandon Berkeley. Another was that the colonel was spending less time with his lawyers in London and more with the courtesans of the theatre.

The end came finally when the pair fought bitterly over the colonel's faithfulness and Maria's almost irrational desire for social prestige.

In mid-1821 the dazzling Maria Foote returned to the London stage where packed houses at Covent Garden and Drury Lane received her with thunderous applause.

She was back in her element with a constant round of social activities and the ever present queues of young blades begging for the honor of escorting her to yet another wild function.

But as far as Maria was concerned it was always the same; the blue-blooded admirers had no money while the wealthy had no titles.

After a season in London she toured Edinburgh and Dublin giving her favors in return for gifts of jewellery and money. But none seemed willing to pay their debt by conferring a title on the lovely actress through marriage.

It was about this time that Maria Foote fell head over heels in love with the notorious lecher Joseph Haynes, who was known as Pea Green from the

The young Queen Victoria changed Britain's moral atmosphere almost overnight. One result was that Maria Foote, now the Countess of Harrington, was barred from court.

vivid color of his splendid coat.

Apart from being a rake, Haynes was London's leader of fashion, an amateur poet and a man of great personal attraction. And if he had no title at least he had a personal income of about $200,000 a year.

In quick time Haynes had installed Maria Foote as his mistress and was boasting that he was "lord of the angel of the British stage".

By now Maria had decided to forego a title in exchange for a husband with $200,000 a year. But when she put the proposal she got the shock of her life. Haynes was not interested.

Apart from that he point blank refused to allow Maria's two children by Colonel Berkeley to visit them at his ancestral estate in Wiltshire.

Realising Haynes was treating her as little more than a common harlot, Maria flew into a rage and issued a writ for $20,000 against her former lover for breach of promise.

But Haynes was far from beaten. Calling all his male friends to his aid Pea Green contacted pamphleteers and had them prepare booklets which his friends would distribute in London.

The little publications shocked even the city which was accustomed to such literary outrages, for in them the writers accused the famous actress of all kinds of unsavory indiscretions.

Meantime, Maria Foote had not been inactive for she too had rallied her friends who also began distributing pamphlets listing many of Pea Green's moral failings. Most were hair-raising.

Now the battle intensified when the warring parties hired choirs of ballad singers to chant the indecent allegations outside the stage door where Maria was appearing and at the entrance to the West End club where Haynes was

The old Drury Lane theatre where the cronies of Miss Foote's former lover, Pea Green Haynes, jeered her from the beginning to the end of the performance.

tippling.

It was no wonder then that when the breach of promise suit came to court, half of London (split into partisan groups) surrounded Westminster Hall cheering or jeering according to their inclinations.

At one stage the Lord Chief Justice was on the point of sending for a company of Dragoons when Bow Street officials charged into the brawling mob with batons and drove it off the streets.

After a two-day hearing Maria was awarded $6,000. But it did her little good for Haynes was a bitter man dedicated to vengeance.

During her first re-appearance at Drury Lane, Haynes's supporters who filled the pit and boxes spent the entire performance hissing and booing her. After that fiasco Maria travelled to Bath to escape her former lover's hatred.

Her premiere performance in that city was on the night of 14 January 1826, and was to develop into the most terrifying experience of her theatrical life.

293

From the beginning to the end of the first act not a word could be heard from the stage as the Haynes group booed, shouted obscenities, stamped their feet and waved canes and hats in the air.

Finally the lovely Maria Foote broke down. She burst into tears and fled the stage leaving Pea Green to march in triumph from his box to his waiting carriage.

Nevertheless Maria still had her supporters who admired her courage if not her morals and accepted her as the most gifted Shakespearean actress in Britain.

Apart from that she had an exceptionally fine singing voice, was a talented dancer and played the piano, harp and guitar with professional skill. When she first appeared in Paris she became the city's idol overnight.

From 1826 to 1830 Maria Foote travelled the enormous distance of 25,000 miles through Britain performing before admiring audiences. Suitors still begged for her favours but there remained a scarcity of titled lovers.

In 1830 Maria was 33 but perhaps more beautiful than ever. It was then that Charles Stanhope, Earl of Harrington, chanced to attend one of the notorious Miss Foote's Nottingham performances.

One look at the ravishing creature on the stage and the earl was hopelessly in love. For six months he followed her from one British town to another as she continued her tour.

Maria was in Birmingham when at last she won the earl's promise to marry her. Only then did she become his mistress. On 11 March 1831, she made her farewell stage appearance.

Just three weeks later, Maria Foote achieved her lifelong ambition. She became, as the Countess of Harrington, a member of the British nobility.

Nor was the countess unduly concerned when she discovered her husband was a man of strange eccentricities. For instance, in memory of Mary Browne, the mistress he had discarded to marry Maria, he insisted all his servants should wear brown livery.

Even his coaches and the horses' harnesses were varnished brown, while the coachmen's top hats were glazed with the same colour.

Then in 1837 Queen Victoria ascended the throne. The gay, abandoned Regency era was over. Dissoluteness was no longer the mark of good breeding. For people with a past like the Countess of Harrington, the royal court was closed.

Almost overnight Maria found herself an outcast condemned to the isolation of her husband's estate while the rest of the nobility strutted like dignified peacocks before the Queen.

Inwardly the Earl of Harrington seethed at this treatment of his countess. And it was obvious to Victoria that the nobleman resented her sanctimonious attitude.

And he got the opportunity to express his feelings when the Queen once told him that she would like to visit his ancestral castle of Elvaston.

Harrington did not mince words. He said the castle was closed to the public but if the Queen wished to put her request as a command he would have no alternative but to obey.

Victoria had to accept the snub and she never did visit Elvaston.

The Earl of Harrington died in 1851 leaving his wife to survive him for 16 years.

She died on 27 December 1867, a still-lovely, and gracious old lady. Only a few of her contemporaries remembered her scandalous past. And those who could not remember revered her.

Anne Oldfield

DRURY Lane Theatre was in uproar one winter's night in 1711. Two periwigged and belaced young gallants, their faces flushed with wine and jealousy had suddenly leapt from their boxes on to the stage. Swords flashed in the candle glow of the footlights. The terrified actors huddled in the wings, while the audience rose to their feet and lustily cheered on the combatants. They fought till one gorgeous youth fell with the blood soaking his flowered silk waistcoat. Desperately hurt he was carried to the "green-room" to die in the arms of Anne Oldfield, the beautiful actress for whose favors the mortal duel had been fought.

The Drury Lane fracas was only one incident in the stormy life of Anne Oldfield, the dazzling toast of the theatre in the days of Queen Anne and the first two Georges.

Her lovers were many, including the brother of the great Duke of Marlborough. But said one contemporary critic, "she was so lovely that even her amours seemed to lose that glare that surrounds other frail members of her sex."

For 25 years Anne Oldfield was unchallenged queen of the London stage, in an age when the theatre reached a peak of wit, fashion and licentiousness such as it has never known since.

And, despite the scandals of her career, she was the first actress in history to be buried with monarchs within the hallowed stones of Westminster Abbey. Three peers were among the pallbearers who carried her coffin.

Anne Oldfield was born in London in 1683. Her grandfather was a wine merchant, her father a disgraced army captain who had gambled away a fortune before he put a bullet in his head.

As a child, Anne was put to work as a seamstress. In her teens, she was taken to live with an aunt who presided over the Mitre Tavern in the fashionable district of St. James.

Anne early developed a passion for the theatre. Between pouring wine she devoured play books, and soon could recite by heart long passages from the famous Elizabethan and Jacobean dramas.

The Mitre was a favorite haunt of aspiring dramatists. Among them were a penniless young Irishman, George Farquhar, and handsome John Vanbrugh, whose Provok'd Wife had just taken the town by storm.

One day Farquhar and Vanbrugh overheard Anne reciting as she scoured an empty wine cask. Her voice, said Farquhar, "rang like a silver bell. She sounded like an angel among the bottles."

The two authors hurried off to relate their discovery to Rich, the manager of Drury Lane. Rich was sceptical, but as a favour to his most popular dramatist he agreed to give the girl a trial.

Thus in 1699, at the age of 16, Anne Oldfield found herself on the famous boards of Drury Lane. Her first appearances seemed to confirm Rich's prediction that her pay of 15 shillings a week was waste of money.

Anne had glowing beauty, but she was completely untrained, awkward and timid. The critics blasted her mercilessly. One said she was "rubbish that ought to be swept off the stage with the dust".

For four years Anne played minor roles in the comedies of Dryden, Steele, Congreve and Vanbrugh. Then, in 1703, came the chance that was to launch her on the road to fame.

The court was at Bath. One night Queen Anne attended the theatre with her lethargic husband, Prince George of Denmark, who, as usual, settled down to sleep comfortably throughout the performance.

At the last moment the leading actress, Mrs. Verbruggen, fell ill. When the curtain rose, the audience were disgusted to see that Anne Oldfield had stepped into the role opposite the celebrated Colley Cibber.

By the end of the first act, the wit and fashion of Bath were cheering, waving canes and handkerchiefs, and applauding deliriously.

The uproar even aroused Prince George, assisted by a smart blow on the head from the queen's fan. Next day, pump room and promenade rang with praises of the lovely Anne Oldfield.

In London, the triumph was repeated. Cibber rewrote his most famous play, The Careless Husband, to introduce a role for her. Rich raised her salary to 200 guineas.

Fame brought wealthy suitors. And Anne, unlike her older stage rival, the cold and prudish Nan Bracegirdle, was warm-blooded and generous with her favours.

Farquhar had been her first lover. Though he was dismissed, Anne remained a generous friend and often sent purses of guineas to the humble lodging where he hid in penury before his death.

By 1706, Anne was the acknowledged mistress of Arthur Mainwaring, the poet, man of fashion and vitriolic Whig pamphleteer, whose political cronies had given him sinecure jobs worth £5,000 a year.

Anne bore Mainwaring an illegitimate son and lived with him "more constant than a wife" till consumption and high living carried her lover to a premature grave.

Mainwaring bought his mistress a mansion in Grosvenor Street, where she lived in state, entertained peers and wits, and was carried to the theatre in a sedan chair with two footmen bearing torches.

Meanwhile storms were blowing up at Drury Lane. The niggardly Rich complained bitterly when Anne demanded a lavish wardrobe, including £10 worth of extra petticoats to wear in the cold winter months.

Rivalry between Anne and Nan Bracegirdle often had the house in uproar. Hired factions crowded the pit to jeer and shout down both actresses. Swords were drawn and blood spilt in the boxes.

The patrons demanded a "contest", with each woman playing the same role on alternate nights. But the ageing Bracegirdle, the "chaste virgin of the theatre", accepted defeat and retired in 1769.

Then the Drury Lane actors revolted against the avarice of Rich and drove him from control. Colley Cibber and Robert Wilks, the most celebrated comedian of the day, took over the management.

They offered Anne a partnership, but she refused. She was already by far the highest paid actress on the stage, and her annual benefit performance often brought in another £500.

Meanwhile Anne Oldfield's parade of lovers went on, though the most censorious critics admitted that she confined herself to unmarried men "whose attentions cost no deserted spouse a tear."

Gossip linked her name with Lord Hervey and many others. But it was the old soldier, General Charles Churchill, who enjoyed the longest reign over her favours.

Churchill was a younger brother of the great Duke of Marlborough, the conqueror of Blenheim, the favourite of Queen Anne, the arbiter of Europe and the most dazzling military captain of the age.

Churchill himself had fought gallantly at Blenheim, commanded the British army in Holland, and later entered Parliament from one of the most notorious of "rotten boroughs".

The general was over 50, but still a handsome and well-preserved figure, when he fell passionately in love with Anne Oldfield.

He bought a villa at Richmond, where they lived in peaceful domesticity by the Thames between her acting seasons, and where she bore him two sons who were later launched on political careers.

One son eventually married the daughter of the all-powerful Prime Minister, Sir Robert Walpole, and was provided with a safe Whig seat in Parliament for 30 years through the Walpole influence.

For years London society buzzed with the rumor that Anne and General Churchill were secretly married. Gossip penetrated the royal court, where Anne was often summoned to give play readings.

One evening Princess Caroline, wife of the future George II, left her whist table and took Anne into an alcove to question her. "They say, madam, that you are wed to General Churchill", the princess said coldly.

"They say so indeed," replied Anne demurely. "But the general keeps his own counsel, and so do I".

As long as Churchill lived, Anne remained faithful to him. But in 1714 he dropped dead of an apoplectic fit, leaving her half his estate—which turned out to be loaded with debts.

Gallants fought duels on the stage for the favours of Anne Oldfield.

Churchill was succeeded by other lovers. Her London mansion and Richmond villa were filled with their gifts of paintings, plate, porcelain and furniture.

Crowds of gallants waited outside the theatre each night to escort her chair through the streets with torches. Poems and songs were written in her honour, and ballads extolling her wit and beauty were hawked in thousands through the town.

Anne was kindly and generous by nature, and even jealous rival actresses found it impossible to quarrel with her.

When the partisans of Mrs. Rogers tried to hiss Anne off the stage, the whole cast refused to continue the performance till the rioters had been caned and thrown out of the theatre.

No actress had ever made so much money as Anne Oldfield. But she used it lavishly to rescue poor actors and authors from debts and starvation.

Her most notable beneficiary was the unhappy poet and hack writer Richard Savage, to whom she gave a pension of £50 a year.

Savage was the illegitimate son of Lady Macclesfield. To conceal the scandal of his birth, she had tried to ship him off to the West Indies and then apprenticed him to a slum shoemaker.

For years, though Savage lived in semi-starvation, Lady Macclesfield refused to recognise him. Only help from Anne Oldfield, Steele, and other fellow-writers kept him from death or debtors' prison.

Henry Benson: King of the Swindlers

ONE day in 1870 a fine carriage came to a halt before Mansion House, the residence of the Lord Mayor of London, Sir Thomas Dakin, and discharged a colorfully-dressed man bearing a gold chain round his neck.

Haughtily approaching a footman, the visitor said he was the Count of Montague and carried letters of introduction to the Lord Mayor from the President of France. He demanded he be shown to the Lord Mayor's private chambers.

A few minutes later the French nobleman stood before Dakin and, with tears in his eyes, told the harrowing tale of the ruin of his estates in the Franco-Prussian War and the misery of the citizens in the village of Chateaudun.

Pointing out that he was Mayor of Chateaudun, he said he had come to London in the hope of raising funds to relieve the straitened circumstances of his villagers.

A man of great charity, Dakin immediately made a gift of $2000 from the city and promised to launch a Mansion House fund for the sufferers.

Next day the embarrassed Lord Mayor of London discovered he had been duped by Henry Benson, a brilliant swindler who was destined to win himself a prominent role in the history of crime.

The details of Henry Benson's birth and early career are shrouded in mystery. But it is known that he was the son of a French merchant and an Englishwoman and that he grew up speaking several languages.

An excellent instrumentalist and singer, Benson moved to Paris in the late 1860s and soon won the esteem of select audiences with his pleasing personality and singing.

Finally, when he had accumulated a little capital, he decided to earn a living the easy way.

Dubbing himself Count of Montague and Mayor of Chateaudun, he found it amazingly easy to persuade banks to advance him substantial sums of money.

Using this money, as well as credit, he set himself up in a mansion in one of the city's fashionable quarters.

Soon he was entertaining on a scale Paris had rarely seen while he became one of the city's sights riding in his gilded carriage with a coat of arms emblazoned on the sides.

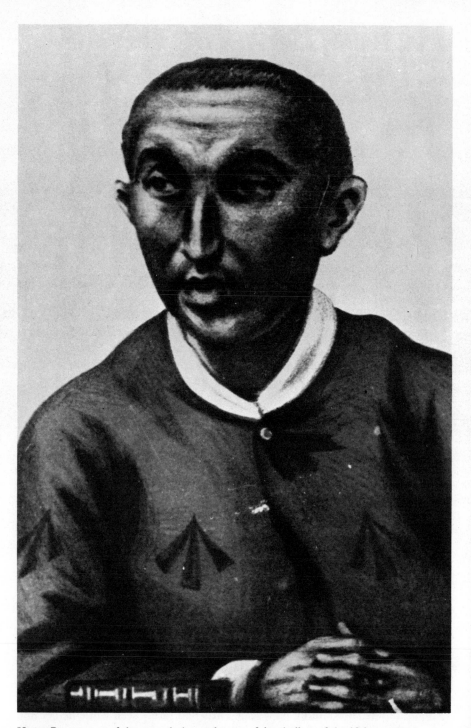

Henry Benson, one of the most daring and successful swindlers of the 19th century.

By 1871 the sands were beginning to run out. The banks were demanding settlement and threatening to impound his possessions.

To ease the situation Benson crossed to London with forged letters of introduction from the Prefect of the Seine and the President of France to London's Lord Mayor.

Immediately he received Sir Thomas Dakin's cheque for $2,000. Benson rode to a bank and cashed it. And while he was doing this Dakin was sending a telegram to Chateaudun asking about its travelling mayor.

When the reply came back it stated simply that no one in Chateaudun had heard of the Comte de Montague.

Scotland Yard was called in and it did not take long to pick up Benson. But the police were mistaken if they also hoped to get the money. The swindler had already buried it in a secret place.

It was ironical that when Benson was committed for trial to the Old Bailey early in 1872, Sir Thomas Dakin himself sat on the magistrates' bench·

The idea of public exposure and a possible long prison term preyed on Benson's mind as he lay in gaol. So one night he set fire to his straw mattress and flung himself in the flames.

By the time the warders succeeded in dragging him out of the cell the whole of the lower half of his body had been terribly burned.

As a result he had to be carried into the Old Bailey over the shoulder of a court attendant and was unable to stand when the judge read the verdict sentencing him to six months' gaol.

Too ill to work, he spent the six months in the prison hospital where his groans of torment horrified other inmates.

Benson was in a pitiful physical condition when he was released in 1873 but his brain was as sharp as ever.

After spending some time with relatives in a London suburb, he assumed the name of G. H. Yonge and advertised in several newspapers offering himself as secretary to a gentleman of leisure.

There was only one reply but it was to launch him on one of the 19th century's most spectacular criminal careers.

The answer came from a wealthy publisher, William Kerr, who, during the interview, was so impressed by Benson's theory on how he could increase his wealth, that he hired him on the spot.

Starting up several bogus investment companies with two other partners, Benson and Kerr fleeced hundreds of small investors.

Then they bribed a Scotland Yard detective named Meiklejohn to keep them informed of developments within the police force.

Several months after their new companies began operations, Benson and Kerr learned from Meiklejohn that the Yard had received complaints about one of their investment enterprises.

This was the Systematic Investment Corporation of Glasgow, which had already absorbed thousands of pounds worth of investors' money by offering high dividends.

Next day the proprietors closed the corporation's offices and, a few weeks later, opened the same company again under another name.

This procedure was to become standard practice whenever Meiklejohn—who was being paid in sums from $200 to $2000—told Benson and Kerr that the Yard was taking an interest in a certain company.

Then in 1875 Meiklejohn advised the two swindlers to ease up on their activities and retire temporarily from the scene.

Wasting no time, Benson moved to the Isle of Wight, bought a large house and hired seven servants.

He also saw to it that the nearby town of Shanklin heard of the wealthy cripple who was a friend of the Empress of Austria and a member of the noble Murat family.

And when he appealed for funds to aid those who were dying of starvation in Austria and France, the locals proved more than generous. Benson was able to use this money to finance his own luxurious way of life.

But this was street begging compared to Benson's money-making ambitions. He decided to return to the world of big business.

Believing Meiklejohn would now need assistance, Benson added two more Scotland Yard men to his pay roll. One was the celebrated Chief Inspector Nathaniel Druscovitch.

With the assistance of William Kerr, Benson published one issue of a racing paper, Sport, with 'a special French edition.'

Among the false advertisements and concocted sporting news items, was a story headed, The Unluckiest Man Alive.

The story told of a man named Montgomery who had hit on an infallible system for backing horses.

In fact the system was so good that he had already won more than $3 million with it.

The article continued: "Many of our readers will wonder why Mr. Montgomery is the unluckiest man alive. The answer is simple. Bookmakers, realising that Mr. Montgomery can always beat them, have refused to take his bets.

'He has, however, found a way of still making bets without the risk of their being refused. Many of his friends are doing the betting for him.

"They take no risks. They merely forward the winnings to Montgomery and receive 10 per cent comission.

'Mr. Montgomery now needs a large number of people to put money on for him.'

This one issue of Sport was sent to thousands of people in England and France. And with the paper went a letter, signed with the name Montgomery and saying the recipient's name had been favorably mentioned to him by the Franco-English Society of Publicity.

The letter then asked the recipient to place bets on Montgomery's behalf. In return 10 per cent commission on successful bets would be paid.

Within days thousands of letters had been received accepting Montgomery's terms.

Benson and Kerr knew how the bettors would react. When the spurious cheques purporting to come from Montgomery were sent to them to place on a horse, they also put their own money on with the bookmaker nominated by "Mr. Montgomery."

The bookmaker, of course, was employed by Benson and Kerr.

The smaller investors never heard from Montgomery again. But the others received their winnings and were led on to heavier investments until in the end they were fleeced of huge sums.

Within three months the criminals had amassed $160,000 and within the year they were getting close to the millionaire class. Then they made their first mistake.

One day a wealthy Frenchwoman, Marie de Goncourt, wrote to the Benson and Kerr bookmaker from Paris and asked him to place $20,000 on a horse in the Ayrshire Handicap which would be run the following week.

One of Henry Benson's last big jobs was posing as the advance booking agent of the famous singer Adelina Patti. He picked up $10,000 before being arrested.

When Benson heard of the huge bet he could not restrain his greed. He sent the woman a letter over the Montgomery signature suggesting she increase the bet to $60,000 as the horse was certain to win.

Her suspicion aroused by the letter, the woman showed it to her lawyer and asked his advice.

The lawyer immediately reported the matter to the Surete who in turn contacted Scotland Yard. And it was coincidental that the man appointed to investigate Sport and its owners was the Kent-Benson hireling, Chief Inspector Druscovitch.

At once Druscovitch warned his colleagues. When they fled, the inspector raided their premises and seized the remaining copies of the newspaper.

Not long after, Druscovitch's superior, Superintendent Williamson, heard the wanted men were hiding in Scotland. He sent Druscovitch to arrest them.

But before leaving for Scotland the detective saw to it that his friends were safely aboard a ship bound for Rotterdam.

Then in the Dutch city a mistake by a hotel owner brought them both to the end of the road.

When the Englishmen handed him a genuine Scottish banknote, the hotel owner, for some reason, thought it was counterfeit and called the police.

Immediately the officers saw Benson and Kerr they knew they fitted the descriptions of two wanted men cabled to them by Scotland Yard.

The Dutch police now advised Scotland Yard that they had the two wanted men. But all that happened was that Druscovitch sent a cable reading: "Two men you have in custody not those we want. Liberate them."

But the Dutch police did not obey Druscovitch's order. They insisted he come over and see the men. He has no alternative but to agree and then arrest the men who so obviously fitted the cabled descriptions.

When Benson was sentenced to 15 years' imprisonment and Kerr to 10, the prisoners shocked all England by revealing the parts played by the Scotland Yard detectives in their crimes.

Delighted at the stir they had caused, Benson and Kerr served their sentence quietly and after their release continued a life of crime in America.

In 1902 Kerr retired and Benson went to South America. There he posed as the advance agent of the singer Adelina Patti on her tour of Brazil, Argentina and several other countries.

After picking up $10,000 in advance bookings he fled to New York where he was arrested and sentenced to 20 years' gaol.

But he did not serve the full term. One day he ran from his guards and jumped to his death down a stair-well.

Dr. Graham's Mysterious Bed

ALMOST 200 years ago when a fertility pill was not even a scientist's dream, Dr. James Graham invented a device guaranteed to produce "beautiful rosy heirs." He called it the Celestial Bed.

It is not recorded if the Celestial Bed did anything for Britain's birth rate. But by earning tens of thousands of pounds it did a great deal for Dr. Graham. Yet the Celestial Bed was not the only money-spinning gadget dreamed up by Graham, that prince of swindlers and quacks.

His other contributions to the art of quackery included his Celestial Throne, his hot mud baths and his Elixir of Life. Although the elixir was guaranteed to extend the life span to at least 150 years, the fact that the doctor himself died when he was 49 disproved the claim.

But by then it was too late for his hundreds of rapidly-ageing clients to do anything about it.

One of Graham's claims to fame was that he put Emma Lyon, later Lady Hamilton and, mistress of Horatio Nelson, before the public for the first time.

Emma, then a pretty nursemaid was induced by Graham to share a hot mud bath with him while he explained to an audience the health benefits to be derived from this unorthodox toilet.

In later years the mud bath part of her career remained a perennial embarrassment to Britain's most notorious woman.

James Graham, the man who turned gullibility into cash, was born in Edinburgh in 1745, the son of a saddler. Despite his background he was given an excellent education and began a medical course at the famed Edinburgh University.

Although it is doubtful if he actually graduated, Graham left the university in 1772 and travelled to Philadelphia in America where he set himself up as an ear, nose and throat specialist.

It was while he was in America that Graham met Benjamin Franklin, then in the midst of experiments with electricity. From the great inventor and statesman, Graham learned the rudiments of the new science.

Soon after returning to England in 1774 and settling in London, Graham met the historian, Catherine Macaulay. It was the support of Catherine that put Graham on the road leading to affluence.

Miss Macaulay was probably the first Englishwoman to experience the tingling sensations of one of Graham's 'electric baths.' And she was certainly the first to be massaged with his Ethereal Balsamic Balm.

Delighted with the treatment, Catherine Macaulay told her friends. And they told their friends. Soon Dr. Graham had netted a small fortune.

Now Graham saw an unlimted future. He rented a mansion in Pall Mall opposite St. James' Palace and set gangs of builders and renovators to work behind barred doors.

In August 1775 London newspapers were filled with advertisements announcing the coming opening of Dr. James Graham's fabulous Temple of Health. Within the temple's portals all sicknesses would be cured. Even age would be conquered.

All these advertisements concentrated on the chamber called The Great Apollo Apartment.

The copy read: 'On entering this, words convey no adequate idea of the vast and awful sublimity which seizes the mind of every spectator'.

What the spectators actually saw when they entered the chamber were numerous papier-mache sphinxes, dragons, nude sculptures and garishly-decorated walls.

The centrepiece was the Celestial Throne, a heavily-decorated chair with wires connecting it to batteries. The throne, it was claimed, would cure anything from mental diseases to ingrown toe nails.

In other parts of the building were numerous bathrooms where clients could bathe in hot mud or milk. Slight electric charges in the baths "recalled youth and rekindled the divine fire of Venus."

When the temple was filled with clients, Graham would lecture them on a pot-pourri of health, religion and sex then sell them his balms, purges and pills at exorbitant rates.

Each lecture invariably ended with the sentence: 'Ladies and gentlemen may be electrified for a small charge of $40.'

The wealthy quack did not mix his famous Elixir of Life with his pills and purges. The sale of this concoction was the subject of a special lecture.

The elixir, Graham told his fascinated audience, was made from a mixture of rare and mysterious herbs from the East known only to the sultans and volupturies of Persia.

Anyone who wanted to prolong life to at least 150 years by taking a full course of the elixir, Graham said, must pay $2000 in advance so the ingredients could be purchased from the East.

Among the scores who paid for a full course were Lady Spenser, Lady Clermont and the Duchess of Devonshire. Even the Duchess de Polignac travelled from Paris in the hope she could retain her already well-preserved middle age.

But if James Graham was 90 per cent quack there still remained 10 per cent of the genuine medical practitioner in him.

Thus there were times when he was able to diagnose patients' complaints and put them on a strict diet. But, of course, they got the expensive electric treatment as well.

He told his clients that while his treatments could cure most ills it was up to them to retain their health. Thus they should drink port and smoke tobacco sparingly. Over indulgence of any of the senses, he said, was injurious to health.

But the time came when the Temple of Health began losing its novelty for the rich of London society. So the proprietor closed it up and travelled to France where he opened a quack practice on a smaller scale.

In 1778, with his mind filled with new ideas to fleece the gullible public, he returned to England.

Emma Lyon began her public career wallowing in a mud bath with Graham and ended it in the arms of Horatio Nelson.

One of the first things he did was to visit a Newcastle glass works and submit an order for a mysterious and complicated array of glass tubes. Not even the glass blowers could understand what they were making.

In 1779 Graham paid $24,000 for a great house on Royal Terrace, Adelphi. And there he opened the Temple of Health and Hymen under the patronage of the Goddess of Marriage.

A week after the new temple opened the foyer was half filled with walking sticks, crutches and even a few wheel chairs. Although they came from second hand shops Graham claimed they had been left by satisfied customers.

The temple's chief attraction was the Celestial Bed, a blazing mass of gilt with a huge golden sun surmounted by a statue of the Goddess of Health, Hygeia, at the head.

It stood on 28 glass legs and was covered with silk damask. Above it was a great canopy fringed with scarlet tassels.

The entire room was lined with mirrors so the occupants could view themselves from many different angles.

Scores of glass tubes from another room piped in soft music as well as "oriental" perfumes. "Celestial fire" came from a cylinder hidden in a cupboard.

Married couples who wished to use the bed so that they would produce "beautiful rosy heirs" were charged $200 a night. But—and here Graham used some applied psychology—they were warned that repeated use of the bed could shorten life.

Also Graham was not particular whether the couples who used the bed were actually married.

Indeed in one of his pamphlets he wrote: 'Neither I nor any of my people are entitled to ask who rests in this chamber which I have denominated the Holy of Holies'.

To make his point even more clear he added: 'Persons wearing masks admitted.'

For two years the Celestial Bed was booked out as were most of the other attractions. Then Graham added another novelty.

This was the pretty nurse-maid, Emma Lyon, a girl of obvious charms the doctor had seen walking in a park with one of her charges.

In the temple's advertisements Emma was described as 'Vestina, the Gigantic, the Stupendous Goddess of Health.'

Nightly Emma, clad in a flimsy dress that daringly revealed her pretty shoulders, was escorted by the Gentleman Usher of the Rosy Rod to the Celestial Throne.

There she endured a few slight electric shocks before wallowing in a hot mud bath with Graham.

As Emma romped in the chocolate-colored ooze, Graham discoursed on the subject of The Cause, Nature and Effect of Love and Beauty.

But if James Graham was making a fortune from London's gullible society, not everyone swallowed his hocus pocus. The famous dramatist George Colman was one who didn't.

James Graham and fleeing lady. The artist did not indicate if the famous quack's intentions were honorable.

Amused by Graham's quackery he wrote an uproarious farce, The Genius of Nonsense, that drew packed houses of the Haymarket Theatre.

In 1781 London was growing tired of Dr. Graham's expensive and unorthodox health treatments. His clientele diminished and he was forced to close the temple. A year later all his apparatus was seized to pay debts.

At the same time he sold his London residence and set out on a lecture tour of Britain. It went fairly well until he addressed an audience in his home town of Edinburgh.

Deciding that his strange mixture of medicine and religion was an attack on the Established Church, the Scots banned any further lectures.

Soon after Graham published a letter which he claimed had been written by Professor Hope of Edinburgh University. The letter backed Graham's medical theories.

At once the professor condemned the letter as a forgery and Graham was gaoled. He was released only when he promised to leave Scotland immediately.

After that he became a sort of mystic and vegetarian. He took to burying himself up to the neck in holes then existing for days on nothing more substantial than glasses of water.

In 1790 he caused a furore in Newcastle when he and a young girl stripped naked and buried themselves up to their necks 'for their health's sake.'

The stunt ended in a complete farce when an onlooker almost drowned the quack with a watering can. The man later explained that he was simply trying to make the doctor grow.

When Graham heard that King George III was suffering one of his regular mental fits, he somehow arranged an interview with the Prince of Wales.

Graham told the Prince that he, too, would be mentally afflicted unless he married a certain princess. Asked the princess's name, Graham said: "Evangelical Christianity."

But if anyone was suffering from a mental sickness it was James Graham. People laughed when he took to wearing sods of earth next to his skin and filling his boots with mud.

When he died in 1796, the inventor of the Elixir of Life was only 49.

The Financier Who Disappeared

DURING the evening of 16 February 1856, John Sadleir, a former Lord of the British Treasury and director of a string of affluent companies, sent his chambermaid to a nearby shop to buy a bottle of poison.

An hour or two later, after giving his servants three letters to post, he quietly left his Hyde Park home and disappeared into the night.

The following morning Joseph Bates, a donkey driver from Hampstead, was wandering over the local heath looking for one of his animals that had strayed from the stable.

Bates did not find his donkey, but he did discover the well-dressed corpse of a man lying in the rain-sodden soil with an empty bottle marked "poison" beside it.

Later John Sadleir's butler identified the corpse as that of his master and a coroner found the financier and politician had died by his own hand.

When the coroner's inquest began London business tycoons had some doubts about Sadleir's honesty. But they were not prepared for the shock discovery that during his meteoric business career he had embezzled more than £350,000.

London had scarcely recovered from this announcement when rumors spread that the body found on Hampstead Heath was not that of the wealthy Sadleir.

It was pointed out that the only person who had identified the body was his butler. It was also noted that while evidence indicated that Sadleir had walked to the heath, the corpse's shoes, despite the muddy conditions of the ground, were perfectly clean.

And there was one good reason why Sadleir should have faked his death.

Although he had robbed investors of hundreds of thousands of pounds he had lived simply and the money must be stashed away somewhere.

For years after, stories of John Sadleir living a quiet but comfortable life on the Continent filtered back to London. But they could not be substantiated.

John Sadleir was born in 1814 at Shrove Hill in the county of Tipperary, Ireland, the son of Clement William Sadleir whose occupation consisted of being an Irish gentleman.

After graduating in law, young Sadleir established a legal practice in Dublin. When the practice grew, he won a directorship with a local stock company

313

and frequently visited England where he encouraged financiers to invest in Irish enterprises.

Sadleir was still only 32 when, realising his business ambitions could never mature in Ireland, he sold his practice and established himself in London as agent for several Irish firms.

The Irishman made an amazing impact on the business world of London. Personable and brimming with aggressive efficiency he soon established himself as one of the city's most important financiers.

Indeed by 1847 he was so well established that he was elected to the House of Commons as Liberal member for Carlow in Southern Ireland.

With his reputation growing continually, Sadleir turned his attention to railway investment.

Unaccustomed to doing things by halves he quickly invested in the Royal Swedish, the East Kent, the Swiss, the Grand Junction and the Rome Line railways.

Nor did he neglect to make his mark in Parliament where his fluency and grasp of economic matters won him many admirers. In fact there were those who believed that one day he would be Britain's Chancellor of the Exchequer.

His next big venture into the field of finance was his foundation of the Joint Stock Bank in Tipperary which he put under the direction of his brother James.

In 1848 John Sadleir reached the summit of acceptance in London's financial circles. He was appointed chairman of the London and County Bank, one of Britain's great financial institutions.

Meanwhile in Parliament Sadleir, despite the unpopularity of the cause in England, was vigorously defending Roman Catholic interests against the onslaughts made against them.

And he retained his dedication even when the Prime Minister, Lord John Russell, introduced the Ecclesiastical Titles Bill which was aimed against the Catholic clergy in England.

Sadleir was one of those who, because of their vigorous opposition to the Bill, won the title of The Pope's Brass Band.

When Russell's Government fell in 1852, Sadleir was offered the post of Lord of the Treasury by the new Prime Minister, Lord Aberdeen, a notorious anti-Catholic.

By accepting the post Sadleir incurred the animosity of the Catholic clergy as well as political supporters at home. Now his parliamentary seat was threatened.

Realising he would scarcely win a vote in Carlow after aligning himself with the anti-Catholic Prime Minister, Sadleir acted quickly.

He nominated for the seat of Sligo—with a small Catholic population—and successfully contested this constituency when Parliament was dissolved in 1855.

Delighted by his loyalty the new Prime Minister, Lord Palmerston, saw to it that he was given back his old portfolio in his Government.

John Sadleir was now at the peak of his amazing career. There was even talk of a knighthood. Then slowly the facade of financial and political solidity he had built about his name began crumbling.

It began when rumors seeped through the Stock Exchange suggesting the business methods of the tycoon, John Sadleir, were not entirely orthodox. There were even stories that his dishonesty had tainted the Treasury.

Lord Palmerston, the Prime Minister who forced Sadleir to resign his position as Lord of the Treasury because of dark rumors about his private financial dealings.

Taking no chances, the Prime Minister called his Lord of the Treasury before him and suggested he should resign immediately. Sadleir took the advice.

After that the thousands of shareholders in Sadleir's string of companies began feeling uneasy. Nor was the staid board of the London and County Bank happy about their chairman's rapidly-dwindling reputation.

Sadleir was called before the bank's board and asked to resign. He had to comply.

And there was good reason for all this fear for at the time the rumors began circulating, Sadleir had already cheated the investors in his various businesses of hundreds of thousands of pounds.

For years he had been issuing spurious shares, forging title deeds to estates and property and circulating utterly worthless securities.

When draft from the Joint Stock Bank in Tipperary were dishonered Sadlier knew his empire would crash about his ears unless he could quickly raise the money to meet the drafts.

The first man he thought of to solve the dilemma was the head of a firm of solicitors and an old acquaintance, Josiah Wilkinson.

Already Sadleir had been advanced huge sums by the firm. In the past Wilkinson had seemed happy to have the opportunity of making loans.

But before approaching Wilkinson, Sadleir decided to see if he could raise the necessary money from other finance houses. He went from one to the other but all refused him. Then he went to Wilkinson.

Sadleir was ushered into the solicitor's office on the morning of February 16, 1856. Wilkinson was not as affable as usual.

Almost frantic now, Sadleir begged his old friend to help the Tipperary bank as "I cannot live to see the pain and ruin inflicted on others by the closing of the bank."

As far as Wilkinson was concerned his client's obvious agitation only confirmed the truth of the rumors he had been hearing.

As a result he told Sadleir that at this stage his firm was not prepared to make any further advance. Further, he was sending the deed he was holding as security against previous loans to Dublin for checking.

Early that afternoon Sadleir persuaded one of his friends, a Mr. Norris, to call on Wilkinson and support his loan application.

Norris told a man named Gurney, one of Wilkinson's partners, that when he last saw Sadleir he was so depressed he was convinced that unless he received the loan he would kill himself.

When Wilkinson interviewed Norris and heard his pleas for his friend, he not only refused the loan again but instructed another of his partners to take the first packet to Ireland to investigate Sadleir's security deed.

At nine o'clock that night Sadleir instructed his chambermaid to post a letter. It was addressed to the wife of his brother James.

He also told the girl that on the way back she was to call in at a chemist shop and buy a bottle of oil of almonds, a poison.

Later in the evening he gave his butler two letters to post to friends. At

12.45 am when the butler went about the house locking doors and extinguishing lamps, he noticed his master had left the house.

A few hours after dawn the butler heard knocking at the door. He opened it to be confronted by two policemen. They wanted him to identify a body that had been found on the heath at Hampstead.

Two days after the butler had viewed the body and identified it as the corpse of his master, a coroner held an inquest into the death at Hampstead.

During the hearing, the letters Sadleir had written before leaving the house were produced.

John Sadleir, politician and financier, was the central figure in one of the most sensational scandals of Victorian England.

In a letter to his friend Robert Keating MP, Sadleir admitted having swindled and deceived and said he alone was responsible for the embezzlements.

The letter to his sister-in-law contained this passage: "My death will prove I am not callous to the agony of the people I have robbed."

In evidence Wilkinson said he had discovered that the security deed Sadleir had given him was a forgery yet he did not believe the former Lord of the Treasury was guilty of other acts of dishonesty.

After that the inquest was adjourned while investigations were carried out into all the companies with which Sadleir had been associated.

All England gasped when these inquires revealed that Sadleir had embezzled £200,000 from the Joint Stock Bank in Tipperary and had issued £150,000 worth of valueless securities in one of his railway companies.

Apart from that he was guilty of obtaining a large number of smaller sums from other companies.

For years later, rumors circulated that Sadleir was not dead and the body found on the Hampstead heath was that of another person.

It was pointed out that he would have had good reasons to fake his death for he was a man of simple habits and most of the money he had embezzled must still be secure.

It was further discovered that because no cab driver could be found to say he had driven a man from Hyde Park to Hampstead on the night Sadleir disappeared, he must have walked there.

Yet despite the sodden condition of the heath the dead man's shoes were perfectly clean.

After that intermittent reports came back to England of Sadleir living in comfortable peace on the Continent. But none could be substantiated. Time finally erased his name from the memory of his contemporaries.